AFRICAN POLITICAL THOUGHT

STEPHEN CHAN

African Political Thought

*An Intellectual History of the
Quest for Freedom*

HURST & COMPANY, LONDON

First published in the United Kingdom in 2021 by
C. Hurst & Co. (Publishers) Ltd.,
83 Torbay Road, London, NW6 7DT
Copyright © Stephen Chan, 2021
All rights reserved.

The right of Stephen Chan to be identified as the author of
this publication is asserted by him in accordance with the
Copyright, Designs and Patents Act, 1988.

Distributed in the United States, Canada and Latin America by
Oxford University Press, 198 Madison Avenue, New York, NY 10016,
United States of America.

A Cataloguing-in-Publication data record for this book
is available from the British Library.

ISBN: 9781787385504

This book is printed using paper from registered sustainable
and managed sources.
Printed and bound in Great Britain by Bell & Bain Ltd, Glasgow

www.hurstpublishers.com

CONTENTS

PREFACE

For the most part Africa had to fight for its independence. Africa entered a world that, even when it sought not to be racist, was condescending. Even Sartre, in his Preface to Fanon's *The Wretched of the Earth*, wrote of the rebellious native with his "mad fury... bitterness and spleen... their ever-present desire to kill us... the permanent tensing of powerful muscles which are afraid to relax", as the evidence of rebellion against colonialism.[1] To the 'native' alone was denied the condition of philosophy. The denial was the condition of thought. Almost 80 years after the process of independence began, US President Donald Trump was still able to call Africa a place of 'shithole' countries and delayed appointing an Assistant Secretary of State for Africa for his first two years of office. By this time perhaps the condition of philosophy had deserted even the White House, but the idea of an engagement in thought with Africa was still absent in most US academic, as well as political, discourse. Africa gained popular prominence in the film, *Black Panther*—a comic book portrayal of the continent filmed largely in Argentina. In that film, a magic mineral equalised Africa in the world, but philosophy did not. Yet the reality of history is that Africa's struggles to take up an independent role have been just as informed by political thought as any other revolutionary movement. So this book is one about liberation, freedom, and political philosophy. It is about the philosophy of politics but also the politics of philosophy—for philosophers spend time in African prisons as much as political leaders once did. It starts with the black quest for freedom in the USA and the idea of a pan-Africa which included the diaspora, and concludes with a meditation on today's Africa where, finally, the 'writing back' to the former colonial and metropolitan powers is in a philosophical language that the West must learn—the traffic has turned—and appreciate it as being as equally directive of the future of the world as its own philosophies seek to be.

Linking the origins of African political thought to roots in the USA has meant an Anglophonic emphasis in this book. But Francophonic and Lusophonic thought is also represented.

The genesis of this book lies in my lecture course at SOAS University of London, *African Political Thought*, and over many years of delivering this course to both graduate and undergraduate students I have incurred many debts to them for their incisive and thoughtful responses and challenging engagements. Many of them came from African countries and, often, they queried my conclusions—even though I myself have travelled in Africa since 1979, and lived there for some years, working as both an international civil servant and academic, having both a public and a private practice that took me from war zones to slums and to high places, from sleeping in bombed out ruins to the mansions of ministers, rebuilding governments and helping liberation movements to become governments; and to sitting on the side of African delegations negotiating trade issues in Beijing and Washington, DC. The fatal mistake would have been simply to humour my students while thinking them wrong. They most often weren't and I am grateful for their gentle and reasoned reproofs. My colleagues at SOAS, and at various African universities, were always kind and helpful—if sometimes impatient with me. I first decided to mount my lecture course after being awarded the International Studies Association's accolade, Eminent Scholar in Global Development, in 2010. It had been awarded the year before to Mahmood Mamdani, whose own course, at Columbia, on African political thought was then the only one in the world. At least, I thought, there should be one on each side of the Atlantic. So now there is. But, as far as I know, still no more—and, if some, not many more. Perhaps this book, as well as its goal of seeking to illuminate sometimes deep and certainly historically important thought, might encourage other professors to finally teach the basic idea that a continent, in seeking freedom and development, does so with thought.

PREFACE

And, because it does so thoughtfully, that thought is able to be critically appreciated, its contradictions and lapses indicated. I did not want to write intellectual hagiographies. By and large, Africa is 70 independent years old. To write about thinking is to remove security and mere heroism.

Pimlico, London, 2021

1

ANTECEDENTS

RACE AND ROMANTICISM

Africa was far from 'discovered' by European missionaries and celebrity explorers. Many of the latter were feted like rock stars in the clubs and learned societies of Victorian London, and deliberately played up the ideas of exotica and backwardness.[1] Africa was not their only subject. The image of the 'noble savage' was drawn from the Maori resistance, of great chivalry, to white settler colonialism. But, whether adventurism in remote parts was condescending or gracious, the end result was all the same: an imperial outreach and a colonialism. The Berlin Conference at the end of 1884 and beginning of 1885 literally divided Africa among the European powers—the political cartoonists of the day portraying it like a knife to a gigantic Christmas pudding. And they were able to do so because the phenomenon of corporate colonialism, exemplified by Cecil Rhodes and his search for gold and other mineral wealth, was confined to the southern part of the continent. Northern Africa, the Maghreb, represented a contestation between established governments and European powers. The bulk of sub-Saharan Africa was valuable but not worth going to war over—thus the carving of the continent like a pudding on the day of Christ's birth.

But North Africa was an interesting case of the continent being far from dark. In the bitter days of English isolation from Europe, when

1

the Protestant Queen Elizabeth sought to face down the armada and pressures from Catholic Spain, her court desperately sought diplomatic allies wherever they could be found. The portrait of the Ambassador to London from Morocco, an Islamic power, still hangs from time to time in the Tate Britain. Shakespeare made a tragic hero of Othello, a mercenary admiral from North Africa serving the Venetian navy. And the British were later hoisted on their own petard as they tried to crush or apply sanctions against the infant United States. The US also sought diplomatic allies from North Africa—for instance, ironically, from what is now Libya.

In fact, Islam had appeared in Africa in the 10th century, well before the advent of European trade missions and slave raids on the continent from the 1500s. Chinese Admiral Zheng He, in his expeditions to East Africa in the early 1400s, was able to make contact with the local population by virtue of himself being Islamic—even if with different customs and laws—leaving behind porcelain cups, fragments of which can still sometimes be found on the shores of Dar es Salaam, and taking home to his emperor a living giraffe. It epitomised an East African coast with an international exchange of ideas and culture well before the advent of European interest.

Islamic powers conducted their own slave trade in Africa, but Western plundering of sub-Saharan Africa for slaves helped populate the Caribbean islands, and led to large black populations in continental America, notably Brazil and the United States. For the most part slavery was abolished as the 19th century wore on: in Europe in the 1830s, Brazil as late as the 1880s; in the US, it was abolished in the 1860s, but it took a bloody civil war and Abraham Lincoln's proclamation of liberty, and by then the idea of 'return' had already set in to the minds both of many members of the black population and their white well-wishers—who, although liberal and well-minded in the terms of their times, often saw blackness as out of place in a vast country with a white vision of its future. The African Americans who engaged with this idea and began envisaging their own future 'back' in Africa were some of the very first black and African people to conceive a politics responding to Western colonisation, imperialism and slavery.

Liberia, for instance—as we shall discuss later—entered the world of formal states by first being a settlement of the American

Colonization Society, who believed black people would enjoy greater freedom and prosperity in Africa than in the United States. The country declared independence in 1847 but did not gain US recognition until 1862, during the American Civil War. Until then more than 15,000 freed slaves and free-born blacks who all the same did not enjoy full rights in the US, and slightly over 3000 people from the Caribbean, relocated to Liberia—all carrying forms of American culture with them, much to the dismay and alienation of those who were indigenous to the territory of the so-called new state. The Liberian constitution and flag were modelled on those of the US The first president was a wealthy free-born Virginian who had not grown up in Africa. Many of the ruptures that still plague Liberia to this day owe to the peculiar form of what was effectively the black colonisation of an extant population. But, even before the efforts of the American Colonization Society, beginning in 1822, the British Crown founded a settlement in Sierra Leone in 1787 in what was called the 'Province of Freedom', in which it intended to resettle some of the 'black poor' of London, including African-Americans freed by the British during the US War of Independence. About 400 blacks and 60 whites reached Sierra Leone in May 1787. Most died of disease or in violent encounters with the indigenous inhabitants. They were effectively replaced in 1792 by 1200 black loyalists to the British Crown, who, after the US War of Independence, had been settled, unhappily, in Nova Scotia. The efforts of the British anti-slavery movement brought them to Sierra Leone where they established Freetown—still the country's capital. They called themselves 'settlers' and built Freetown in the style they knew from America and continued American fashion and American manners. In addition, they established Methodism in Freetown. Again, many of today's problems in Sierra Leone stem from the imposition of a black colonialism on a pre-existing population—although the British did not grant independence until 1961. Many in that population today remain Islamic, so the mix is about 21% Christian and 78% Muslim. Already, at the time of the foundation of Liberia and Sierra Leone, as we shall see later, people like Edward Blyden were writing about the two religions and the tensions within their African relationship.

The Exception of Ethiopia

If certain currents of thought and practice to do with 'return' were already being put into place by the time of the 1884–5 Berlin Conference, that conference saw Africa as a site of Africanness and blackness certainly but, all the same, with white overlords of territories formalised according to European preferences. This did not mean that Africa was necessarily acquiescent in its own colonisation. This was most apparent in the Italian effort to conquer the independent kingdom of Ethiopia and the fierce war of resistance that greeted the Italian armies. The Ethiopian struggle became emblematic of the efforts of the wider continent, so that Addis Ababa was a natural choice for the location of continental African institutions.

Ethiopia or Abyssinia had been the stuff of legend and wonder for millennia. For a long time, it—or an image of it—was all that was known in Europe of sub-Saharan Africa. In Homer's epic poem of the *Odyssey*, written some 2,700 years ago, the Greek hero Odysseus, having devised the plan whereby Troy was overthrown by the stratagem of the Trojan Horse, was waylaid from returning home by the vengeful god, Poseidon, who had supported the Trojans. His detention was not unpleasant, being confined to an island for almost a decade in a conjugal relationship with the beautiful goddess, Calypso, but he longed to escape home to Greece. His chance finally came when the Ethiopians threw a party for Poseidon.

> But now Poseidon had gone to visit the Ethiopians worlds away,
> Ethiopians off at the farthest limits of mankind,
> A people split in two, one part where the Sungod sets
> And part where the Sungod rises. There Poseidon went
> To receive an offering, bulls and rams by the hundred—
> Far away at the feast the Sea-lord sat and took his pleasure.[2]

There, Ethiopia was an image of sub-Saharan Africa as a whole, exotic and unknown—although seemingly on good terms with the gods. But the various legends that accrued around Ethiopia are augmented by the Ethiopians themselves, who claim that the Queen of Sheba was one of theirs and, as the wisest woman of earth, set out to test her knowledge against that of Solomon. The more substantiated claim is that the Ethiopian Coptic Church has the world's oldest Christian liturgy and, although it was established at about the same time as the Catholic liturgy, was not bound by the imperial need to make Christianity into a religion palatable to the vast Roman Empire. The claim is therefore that of a form of worship closer than any other to the worship of the Apostles. The other major claim that Ethiopian emperors were descended from King David continues to fuel Rastafarian belief today. But, certainly it meant that at the great Battle of Adwa between the Ethiopian and Italian forces in 1896, both sides claimed to be Christian armies. To this day, in the street markets of Addis Ababa, one may buy paintings both of Sheba, in the Ethiopian version named Magda, visiting Solomon, and of the Battle of Adwa. In the latter, St George rides with the Ethiopians—but both sides have Red Cross tents, and both sides have modern armaments. In fact, the Ethiopian army was a mixture of traditional warriors and rifle-bearing soldiers—some 20,000 spearmen, including mounted cavalry, and 80,000 rifles. The army seemed to have included women, as some were named as figures of great heroism. The battle, in which the Ethiopians did claim their Christian roots as inspirational, attracted international sympathy for them, as well as recognitions of legitimacy as an independent country. The Italo-Ethiopian war of 1895–6 was won by the Ethiopians, but this did not mean that the Italians ceased their efforts to colonise the country and other parts of the Horn of Africa.

The second Italo-Ethiopian war in the era of Mussolini was one of two key factors in the demise of the League of Nations, established at the end of World War I, as Haile Selassie's 1936 plea in front of the League saw no response that could stop the Italian invasion. Similarly, China's plea to the League to halt the Japanese invasion of its territory met with no effectual action. Mussolini's forces took Addis Ababa, but in this second war the Ethiopians were able to field, although to no avail, 400,000 rifles, 234 artillery pieces, and a small array of tanks and armoured cars. The liberation of Addis Ababa in 1941, by Ethiopian and Commonwealth forces, was greeted in a London still reeling from the Battle of Britain in 1940, as a key blow against the Axis powers—and this meant a curious map of post-war Africa, with the main actors in Rhodes's south having dominion or self-governing, effectively independent, status under white governments; a North Africa with a long if problematic relationship with Europe—and indeed in ancient Tunisia, then Carthage, an attempt to conquer Rome—and a vast sub-Saharan land mass in which only Liberia, founded, perhaps colonised, by freed American slaves, and Ethiopia were recognised as independent states.

The Father: Edward Wilmot Blyden

Return, education, and the need to understand Islam informed the work of someone who should be regarded as a key founding father of modern thought—by that I mean thought intended and able to render itself in terms of hegemonic modernity, speaking back but also able to speak forwards—in Africa. Edward Wilmot Blyden was born in 1832 in St. Thomas, now in the US Virgin Islands, and was of Igbo (eastern Nigerian) descent. He was refused admission to Rutgers University because of being black and accepted encouragement from the American Colonization Society to go to Liberia, where he arrived in 1850.

Blyden had been mentored in his youth by a white US preacher, the Reverend John Knox, and from him learned Latin and Greek. Once in Liberia, he spent time both there and in neighbouring Sierra Leone, both with similar histories of settlement by foreign blacks. He worked as a journalist in both as well as in Nigeria, became editor of the *Liberia Herald*, and also published in the organs of the American Colonization Society. But it was in education, politics and diplomacy where he chiefly made his mark. He became Professor of Greek and Latin at Liberia College in 1861—and he would become president of the college in 1880. Before then he became Liberian Secretary of State (1862–4), and later combined being college president with being Minister of the Interior (1880–4). He was ambassador to Britain and France and returned for a lecture tour of the USA. From the turn of the century, Blyden lived mostly in Sierra Leone, where he directed the education of Muslims. That country, with its own black settlers, took education very seriously, establishing Fourah Bay College in 1827—the first university in sub-Saharan Africa, now part of the University of Sierra Leone—predating the foundation of the University of Cape Town by two years. Blyden died in Sierra Leone in 1912.

His lectures in the USA were about a 'return' to Africa as the essential means of avoiding racial discrimination, but his intellectual legacy resides in his book, *Christianity, Islam and the Negro Race*.[3] When it was published in 1887, many readers did not believe it could have been written by a black man, this in itself a demonstration of the discrimination against which Blyden warned. He remained a Christian, although accounts about that vary, but his argument was that Islam was a unifying force for black people—not being part of the white project of subjugation, and also having been present in Africa for many hundreds of years. It was in these respects more authentic as a religion for black people. The influence his work had can be seen in the continued sense of a homeland for those of African descent—those in a diaspora—and the advent of a form of black Islam in the USA during the civil rights era of the 1960s, most famously involving Malcolm X, as a counterpoint to the crusades of people like Martin Luther King, a Christian minister who was seen by many to be too moderate. Clearly, however, Blyden was unaware of Ethiopian Christianity and, in the Americas, it took the Rastas to highlight its existence while the US Nation of Islam continued its counterpoint to the mainstream civil rights movement.

Blyden stood unsuccessfully for the Presidency of Liberia in 1885. Only 2,310 votes were cast, the franchise being restricted to registered landowners and not available to the 'native', non-settler populations of the Liberian hinterland outside Monrovia.[4] The question mark over Blyden's thought was to do with what made one both an emancipated and civic black. Was it blackness in itself? Or was it qualities that came from education and private ownership of property? Communal ownership and indigenous religions that were not Islamic (or Christian) did not equip one for citizenship. Women of course, as everywhere in that period, achieved the franchise only slowly and, in Liberia, in a fragmented fashion. Blyden's later life in Sierra Leone, educating black Muslims, was as much therefore a project in citizenship as in education itself. To be fair, in the UK, 1885 marked the start of an era in which electoral reform was slowly being achieved, and still had ownership protocols as part of the eligibility to vote. Liberia could say it was near the forefront of modern practice. But it was not leading it. Freedom from discrimination for some meant discrimination for those who had lived in the land for centuries before the arrival of the American Colonization Society. Again, Liberia was hardly alone. Indigenous Americans did not achieve the franchise in the USA until 1924, and first-generation Asian immigrants could not achieve citizenship until 1952.

As for Islam, what Islam precisely did Blyden mean? Was there an African Islam of which he was aware, and was this cognisant of the extraordinarily rich and diverse forms of religious organisation and governance this could entail in both nomadic and sophisticated urban life; its historiography and genealogies; rituals and culture?[5] In Blyden's time, this richness was largely unknown in its detail to Western scholars.

So there is something curiously partial about the work of a man who, all the same, pioneered the sense that black freedom and black pride could be achieved through black 'authenticity' in a black continent with, if not a black religion, a less white one.

The Acknowledged Giant: W.E.B. Du Bois

Born in 1868 in Massachusetts, just after the American civil war which had been fought over slavery, William Edward Burghardt Du Bois (who refused to pronounce his name in the French manner, preferring 'doo boyz') achieved distinction by becoming Harvard's first black PhD. It was that kind of distinction that, for all his pioneering work, marked him. He essentially saw a future whereby black Americans would be mentored and taken forward by their own intellectual elite, what he called 'the talented tenth', and the means behind this would be education. By this he meant a full 'classical' education, not one confined to vocational or industrial training. He was opposed therefore to the so-called 'Atlanta Compromise' put forward by Booker T. Washington—whereby, in the southern USA, blacks would accept continuing white superiority on the condition that educational (largely education in industrial pursuits) and economic opportunities would be accorded them—a gradualist approach to equality based on education. Du Bois was against any gradualism that retained inequality. Full civil rights was a precondition for Du Bois for any possibility of black advancement. Within these rights, the 'talented tenth' would tow the 90% forward towards the fulfilment of opportunities within an already achieved equality.

Du Bois was an activist, vocal against the discriminations and lynchings in the south. He documented discrimination against black soldiers during World War I—and he partook in a full range of movements that were not specific to the black American condition: he believed capitalism lay behind racism, he was a peace activist and, in his later life, was in favour of nuclear disarmament. The FBI had a 750-page file on him as his work impacted upon a USA in the throes of the McCarthy anti-Communist witch-hunt era. Above all, he became renowned for his support of the pan-African Congresses that, in an increasingly influential and mobilising series, helped establish both black nationalism and the possibility of a pan-Africanism on the African continent. He was a primary organiser of the early congresses and attended the most influential one in 1945 in Manchester. We discuss these congresses below. He travelled to Asia, Europe and Africa and, in fact, died in Accra, Ghana, in 1963, at the grand age of 95, a year before the Civil Rights Act—for which he had long campaigned—finally came into force in the USA.

Of several books that he wrote, the most influential was *The Souls of Black Folk*, which appeared in 1935.[6] This had a profound effect on its readers, both at the time and later. As we shall see, South African President Thabo Mbeki's thought owed much to this book. It was a book of essays, many of which had been published in journals like the *Atlantic Monthly*, and was not an academic work of sociology so much as a direct statement from a sociological group undergoing change. The essays are on different themes but, insofar as they may also be said to be variations of an image, they concern a colossus of great cultural history, expressed very much in classical terms to do with African civilisations, seeking to march into the future. That future is one of equality, expressed curiously in epigrams to each chapter, utilising work by largely European poets set to music drawn from 'Negro spirituals'. (The actual musical notation is given, so it is clear which 'spirituals' are meant.) But music is of importance in the book. In a chapter devoted to the 'spirituals', they are described as songs of sorrow. For Du Bois, the songs of hope lay in education, and the book deals at length with this key concern, and includes his quarrel with

Booker T. Washington.[7] Du Bois wanted education up to the highest level—he himself being the first black man to take a PhD in the USA (at Harvard)—whereas Washington's was a more gradualist approach.

But education was critical primarily so that black people could be reconciled within a double consciousness, and emerge from it—a consciousness of their own perceptions of themselves, and a consciousness as to how they are seen by others, i.e. by white people. The equality of perceptions, so that no one would consider they were being perceived with condescension, was a critical ambition for Du Bois. The reconciliation of self with Africanness became a key motif of the later work of Africa's independence leaders such as Kwame Nkrumah, Kenneth Kaunda, and Julius Nyerere. All had a different vision of what this meant and how it could be achieved. Nkrumah aside, the others owed no direct debt to Du Bois, but the perceptions he discussed in his book entered a general sensibility of what was required for black advancement. Part of the dissemination of this sensibility was due to the Pan-African Congresses.

The Pan-African Congresses

There were six of these congresses from 1900 to 1945. They were animating and formative of both black and wider public opinion, including in the formulation of the sense of a unifying blackness and Africanness; and the one in 1945, coming at the end of WWII, was decisive in the direction it achieved for nationalism and the drive for independence.[8]

In 1900, Henry Sylvester-Williams, a lawyer from the Caribbean, organized the first pan-African meeting in London. It was attended by 30 delegates, largely from the Africa diaspora. Most were from Britain and the Caribbean, but W.E.B. Du Bois came. Despite the small number, this was the first time opponents of colonialism had assembled in an international meeting. The term, pan-African, was probably coined there—or certainly the press, which covered the meeting, disseminated the term so that it began its entry into popular speech. This gathering was called a conference, and successor meetings were described as congresses—thus the confusion as to whether there were five or six congresses, but the London meeting should be considered a progenitor of those that followed, so six is a just number.

Du Bois essentially became the intellectual lead at the London conference. Papers were presented on the economic condition of the diaspora; on the few black independent states such as Ethiopia, Haiti and Liberia; on slavery and imperialism; and on the impact and role of Christianity. But it was a committee chaired by Du Bois that composed a document entitled, 'To the Nations of the World', which demanded reforms in colonial Africa.[9] The document asked that the USA and Europe protect the rights of people of African descent, and respect the integrity of the few black states—but it stopped short of a programme for decolonisation; it stipulated no timelines for independence and made no suggestions for government or governance of black states. It was basically a statement of 'here we are in international relations' and a request for acknowledgement that this was so. This document made no impact at all on the colonial powers, but the conference did agree to continue the project of a pan-African grouping—and this came into its own after WWI, when it sought, under Du Bois's guidance, to impact the Versailles peace conference of 1919 where all the great powers were gathered—Du Bois attending as the special representative of the NAACP (National Association for the Advancement of Colored People).

He made an impassioned appeal to President Woodrow Wilson[10] and, although it is a matter of conjecture whether Wilson's vision for a post-war future, the famous Fourteen Point document, was influenced by Du Bois, it did call for a review of the colonial project and spoke of an impartial adjustment of this project based on the claims of the people affected. Although Du Bois also asked Wilson to look at how poorly black US soldiers had been treated in WWI, it remains the case that no one else addressed the president on the question of an end to colonialism. Given the importance of the Versailles meeting, it was decided to hold a Pan-African Congress, also in Paris, in 1919. This time, 60 delegates attended.

They came from 16 nations, though few were from Africa itself. Many delegates had no direct knowledge of Africa, though they were studded with educational luminaries and others who had made a mark in the world. But they expressed strong concern over the excesses of colonialism in Africa, especially in the Belgian Congo. They wanted supervision of the colonies by the newly formed League of Nations, and an abolition of slave conditions and capital punishment on colonial plantations. They insisted upon the right to education. But, again, there was no programme or timetable for decolonisation. The irony is that, although Du Bois was antipathetic to Booker T. Washington in the US context, it could be said that it was exactly a Booker T. Washington vision that delegates had for Africa. Education was a priority and, until it achieved its goal of upliftment for all, the colonial project would continue. Even so, the great powers at Versailles were unimpressed.

The 1921 and 1923 congresses were both held in London with spill-overs on to Brussels and Lisbon respectively. Self-government of the colonies became a theme, as was the reaching out by the black intelligentsia to white thinkers. At the 1923 congress this became a reality as H.G. Wells and Harold Laski both attended the London segment. Laski, in many ways, the intellectual animator of what became the British welfare state, would have a significant influence on Kenneth Kaunda's vision of a humanistic Zambia.

By the fifth Pan-African Congress in New York in 1927, 208 delegates from the US and ten other countries attended. Still Africa was not heavily represented, except from West Africa, including Liberia. Colonial travel restrictions were a large factor in the sparse attendance as, by now, the idea of an independent pan-Africanism was seen, even by colonial authorities, as taking root and was regarded as dangerous.

There were no further congresses until 1945, firstly because of the global financial crisis that erupted from 1929 to 1939, followed immediately by WWII in 1939. That war, however, was something of a turning point for Africa. Many soldiers from the continent participated, not just in Ethiopia, but well beyond. Battalions from what is now Zambia fought in Myanmar (Burma) as frontline troops for instance, not just as porters and support personnel. But the effect of the war in terms of the Francophonic colonies and their relationship with France was immense. General De Gaulle, who escaped France as it fell—having himself commanded the only French counterattack of merit—confronted Winston Churchill and sought recognition of himself as leader of the Free French. Churchill, in an unkind manner, asked him of what he was any longer the leader: France had fallen. To this, De Gaulle said that the African colonies had stood firm and were with him.[11] Insofar as they did indeed continue allegiance to France and did not offer it to the Vichy government installed by the Germans, the nationalist leaders of the French colonies in West and North Africa had leverage in talks for independence when the war ended. Indeed, even thinkers who later became the flag-bearers of liberation, like Frantz Fanon, fought in the field for France. (Fanon was wounded, and decorated for gallantry.) This contributed to a general sense as the war ended that independence was nearer than once hoped, and this sense imbued the 1945 pan-African Congress in Manchester.

Du Bois was there but, finally, for the first time, so was significant representation from Africa itself. The agenda was no longer about the reform of colonial regimes, but the end of colonialism.[12] George Padmore from the Caribbean signalled the change in emphasis and it was taken up by delegates that included future leaders or key political figures of new states. People such as Kwame Nkrumah (Ghana), Jomo Kenyatta (Kenya), Nnamdi Azikiwe, Obafemi Awolowo (both Nigeria), and even the conservative figure of Hastings Banda (Malawi) all demanded a new world order of independent states— with African states—and urged a sense of pan-Africanism. Their deliberations and declarations were supported by cultural figures such as the opera singer and actor, Paul Robeson, who, having come to London to escape racism in the USA, had added to his sense of blackness by an appreciation of Africanness by studying African languages at SOAS University of London. The appeal for independence and self-determination was expressed as a desirable goal not only for Africa but the rest of the emerging world. In a way, it laid the ideological groundwork for the Bandung Afro-Asian Conference of 1955—which in turn laid the groundwork for the future Non-Aligned Movement, and also saw the introduction of China into the fortunes of Africa in the form of Premier Zhou Enlai's Bandung speech pledging assistance and non-intervention. But there was another backdrop to Manchester, and that was the romanticised appeal of Africa to the diaspora as expressed by figures like Marcus Garvey—someone not liked by Du Bois (they were of the same generation)—for reasons expressed below.

Marcus Garvey: The Black Moses

Garvey, 1887–1940, of Jamaican/American origin, was flamboyant. He dressed occasionally in a concocted ceremonial military uniform as if he were a reborn Toussaint l'Ouverture, the leader of the Haitian uprising against French colonialism,[13] but was not himself interested in building a nation as much as imagining a great omni-nation, geographically as great as continental Africa, inhabited by a race of 'pure' Africans. This inflected upon his views of Du Bois, whom he described as only a "little Negro" and was basically a "mulatto" and a "monstrosity". Du Bois responded in kind, describing Garvey as "a little, fat black man; ugly, but with intelligent eyes and a big head." Apart from the eyes, Du Bois did not overly impute intelligence to Garvey and his thought.[14]

Garvey, a Jamaican immigrant, didn't think whites would ever come to accept blacks—but this was a result of a sense of whiteness as purity, to which Garvey proposed a sense of blackness as purity in its own right.

> I believe in a pure black race just as how all self-respecting whites believe in a pure white race, as far as that can be. (Notwithstanding historical intermixing of races) ... we believe we should now set out to create a race type and standard of our own which ... could be recognised and respected as the true race type anteceding even our own time.[15]

He proposed that black people in the US should return to Africa, where they would be the majority population with real political power. Accordingly he created and sold shares in the Black Star Line. This was meant to be a fleet of ships that would eventually sail black people from the USA back to Africa. In a way it was a rerun of the thought of the American Colonization Society, without any sense of respect for the separate identities and cultures of African populations throughout a vast and pluralistic continent. And it was certainly very different thought from that of Du Bois, who saw an equality throughout the world, rather than a separation into different parts of the world. Even so, as we shall see, Garvey had an influence on Kwame Nkrumah, who had been a university student in the US when Garvey's influence was at its height. Nkrumah had attended black universities and worked to support himself as a kitchen hand—so would have seen discrimination up close. His later work of 'consciencism' would reflect some of both Garvey and his own knowledge of barriers in the US and how they imparted a sense of inferiority to black people who, at best, would manage and navigate a double consciousness of the sort Du Bois described. Breaking out of double consciousness altogether by one powerful remedy was what Garvey proposed.

But the flag of independent Ghana features the black star from Garvey's never-realised Black Star Line. The national football team is called the Black Stars. Nkrumah's early advocacy of a united Africa is an echo of Garvey's sense of one pure Africa. As we shall see, being both a nationalist and a continentalist was a double consciousness of its own. But, if the Garvey project did not in itself bring black people across the Atlantic from the USA to Africa, the loop back of African influences to the USA had a profound genesis in the elite intellectual circles of France.[16] Fanon is included in this sense of inspiring back across the Atlantic from France, but the black intellectuals of post-war France took to French culture and intellectual and cultural life at high level, used its methodologies to express black culture and thought, and made blackness seem part of a profoundly emerging intellectual world that was not purely white. It was not just Africa and France: Ali Shari'ati from Iran was, like Fanon, someone who was a part of Jean-Paul Sartre's circle (Sartre wrote the prefaces for both their great books).[17] And the openness of Parisian society to a slightly later figure like Miles Davis echoed even more in terms of an example to the USA than Paul Robeson's adoring reception in circles of the left in London.[18]

Paris: Becoming Equal By Becoming Better

The sense of achieving equality, not separation was expressed in a typically poetic French by Aimé Césaire, that there was a place for all at the 'rendezvous of victory'. While black American voices were increasingly articulating the aspiration to equality and freedom, in parallel with the pan-African movement among nationalist leaders of the British colonies, French African ideas of black identity were emerging that arguably triggered the continent's decolonisation.

15

Césaire coined the term' negritude' and disseminated what it meant with Leopold Senghor[19]—the two became staunch allies in Paris although Césaire had come from Martinique—itself siding with De Gaulle's free French during WWII—and Senghor from what would become Senegal. Both studied at a very high level at elite institutions in Paris, and it was particularly Senghor's recorded brilliance in gruelling exams that helped catapult him into high French cultural, academic and political society. He became a member of the French National Assembly (parliament) and even a minister in French governments.[20] His method of achieving equality was not a separation, and not a double consciousness, but a reconciliation of opposites. Firstly, however, both sides of the opposition had to be equal—thus negritude, which has often been misunderstood as the celebration of something in which spontaneity excused a lack of expressible and measurable depth. "The African can dance and sing and recite poetry but cannot build a spaceship." But even the song and poetry are not as complex as a symphony or Shakespeare. It was into this ground of what seemed stark opposites, a binary that was asymmetrical, that Senghor intruded. Senghor, however, had taken his *aggregation* (the highest French degree with a complexity unparalleled in the Anglophonic university world) in Grammar. Ebou Dibba reminds us that Senghor's poems, praised for their beauty, were also exercises in grammar. "There is an abundance of figures of speech: hypallage, hendiadys, "astuce", asyndeton and what he calls *symetrisme asymetrique.*" Senghor himself wrote of a vision all the same of symmetry, despite asymmetry within each or all of the 'opposing' sides, provided the end result was an equality: "I speak of a Word like a simultaneous new vision of the universe and pan-human creation: of the *fecund Word*, finally, because it is a fruit of different civilisations created by all nations together on the entire surface of planet earth."[21]

The emphasis was on an equality of cultures, both in terms of aesthetic sensibilities that were cultivated and nuanced, but also in terms of complexity. From this arose an equality in terms of beauty.

To an extent Paris was a fecund place for such interaction. The influence of African art on figures like Picasso during his Parisian period is well known. The advent of jazz as a cultural force, not just New Orleans jazz but Racing Club Paris jazz—in a city with many more recent migrants and visitors from Africa than was the case in New Orleans—and the exchange of techniques and motifs meant an interaction that was accepted in Paris. And one of the great musical stars of the period was Josephine Baker, accepted as a great *chanteuse* despite being black; all this signalled an openness rather than any strict separations. Paris in the post-war years was also the magnet that brought aspiring artists and literary figures from around the world— people like Ernest Hemingway—and inspired films like Gene Kelly's 'American in Paris'. It could not be a city of dichotomies in the way Garvey saw the USA. Thus Césaire's aspiration that there could be a rendezvous of victory for all.

It is often suggested that Marcus Garvey and his involvement in the Harlem Renaissance, the great explosion of cultural expression in New York, was the prefiguring of the 'black is beautiful' movement in the 1960s. Ali Mazrui, however, sees it as a trans-Atlantic loop in which Africa impacted upon the USA via France.[22]

France was, as suggested above, ready to concede independence to the black nationalist movements of the Francophonie—although they inserted into that independence a vast number of particularly economic ties to France. But the movement of France towards an economically contingent decolonisation—notwithstanding huge problems to accomplish this in Algeria, Fanon conspicuously taking the side of the Algerians—also impacted upon the United Kingdom. Before the war, the hopeful outlook was independence for Africa by the 1980s. The author of that projection, a young civil servant at war's outbreak, Malcolm MacDonald, son of Ramsey, told me that after the war Britain, notwithstanding anything else, was simply too weary to continue the colonial project.[23] And the French were moving anyway. So independence began to come to Africa, with Ghana in 1957, a mere 12 years after the end of WWII, and a rush of independences of both Francophonic and Anglophonic colonies from 1960 onwards—all of which was couched on the British side at least in a 'winds of change' rhetoric, but all of which had also been contemplated and anticipated by many long years of intellectual history in which black intellectuals were differently dreaming, organising, and thinking about the moment of freedom.

2

NATIONAL CONSCIOUSNESS, INTERNATIONAL STRUGGLE

CABRAL, KAUNDA AND THE THOUGHT OF LIBERATION

As independence began arriving in Africa, it did so unevenly. White minority rule persisted in the south of the continent and in the Portuguese colonies of the east and west. The world was engulfed in a Cold War between East and West, with the constant threat that it might turn thermo-nuclear hot. The two independence leaders discussed in this chapter were both trying to forge a national identity for their peoples, while also conceiving a politics of solidarity with the struggles going on around them. Kenneth Kaunda, the first leader of independent Zambia, had to reconcile his pacifist ideology with the continuing struggle for black freedom in neighbouring countries; we will meet him later on in the chapter. And Amílcar Cabral, the liberation leader of Portuguese Guinea and Cape Verde, had to elaborate a theory of history that could at least seem to draw on Marxism while staying relevant to Lusophone African society.

Cuba was a central actor in the uneasy balance between hot and cold. It was led by Fidel Castro, who had come to power in a guerrilla insurgency against a US-backed government. The US never found a way to tolerate what it saw as a Communist-supported presence in its Caribbean backyard—despite intellectuals like Susan Sontag cel-

19

ebrating the cultural vibrancy she found there both before the 'Cuban missile crisis', and afterwards.[1] The geopolitics of the situation—a supposed outpost of Moscow, militant and suspected of exporting revolution internationally, including to Africa—was too much for the US administration to bear. This was especially true after the humiliation of its own CIA-sponsored effort to invade Fidel's Cuba in 1961, by means of a rebel army, which had failed dismally at the Bay of Pigs on the southern coast of the island.

Among others, the 1962 Cuban Missile Crisis which came after the Bay of Pigs did three things. Firstly, in the West at least, it made a legend of US President John Kennedy, not least because the steps and decisions he took to face down the Soviet Union in its effort to ship missiles to Cuba was memorialised by his own brother—who was Attorney General in his cabinet.[2] Secondly, it inspired the seminal account of foreign policy making by Graham Allison, with types of foreign policy responses modelled on this crisis.[3] Thirdly, even though the Soviets seemed to have pulled back their ships bearing what were thought to be missiles to Cuba, it made the Cubans themselves seem like heroic underdogs who had sought only a means of defending themselves against huge US might.

This reputation of defying US might was augmented when a key person in the Cuban Revolution, Che Guevara, went to fight (unsuccessfully) in what is now the Democratic Republic of Congo in 1965—in the midst of the chaos and anarchy that had descended upon the country after its fraught independence in 1960 and the 1961 assassination of founding Prime Minister Patrice Lumumba.[4] Cuba, for many in Africa, began to seem like a patron and ally—especially, in the Portuguese colonies, where there was no prospect of independence from a conservative and stubborn government in Lisbon. The early Cuban poet, Jose Marti, who died fighting in 1895 in a war against Spanish colonisation of Cuba,[5] was an inspiration to revolutionary leaders and poets like Angola's Agostinho Neto, who became the first president of Angola in 1974 after a bloody war of liberation from the Portuguese. Some of Neto's favourite lines from Marti were:

Do not bury me in darkness
To die like a traitor
I am good

And as a good man
I will die facing the sun.

And there is recognisable echo in Neto's own poetry:

In me exist lives which never were
I see light where there is only darkness.[6]

Apart, however, from expansive Portuguese colonial territories in Angola and Mozambique, where wars of liberation raged, there was also uprising in the smaller territories of Cape Verde and Guinea-Bissau on the western side of Africa—militant in the case of Cape Verde, but military in the case of Guinea-Bissau. There too, leaders of rebellion turned to Cuba. But the two territories had very different histories and demographics. Cape Verde consists of ten volcanic islands in the Atlantic, totalling 4,000 square kilometres (1,500 square miles). It was uninhabited till the 15th century when it became a base and haven for pirates, privateers and their slaves. Guinea-Bissau, by contrast, was historically part of the deeply structured Mali kingship, and covered 36,125 square kilometres (13,948 square miles). Local rulers benefitted from the slave trade and were powerful enough to confine the Portuguese, their customers and would-be colonisers, for some time to the coastline before Portuguese strength was able to dominate the territory.

Portuguese colonialism was more like the French than the British system. The colonies were technically regarded as parts of metropolitan Portugal with certain limited political rights conditionally accorded to some adult inhabitants. The process of assimilation, engineered primarily through education, and which included membership of the Catholic Church and the acquisition of Portuguese habits and values gave, very unevenly, various recognitions—but almost never full political rights or political equality. It was much less than the French accorded the elites that had gone through a Francophonic formation, as evidenced in the case of Senghor. Even so, this did echo a restricted but relatively liberal history of racial interaction whereby, even in Portugal itself, a black person could exceptionally rise to knighthood and courtiership in the king's court. João de Sá Panasco in 1535 accomplished this—but he did have to start as the court jester.[7] And, although a country like England hosted an ambassador from Morocco during the reign of Queen Elizabeth I, and Shakespeare cast Othello as a tragic mercenary admiral in Venice, there is no uncontested record, notwithstanding conjectures, of a black knight or nobleman in Britain itself.

But insofar as education was a key indicator of whether a person could aspire to an approximation of rights in Portugal there was, as in France, access given to metropolitan universities in Portugal to those from the colonies. Thus Neto studied medicine in Lisbon, and Amílcar Cabral, who came to lead the independence struggle in Cape Verde and what is now Guinea-Bissau, was born in Cape Verde and went to Portugal to study agronomy. It was, to be sure, a form of elite formation for purposes of assimilation, but it also produced a handful of liberation leaders who were highly educated. And it still meant of course that the vast bulk of the population in the colonies remained without rights. There was vast inequality in terms of income and rights to control production for distribution—and, forms of inter-racialism and miscegenation notwithstanding, persistent racial discrimination.

But the university education in agronomy meant that Amílcar Cabral conducted a liberation struggle that had a technocratically thoughtful character that was unique at the time in all parts of Africa.[8] That education, in Lisbon, was meant to facilitate assimilation into Portuguese customs and inculcate a sense of being Portuguese even in Africa. But, in bringing students from different locations together in a vibrant city that, all the same, was under a national conservative dictatorship, what it did was to encourage a Lusophonic (Portuguese-speaking) pan-Africanism. It also brought the African students into contact and collaboration with Portuguese students who were profoundly antipathetic to the right-wing government. Cabral met Neto in Lisbon and, with him, later helped found the Movimento Popular Libertação de Angola (MPLA)—so, although liberation movements were founded with specific territories in mind, the idea of liberation was one of a collaborative struggle or, at the very least, struggle in solidarity with other struggles. Back in Africa, Cabral founded the *Partido Africano de Independência da Guiné e Cabo Verde* (PAIGC) in 1956—the same year as the foundation of the MPLA—so liberation in different parts of Portuguese Africa had a common genesis.

From 1963, the PAIGC waged war against the Portuguese colonisers in Guinea-Bissau, then Portuguese Guinea. The rest of Africa had, by that stage, begun achieving independence. The first post-war independence was that of neighbouring Ghana in 1957, and Kwame Nkrumah gave permission to Cabral's guerrillas to establish training bases in Ghana. The training was not only military. Cabral saw the importance of good communications with people living in contested territories—and particularly with local chiefs. How to speak to chiefs became part of the curriculum. But, above all, he taught his commanders and soldiers how to educate and encourage local farmers in better agricultural techniques. The guerrillas would also help the farmers in ploughing their land. The increased produce was distributed throughout the rural areas on a trade-for-barter basis and used a pricing system that was more competitive than that of colonial stores. Travelling doctors also tended to the population.

The result of this kind of thoughtful approach meant that Cabral's PAIGC was able to control a large part of Guinea-Bissau—not just in terms of denying control to the colonial administration, but in terms of a form of sustained public administration.

Cabral travelled to many foreign countries seeking support. One of these was Cuba. It is the speech he gave in 1966 to the first Tricontinental Conference of the Peoples of Asia, Africa and Latin America in Havana that led many people to identify him as a Marxist. Other speeches and writings followed, but the lengthy Havana speech seemed defining. It was entitled, *The Weapon of Theory*. It might have equally been entitled 'The Pragmatic Use and Nuancing of Ideology', for, when analysed closely, this is what the speech did. But it, above all, cemented his reputation as an intellectual as well as a fighter. Fidel Castro hailed him at the same conference as "one of the most lucid and brilliant leaders in Africa [...who has] instilled in us tremendous confidence in the future and the success of his struggle for liberation."

Cabral began his speech with a conspicuous courtesy.[9] Instead of asking Cuba for help at the outset, he offered to help the Cubans. The Cuban missile crisis of 1962 was still painfully remembered in Cuba. It had already overcome the botched CIA invasion at the Bay of Pigs. Cuban solidarity with others was in a sense a weapon against siege.

And a weapon against the effects of exodus as many Cubans fled across the sea to Miami and other parts of the USA, taking labour capacity and expertise with them. Cabral said, "we guarantee that we, the peoples of the countries of Africa, still completely dominated by Portuguese colonialism, are prepared to send to Cuba as many men and women as may be needed to compensate for the departure" of such people. Cabral spoke of people from Guinea-Bissau and Angola who were slave-shipped to Cuba, but the new generation would come to help Cuba as free people. The *politesse* of the offer was, of course, to establish a sense not just of solidarity but historical kinship. Africa, but particularly Angola, would in the 1970s and 80s come to depend on the Cubans, particularly for military support to roll back the juggernaut of the South African Apartheid armies.

Cabral then pointedly said that he would not rail against imperialism. Words and insults would not defeat imperialism. Struggle would. But he then said that a fundamental part of that was a "struggle against our own weakness"—and that weakness was established on "the expression of the internal contradictions in the economic, social, cultural (and therefore historical) reality of each of our countries." This allowed him, in a very carefully prepared speech, to elide into an analysis of Guinean class formation in a peculiar history. It allowed him to use a Marxist vocabulary to describe something uniquely Guinean, and something pertaining to a "national" liberation, a term which he emphasised, and what was "national" required "detailed knowledge" of it. One might admire the "fine and attractive" accomplishments of other revolutions, but national liberation and revolution were not "exportable commodities". His courteous genuflection to Marxist vocabulary allowed him to express a fundamental humanism within a specific history and a specific approach to liberation.

The Marxist approach to revolution is predicated on three key factors: the means of production; the formation of classes determined by access to and control over production; contestation among these classes with the mass mobilisation of the 'working class', as the key engine of productivity, leading to revolution. The concept and widespread practice of production is essential in all three factors. By production is meant industrial production, or production with forms of organisation associated with industry. Class formation is determined by control and subservience in the production process. At stake are control and lack of control over material inputs and material benefits from production. And contestation involves a search by the mass of hitherto subservient workers in the industrially productive process to reap fair material benefit against smaller classes that are exploitative by reason of their acquiring greater rewards from the productive process than is warranted by their input which, in any case, relies upon coercive lessening of rewards to other classes. The basic Cabral argument was to do with, in Guinea-Bissau, with its subsistence agricultural economy and the lack of industrial productivity in any properly recognisable Marxist sense; the lack of material rewards in the absence of uniform and recognisable forms of exchange; and the lack of class formation with recognisable forms of economic exploitation, and material deprivation of others. In a subsistence economy there are, in fact, none of the artefacts and mechanisms of a formal economy which demarcates the processes of production, acquisition and deprivation. Input and output are not measurable and have no critical mass. Analysis becomes anecdotal.

Cabral proposed an entirely new approach to class and class formation.

> Does history begin only with the development of the phenomenon of 'class', and consequently of class struggle? To reply in the affirmative would be to place outside history the whole period of life of human groups from the discovery of hunting, and later of nomadic and sedentary agriculture, to the organisation of herds and the private appropriation of land. It would also be to consider—and this we refuse to accept—that various groups in Africa, Asia, and Latin America were living without history, or outside history, at the time they were subjected to the yoke of imperialism. It would be to consider that the peoples of our countries, such as the Balantes of Guinea, the Coaniamas of Angola and the Macondes of Mozambique, are still living today—if we abstract the slight influence of colonialism to which they have been subjected—outside history, or that they have no history.

This does not mean there are no productive forces or modes of production. It means that class formation does not have to be tied in any absolute sense to the model derived from European industrial economic and productive history. To insist that it should would be another form of imperialism in itself. But the major radical element of Cabral's view of history lies in the development and the roots of class in Guinean society—away from the bulk of the population living a subsistence existence in the countryside—roots within an urban petty bourgeoisie, both of bureaucrats and those assimilated into the formal commercial sector. Without this development, there could not be the subsequent development of an urban working class. The latter is generated by the former. Similarly, as the formal economy spreads to the countryside, the development of private agricultural property generates the development of a rural proletariat. Both phenomena go hand in hand with an increase in productive forces and, in this way, classes and class struggle can be born. This does not follow the pattern in European economic and industrial history and, indeed, the process may never become industrial. But, as Cabral said, it is the "inalienable right of every people to have its own history, and the objective of national liberation is to regain this right usurped by imperialism, that is to say, to free the process of development of the national productive forces." Without this objective, a liberation movement may be anti-colonial and anti-imperialist, but will not be struggling for national liberation.

But this view has a major implication. If it all depends on the generative power of the petty bourgeoisie, it is the role of the revolution firstly to encourage its formation as a class, and then drive this bourgeois class to a crossroads. It must develop to a sufficient extent, and itself help generate a working class that will, at a certain point of its development, seek revolution and liberation. At that point the bourgeoisie must either oppose revolution or join it—committing suicide as a bourgeois class as it does so.

What Cabral does not deeply argue in his speech is the articulation of interaction between the imperial power and these processes of development. The imperial power certainly seeks to use the bourgeoisie as its instrument and as something to serve its administrative requirements for successful colonialism. But it too seeks a role in the history of the nation it has colonised. It is not, at any stage, an unchaperoned development of the working class. In fact, in the case of Cape Verde and Guinea-Bissau, two things happened. Firstly, it was people like Cabral himself, highly educated, who could call themselves members of the bourgeoisie that had decided to commit suicide, if not of an entire class, of themselves as members of that class. But Cabral had reached that position by studying in the imperial metropole, and it was his liberation movement that developed the peasants, through modern agricultural knowledge, into a productive force. Secondly, insofar as the produce of the peasants was exchanged, not for money so much as in a trade and barter system, there never really was any development of a formal means of exchange. So the idea of productive force was never measurable in economic terms, but was a social phenomenon. And it was, in any case, the bourgeoisie—people like Cabral—who led the peasantry in quite a short struggle for liberation, rather than developed in any long process of history.

Within Cabral's own thought and work were contradictions. But the use of a Marxist-seeming vocabulary to impersonate Marxist stages of history while begging to differ from its traditional actuality was, in Cabral's case, a presentational master-stroke. Fidel Castro, who would have faced a not-dissimilar situation in his Cuban revolution, might well have appreciated a simulation of Marxism that, all the same, depended on the leadership and education of a bourgeois elite. He himself had been a lawyer; his legendary comrade, Che Guevara, had been a medical doctor. What made it all stick together in Cabral's case was his insistence upon the role, not just of local productive forces, but his location of them within culture.

He might have discoursed on The Weapon of Theory in Havana but, a little later, in 1970, he perhaps more properly spoke of history as a weapon—by which he meant the history of a nation's own culture and its role in national liberation.[10] This speech was delivered at Syracuse University in New York State and was startling for the stark dichotomy with which it began. But, even before the dichotomy, he drew a stark comparison between the colonial master and Goebbels, the Nazi master manipulator and suppressor of truth and culture. Cabral said that the colonising power, in order to retain everlasting control, had only two choices: either a genocide of all subject peoples to prevent any possibility of resistance and rebellion—the method of Goebbels—or to assimilate cultures of subject peoples into something that exists in harmony with metropolitan modes of colonial domination—a culture not only of compliance but one that actively seeks to be like that of the coloniser.

The quest for education to accumulate marks of progress towards being awarded political rights, rights that invoked the political performance of loyalty, was what Cabral lamented. He would have been against the Booker T. Washington model, the so-called 'Atlanta compromise', that accepted, for the time being, second class citizenship if education was guaranteed. But would he also have been against Senghor, his contemporary, so immaculately educated in the highest style of France that he became a French government minister? Yet Senghor led his country to independence. And, of course, as intimated earlier, it begs a question of Cabral himself, of Neto, as to how far one becomes educated in a metropolitan fashion, how far one becomes assimilated at least into a professional mode of conduct—before one is rescued by the declaration and practice of self as a rebel and as a liberator.

But Cabral is not saying that the metropolitan culture of the colonial power is in itself bad; he is saying that the culture of those who by right own the nation should be elevated into something better—not something inferior. The 'negritude' of Senghor and Césaire tried to do this, but sought to do so as a demonstration of depth in culture as culture. Cabral relates culture to forces of production, and thus makes it part of his theory of history. He noted that production can only be related to cultural impulses and structure, so these things go hand in hand. To own one's own culture therefore means that one owns one's own productive capacity and one's own development. It is within this that national liberation resides and, in this conjuncture, there resides a profound humanism as opposed only to a materialism.

Cabral was assassinated in 1973. Speculation still abounds as to the identity and origin of the assassins—whether rival elements within the PAIGC or Portuguese agents. Eight months later, Guinea-Bissau declared independence. Cape Verde became independent in 1975, along with Mozambique and Angola, following the Portuguese revolution that overthrew the Salazar regime that had insisted upon retaining the colonies. But it meant that the two countries, part of one liberation struggle—that, all the same, always had its military epicentre in Guinea-Bissau—were never united in independence but entered international relations as two separate states. Cabral had been a Moses figure, dying on the banks of the Jordan before being able to set foot into the promised land—but the promised land itself became sub-divided.

Having said that, there is an often overlooked or under-emphasised aspect to the effect Cabral had—and that was not on African or Cubans, but upon Portuguese conscripts called up to fight in the colonial wars. With strict censorship, no one in Portugal knew how many young soldiers were dying—although anecdotal evidence from village after village, tales of sons of the village coming home in body bags, began to mount. But, while a student in Lisbon, Cabral had associated not only with other members of the African diaspora, but also with student groups opposed to the conservative regime of President Salazar. It was a regime that was at least proto-fascist, if not actually fascist, and liberties at home were strictly rationed. Portugal was the poorest country in Western Europe. It was regarded as the economic basket-case of its day, the most backward and least modern country of Europe. The call of the Africans for liberty echoed in the thoughts of disgruntled young Portuguese students and workers and, above all, in the thoughts of young army recruits sent to the African wars. The Movement of the Captains that led to the 1974 coup, the Carnation Revolution that overthrew Salazar, was profoundly influenced by the thought and writings of Cabral with their clear modern ideological reference points, their concepts of national class development, and their application in the productive forces within territory he took from the Portuguese. The young captains knew they were fighting against an intellectual and his words on national liberation were a spark to their own desires for national liberation in Portugal.

Without Cabral's metropolitan formation, his words would not have been expressed in terms that were meaningful to the young captains. But this emphasises once again that Cabral was a man who traversed cultures Finally, the national culture of liberation was an international culture of liberation. One of my former colleagues, Professor David Birmingham at the University of Kent, wrote copiously and deeply about Portugal and the nationalism of the colonies.[11] When he heard that the Carnation Revolution was under way, he immediately smuggled himself into Portugal where, trying to appear inconspicuous in the Lisbon crowds, he was astonished that the young soldiers riding by on their tanks were throwing into the crowds hastily translated copies of his own writings, including on Cabral. "Here is the truth!" And this added to the sense of internationalism. To speak as he did in Havana and Syracuse, to inspire a successful uprising in Guinea-Bissau, to help inspire a revolution in Portugal, Cabral was simultaneously a man born in Cape Verde, who fought in Guinea-Bissau, but whose African political thought spoke a global as well as local language.

Insofar as Cabral used a language that was simultaneously international and local, while claiming the primacy of the local, he was not alone in what might be called a humanism in which, as in his Havana speech, he refused to throw rhetorical rocks and insults at imperialism and the agents of imperialism. This refusal to do so was in part what earned him respect from the young Portuguese captains. The revolution had to be won across a number of fronts. But he was not alone in beckoning towards inclusiveness, as the case of Kenneth Kaunda in Zambia demonstrates.

The Contradictions of Militant Pacifism

Although Guinea-Bissau is ethnically diverse, two specific groups—Fulani and Balanta—constitute 50% of the population. Three other groups constitute almost 30% of the rest, so that the smaller ethnic groups are for the most part each under 3% of the population. However, a significant unifying factor was that Creole was spoken as a first language by about 50% of the population, and as a second language by almost everyone else. Also, given that Cabral, with his emphasis on productive forces implied at least in part a common material basis to culture, he had entry points to all groups.[12] Critically, the Portuguese idea of assimilation, whereby selected Africans were offered high levels of education, meant a technocratic leadership that was able to suggest at least, if not offer, a sense of progress with liberation. There was no such impulse towards assimilation or advanced education in Zambia. It would have been harder to do in any case. The contrast with Zambia and its 72 ethnic groups, and 72 languages,[13] spread over a larger overall population and a much larger geographical area is immense.

Northern Rhodesia, as Zambia was called in the colonial era, was the product of the corporate colonialism of Cecil Rhodes. Chief among Rhodes's objectives was to secure mining revenues. There was no policy or effort of elite formation and assimilation, and the 'natives' were treated essentially as a labour reserve, educated to the level where they could be of service to the white settlers who came, in part to Northern Rhodesia, but mostly to Southern Rhodesia (now Zimbabwe), where there were rich farmlands, even if not the scale of mining possibilities Rhodes had found in South Africa. The Rhodes corporate colonialism extended northwards across all three countries of what are now South Africa, Zimbabwe and Zambia. The mining potential of Northern Rhodesia, however, was only partially realised because of infrastructural and access problems—so even the provision of limited education to service the mining sector was not vigorously pursued as any sort of national priority. Zambia came to independence in 1964 with between 99 and 109 university graduates, and a secondary school system that was two-tiered and biased against equal treatment of those black students who had made it through to that level—with, in any case, only 0.5% of the population having completed primary school.[14] In such a situation, someone who had attended teacher training college was an intellectual.

With 72 ethnic groups, not counting white settlers and the descendants of Indian indentured labourers, without a national elite or petty bourgeoisie, the independence president, Kenneth Kaunda, had no choice but to develop a set of values which he called national, saying they were derived from common practice, but which were designed to transcend many cultures and divisions.

In Northern Rhodesia, compared with Southern Rhodesia, the future Zimbabwe, there was little overriding sense of being part of Britain. Notwithstanding an appeal to British 'standards' and habits, born as much out of nostalgia as metropolitan loyalty, the outlook of white settler communities was that they were forging a new land. And they were fortified in the sense of white community in any case by the greater number of white settlers in Southern Rhodesia, and the clear sense of a whites-only government in South Africa—and to a lesser extent by the Portuguese colonies of Angola and Mozambique that flanked Northern Rhodesia west and east. In short, the sense of white supremacy could be given reinforcement in the most literal sense at short notice. Cecil Rhodes had built a road and rail network that linked the north and south of all three countries of Northern Rhodesia, Southern Rhodesia and South Africa. These were vertical networks, i.e. Northern Rhodesia, for its contacts and exchanges, its trade with the outside world, was dependent on the goodwill and transport cooperation of the white south.[15] Even if there had been lateral networks, Angola and Mozambique remained—despite wars of liberation—governed by a stubborn Portugal at the moment of Northern Rhodesia's independence as Zambia in 1964. But all this meant that Kaunda had to forge a national black unity in the face of a resident united white identity. He had been able to achieve independence without a liberation war—although strikes and street demonstrations certainly featured. His leadership of the nationalist movement was recognised by the colonial authorities and the actual transition to independence was, certainly by comparison to the Portuguese territories, calm.

The deeper sense of national culture that Kaunda, as founding president, sought to inculcate will be discussed more fully in the next chapter, where his sense of culture—and, above all, autochthonous culture that was truly independent, truly home-grown and authentic—will be compared to the national culture Julius Nyerere sought to elucidate and instil in Tanzania. In 1964, however, storm clouds were already looming over the moment of Zambian independence, and they spoke of white rebellion and insurrection against the British Crown in Southern Rhodesia—wishing to follow continued white rule as in South Africa, rather than give way to black majority rule as in Zambia. White rebellion meant military means to avoid all obstacles and reprisals. So, a mere year after independence, Zambia faced an armed south that could also, by means of control of transport links, economically squeeze Zambia into acquiescence. In fact, this aided Kaunda in his project of a national culture and added to it a sense of a national liberation that could not be regarded as complete until the neighbouring countries had also been liberated. National purpose and consolidation came about to a large extent because of defiance against the values of white supremacy.

But the new Zambia had no real armed strength to speak of. The army and, above all, the air-force were in a rudimentary state. A firefight with the white south would leave such Zambian forces (as existed) defeated. If we treat Southern Rhodesia, simply known as Rhodesia after the white Unilateral Declaration of Independence in 1965, as part of the project of liberation, then, like Cabral, Kaunda had to fight a most thoughtful war of liberation.

It was an adroit combination of tactics and stratagems that Kaunda used.[16] Firstly, although he did increase the size and capacity of his defence forces, they were ordered, despite any provocation, not to fight or fight back against the Rhodesians. They were a deterrent in name, although scarcely in practice—with notable exceptions as we shall see later. Secondly, he offered to host the exile headquarters of liberation groups from Rhodesia, South Africa and South West Africa (now Namibia, then governed with the practice of racial discrimination by South Africa). This was a point of principle to assist liberation—although the size and activities of these groups were closely monitored, certainly at first. Even so, the exile offices were of great benefit to Joshua Nkomo's branch of the Zimbabwean struggle, and Zambian soil was used as the base for his Soviet-supplied and equipped guerrilla army; to South Africa's African National Congress (ANC) as a genuine point of regional coordination (Thabo Mbeki visited often to accomplish exactly that); and to the South West African People's Organisation (SWAPO), the Namibian movement, who established, through the UN, its university-in-exile in the Zambian capital of Lusaka.

Thirdly, although Zambia suffered military reprisals from the Rhodesians, Kaunda's adroit diplomacy and mobilisation of international support ensured pressure on the South Africans, and through them the white Rhodesians, to limit the scale of their reprisals—economic as well as military—against Zambia, for fear of a regional conflagration and, above all, for fear of reducing the diplomatic support upon which Apartheid South Africa subsisted. That support was tied to Western interests in South African minerals and the country's strategic location, commanding the waters around the Cape of Good Hope in the Cold War years with their competitive posturing between NATO and Soviet navies.

Fourthly, the Zambian role in the region was framed in terms of moral and political philosophy. Kaunda cloaked all this, partly out of pragmatism but certainly out of belief, in the ideology and 'national culture' of Humanism—which we shall discuss in the next chapter—but which sought in his foreign policy at first to marry principle, in the face of military pressure, with pacifism. What was the source of his pacifism—if not only in pragmatism? Kaunda had a profoundly Christian upbringing. Even so, the example of India's successful struggle for independence rang loudly to him, especially its largely pacific nature. Zambia had an Indian population that, as in many East African countries, was descended from indentured labourers and later migrants. In Lusaka, the Indian community clustered together in a suburb known as Kamwala—on one side of the rail tracks near what is now the centre of the city. At one stage when Kaunda was on the run from the colonial authorities—he had been imprisoned more than once for distributing 'seditious literature'—he was offered shelter amongst the Indian community in Kamwala. It was the last place the authorities thought of searching—there was meant to be a social distance and a degree of mistrust between the Indian and African communities. The legend was that, hiding under a safe-house bed as the police patrols nevertheless rolled by, Kaunda was given reading material—and this included works by Gandhi.

This was far from a fanciful story. I once questioned him directly about this and he affirmed it without mentioning the bed. Gandhi, despite recent revisionism that touts his supposed racism when in South Africa, had a profound influence in the region. Moeletsi Mbeki, Thabo Mbeki's brother, told me that, in his family's house, their father Govan had two portraits on the mantelpiece: one was of Marx and the other Gandhi. The influence that Gandhi had on liberation activists and thinkers was immense, not least because he had defeated British colonialism, but had done so within recent memory, winning independence from Britain in 1947, and was therefore an immediate inspiration. But the way he did it was profoundly important to Kaunda. Could he fight, as much and as far as possible, a pacific liberation? The Gandhian philosophy and methodology of *Satyagraha*, passive as well as nonviolent resistance, was a product both of thoughtful belief on Gandhi's part, and also one of the basic calculation that he could not defeat superior British military force with force of his own. The literal meaning of the term, *Satyagraha*, involved a holding steadfastly onto truth, but was also meaningful in giving Gandhi's followers a sense of moral courage. Their cause was a moral and truthful one.

Before discussing whether he could or not, there is the important note that Kaunda was grateful to the Indian community. Unlike in many other African countries, there has been no significant hostility towards Indians in Zambia. Kaunda ensured there was an Indian minister in his cabinet, and successive government cabinets have regularly had ministers of Indian descent. This is not unlike what has occurred in post-Apartheid South Africa, with its immensely inclusive national constitution, conferring a range of equalities unlike those seen in any other constitution in any other part of the world or at any time up to the present day—including to those of different sexual orientations. Perhaps some part of this derives from Mandela's time on the run, when he was sheltered by a gay man and the escape route was manifested under the guise of Mandela as the chauffeur for his white (gay) limousine-owning 'employer'. National liberation was for equality that went way beyond black and white.

The end of white rebellion in Rhodesia, which started in 1965 with the Unilateral Declaration of Independence and the statement by rebel Prime Minister Ian Smith that "never in a thousand years" would there be black majority rule in his country, came in 1980. Military stalemate and encroaching guerrilla victories drove Smith to the negotiating table and, at Lancaster House, London, at the end of 1979, a formula was found for majority rule elections in early 1980. The precursor to Lancaster House, a Commonwealth summit in Lusaka earlier in 1979, saw Kaunda at his diplomatic best in cajoling Margaret Thatcher and other Commonwealth leaders to agree possibly peaceful means to end the military struggle. That was hardly Kaunda's first effort at mediation and negotiation. The 1975 summit between himself and the South African Prime Minister Vorster, in a railway carriage parked across the border line on the Victoria Falls Bridge that linked Rhodesia and Zambia, with the border painted half way down the length of the carriage, with neither leader crossing onto the other side, was famous for its symbolism but produced no tangible result.[17]

A bitter war of liberation had been fought from the 1970s, but particularly in the second part of that decade, with two liberation armies representing different nationalist parties in the field. Robert Mugabe's forces operated out of Mozambique, after that country's own fought-for independence from Portugal—the 1974 Carnation Revolution in Portugal giving independence in 1975 to Mozambique as well as other territories such as Angola and Cape Verde, and recognising the self-declared independence of Guinea-Bissau. Joshua Nkomo's forces operated out of Zambia, with a higher grade and range of equipment than that possessed by Mugabe's soldiers, capable for instance of shooting down airliners—which occurred with much loss of civilian and non-combatant life. The violence of the years of Liberation struggle in Zimbabwe—military war, loss of innocent life, the hosting of armed liberation groups—offered huge contradictions to Kaunda's ambition to fight pacifically.[18]

It also caused resentment and occasional defiance within his own armed forces—by now very much less rudimentary than they had been at independence. There was now an airforce with modern warplanes, but the pilots were expressly forbidden from taking off to engage Rhodesian planes attacking targets on Zambian soil. The most infamous attack came in 1978 and wiped out at least 1,500 guerrilla soldiers. A Rhodesian wing of Hawker Hunters circled over Lusaka airport, and its commander, identified as 'Green Leader', courteously requested air traffic control that no Zambian interceptors should engage his planes. Some of the pilots in his wing were less courteous, hurling accusations of cowardice at the Zambian pilots. The Zambians obeyed orders but were so incensed that afterwards the air force commander, General Hananiah Lungu, took off alone in his own fighter-bomber, flew across the border, and dropped smoke bombs the full length of the Rhodesian military airfield—very much as a "we would have taken you on if we had been allowed to" gesture of defiance.[19]

Zambia suffered not only from such military incursions, some of which hit central Lusaka directly—in the form of commando raids as well as air strikes—but suffered huge deterioration of its economy. British and international economic sanctions against Rhodesia were passed directly on to Zambia. Importing food from the white south whenever Zambia's harvests failed or were erratic became a Rhodesian and South African means of leverage against Zambia. Internal development slowed down. Richard Hall called it "the high price of principles".[20] Navigating all these pressures, contradictions, choices and policies—and turning a blind eye to General Lungu's solo expedition (in fact, Kaunda later quietly awarded him a promotion)—involved a moral contemplation best expressed in his book, *On Violence*, which was published in 1980, after Zimbabwe finally achieved its independence.

Zimbabwean independence didn't mean an end to the challenges facing Kaunda and his pacificism. South Africa was still ruled by Apartheid. The ANC cadres living in Lusaka were still subjected to hit squads. My own was itself part of the safe-house network when ANC intelligence had word of an impending commando raid. Zambian soldiers were involved in engagements with South African troops crossing Zambia from the Caprivi Strip into Angola, still riven by civil war, in order to outflank MPLA positions. Zambian soldiers told me then that they went into battle hyped on mustard. Swallowing a lot of it made you angry and fearless, just as US troops in Vietnam used amphetamines to heighten their responses and Mugabe's liberation soldiers used marijuana to calm their nerves (the marijuana being distributed on one occasion by General Solomon Mujuru, the guerrilla field commander, himself).[21] War never went away as stories of military engagement continued to swirl in Zambia. And, at the moment finally of possible Namibian independence, under a fragile plan painstakingly brokered by the US and UN, everything was placed in imminent peril of unravelling as South African troops engaged SWAPO guerrillas whom they viewed as breaking the ceasefire in 1989. Zambian troops had been unofficially embedded with the SWAPO guerrillas so that Kaunda could receive first-hand reports of whether or not the peace plan was working, and many died. The stories of the survivors again added to the constant whispers that war was not over. Even so, with adroit UN intervention, Namibia did achieve independence in 1990.

In 1984, in Lusaka, carefully planned negotiations of a confidential nature began between South African emissaries and the ANC. Kaunda knew what was going on and encouraged the process. But it was not till 1988 and the Cuban victory at the Battle of Cuito Cuanavale in Angola and the withdrawal of the South African army from that country, that talks about transforming the region from its violent past began—and Kaunda was the first to meet, in August 1989, the new South African leader, F.W. de Klerk. Their meeting was not on a bridge this time but on the Zambian side of the Victoria Falls. Nelson Mandela was released soon after in February 1990.

In all of this volatility and the comings and goings that prioritised negotiations, but which were very often far from pacific, Kaunda's book on violence is a signal testament to his attempt to think his way through the moral contradictions he had to navigate on a policy basis every day.[22]

The book was not well received internationally; some reviewers regarded it as trite.[23] Even the *Christian Science Monitor*, in its attempt to endorse the book, could only appear lukewarm.

> Still, it is beneficial to all humanity when a world leader seeks to sort out his thoughts on an important subject and give them systematic expression. Given the rhetoric of last year's presidential campaign, Americans might wish their leaders were moved to make similar attempts.[24]

Part of the problem was Kaunda's effort to declare an African ethics while also using the language of Christianity—of which he was a devotee. So the rigour of definitional work was largely lacking from this book, as the *Christian Science Monitor* pointed out.

> Dr Kaunda restates the proposition that, when applied as policy, racism and colonialism are forms of violence. Not only are they supported by symbols of legitimacy (however fictitious), by legal systems, and by police forces; they also do violence against subject peoples through assumptions of superiority and control of the news media and the educational system. The Zimbabwe situation showed Dr. Kaunda that subject peoples can challenge these subtler forms of violence only by the crude form of guerrilla warfare.

> If Dr Kaunda were an academic, some of his ideas might have been tested by criticism as well as events. Had that happened, his notions, for example, about when a guerrilla is or is not a terrorist would be more precise.

> And there might be more clarity in communicating across the cultural gulf. He does say: "If there is one thing the African people are good at, it is forgiving their enemies," but this is the one moment when he allows himself to suggest the important cultural differences between

Africans and Westerners. More attention to these differences might have made the book more useful to American readers.

Having said that, Kaunda did use generalised class terms to make a key point: namely, that colonial ruling classes imagined themselves as somehow heroic while laying "a grievous burden... on the rest", meaning the colonised.[25] This leads to the essential dichotomy expressed in his book, one based on self-imagination, and the imagination of the rest of the world in terms of oneself, and the refusal to emancipate the rest of the world because it would first require a breakout from the narrowness of oneself. Here he uses a central case example of the World Council of Churches and its 1970 decision to give grants to liberation movements engaged in militarised struggle.[26]

It is important to note that this WCC decision gave Kaunda his own self-justification as to why, as a pacifist and a Christian he had decided to support, although not directly himself, wage war. It was, as it were, an institutional approval for his decision as a Christian to support liberation movements at close quarters, and also to invite in effective terms military retribution that impacted on his own people and economic retribution that impacted upon his entire country. But, having thus made use of the WCC decision, Kaunda then proposed his thoughts on moral dichotomy—not in fully defined and academic terms, but in robust and immediate terms to do with what he and his citizens faced and endured. To this day, Cabral is debated in university classrooms, but Kaunda is not. Regardless, both were liberation leaders in a real sense.

Kaunda lambasts Western 'myths' about the liberation struggle in Southern Africa. "I rejoice in that WCC grants are helping to combat the notion that the white minority government, in trying to exterminate the freedom fighters, is defending Christian civilization against a militant paganism that has spread across the rest of Africa. According to this fairy tale, Pretoria is a besieged fortress from which a holy war is being fought to uphold Christian values and standards."[27] So, for Kaunda, the WCC established not only a proper outlook but a powerful corrective of what was really Christian and what was not.

Essentially, Kaunda proposed that the weight of moral force towards pacifism was finally less than the weight of the moral impact of suffering caused by lack of liberation. The moral relativity here becomes a question in a proper Christianity. Even so, the decision to move from a declared pacifism to open support for wars of liberation had been a painful one for Kaunda. Again, he proposed a counterweight to himself: "I believe my country has been betrayed and tricked and misrepresented so much during the UDI conflict that had I not had a reservoir of idealism on which to draw when the going was toughest I would by now be so bitter as to be in danger of losing my very soul let alone my fitness to be a national leader."[28] Here he means that duplicity, largely on the part of the British, was a much greater moral failing than his decision to abandon the moral principle of pacifism. He emerges more moral, at least in relative terms. But he was absolute on a key principle as he justified his support for both the liberation war in Zimbabwe and the continuing struggle in South Africa: "We will never, never rest until Africa is wiped clean of the foul stain of apartheid. We cannot live with it, or come to any accommodation with those who impose it on the black masses of South Africa."[29]

Kaunda himself never wrote poetry. But the South African exile, Lewis Nkosi, who lived in Lusaka in the 1980s, did.[30] As a man of letters, Nkosi did not specialise in poetry, but one of his seven extant poems, *Images of a Nation Yet to Be*, was published in *Sechaba*, the ANC literary journal. In it, he praises Lusaka as the host of liberation movements:

> They came to Lusaka
> Amandla came
> They came to Lusaka
> Power to the People!
> They came riding on a wind of fire
> …They came
> The wizards of an unstoppable army.[31]

But, if writers like Nkosi and ANC fighters were grateful to Zambia, Kaunda himself sought to reconcile his contradictory outlooks. Almost as if to redress his moral lapse in condoning and supporting war, he reverts to a Christian forgiveness at the end of *On Violence*, almost a sanctimoniousness. It is an anti-climax. "So unless we are able to forgive the enemies who cannot possibly make up to us for what they have done we go stark raving mad with bitterness and hatred."[32] But, again, it expresses a simple dichotomy—bitterness or forgiveness—and, in a sense, forgiveness is proposed not only as the restoration of a Christian virtue, but simply as something easier to do.

Basically, Kaunda uses dichotomy as a form of moral reasoning; he considers dichotomy as a philosophical method, even if others saw it as a generalised and simple one. In a very real sense, it was an almost fundamental, or fundamentalist, rendition of Christianity with its foundation attributes in the Book of Genesis of Good and Evil, and its later Middle Ages rendition as the Manichean 'heresy'—in which God and Satan co-existed and the universal struggle was in terms of being pulled relentlessly between the two.

But Kaunda did not simply have his dichotomous categories as static oppositions. They were dynamic. And, in terms of the dynamism of colonised people, the sophisticated part of Kaunda's work is the notion of how one creates an imagination of oneself. The African as free and the African as authentic in culture and capacity as the foundations to being free—these were key elements in Cabral's thought, also. But, after liberation has been won and independence established, can this be done within a national (and therefore institutional and public administrative) context? Or does this finally lead to the greatest contradiction of all—the collapse of a certain self-imagination, as it is suppressed by national order? Or does, at that point, a pragmatism take place—a pragmatism which was always a background value, a recourse when thought led one into too many contradictions? We will approach answers to such questions in the next chapter.

3

THE NEW AFRICAN MAN

THE POLITICAL THOUGHT OF TRANSFORMATION

The new African 'man' because, at the moment of independence, the role of women was not conceived as on the verge of radical change, except that women would partake in the new directions and destinations to which men led. No great African leader of the mid-20th century proposed a radical agenda for equality between men and women. (The continuing need for such an agenda is discussed later in this book.) Even so, the impulse was one of transformation, particularly given the sense of escaping from the 'civilising' strictures of colonialism. In their place was to be a new capacity for individualism and a new capacity for community that was not Eurocentric.

In this chapter, we shall look at transformational trajectories in independent Ghana, Tanzania and Zambia—led by leaders with distinct but, in many ways, similar philosophies, all of which they sought to express in writing. There will also be a brief look at what was attempted less successfully in Uganda. But all three main examples finally were unsuccessful. They were all noble and pioneering, but all relied on a process of enforcement, whereby philosophy and one-party state coercion and restrictiveness became uneasy bed-fellows. Ghana was the first to become independent in 1957—leading the way in all sub-Saharan Africa with the exceptions, as we have discussed, of Ethiopia and, problematically, Liberia. Tanzania became independent in 1961, Uganda in 1962, with Zambia following in 1964. In that same year of 1964, Ghana became a one-party state, but it had been preceded in doing so by Tanzania in 1962. Zambia became a one-party state in 1967, two years after the white Rhodesian Unilateral Declaration of Independence and the beginnings of the state of siege described in the last chapter.

Ghana's Nkrumah called his philosophy 'consciencism'; Tanzania's Nyerere called his *ujamaa*, and Zambia's Kaunda called his 'humanism'. Their examples in Africa, about morality and the value of an individual as well as communal personality, were not alone in the world. *Ujamaa* (Swahili) may be translated as 'familyhood' or 'brotherhood', but the detailed enunciation of *juche* (self-reliance) in North Korea in 1965 spoke to a widespread effort to reconfigure human experience, orientation, and community along autochthonous lines. The Cultural Revolution that began in China in 1966 demonstrated the desire to re-establish not just human philosophy but the cultural foundations of human experience. And, of course, there was the immense precursor of Gandhian philosophy to do with truth and non-violence that defeated British colonialism in 1947; not to mention the earlier effort at Soviet Marxism-Leninism that, no matter how totalitarian it became, thumbed a nose at the hegemony of Western thought and ethics.

The independence leaders of Ghana, Tanzania and Zambia had different backgrounds. Insofar as Nkrumah's overlapped with the USA of W.E.B. Du Bois and Marcus Garvey, and was deeply inflected by his experience of racial discrimination in the USA and his observations of how black Americans had struggled against it, not just in the politics of civil rights but in the cultural expressionism of the Harlem Renaissance, his thought echoed Garvey's ideas, and to an extent, Césaire and Senghor's sense of cultural negritude in a way that was not apparent in the work of Nyerere and Kaunda—both of whom were influenced by British intellectual currents, notwithstanding their declarations of authentic thought. Indeed, the British left greatly admired Nyerere and Kaunda's efforts, as did the Scandinavian countries who supported Tanzania even when *ujamaa* was manifestly failing—the Swedes in particular because they saw a similarity with their own senses of centralised social democratic provision—and, in Britain, influential members of the Labour Party and *New Statesman* groupings, i.e. particularly therefore the Fabian wing of the Labour Party, such as Lord John Hatch, redirected the term used by Plato, 'philosopher king', to refer to Nyerere and Kaunda. It was almost as if there was a mad rush to reverse, in one fell and unthinking (certainly uncritical) swoop, some centuries of perception of hearts of darkness and savagery. Having said that, at the time, Nkrumah, Nyerere and Kaunda were all widely considered to be thinkers as well as leaders.

Nkrumah

In 1935, Italy once again invaded Ethiopia, having been earlier defeated in 1896 at the Battle of Adwa. Now, under the rule of the ambitious Benito Mussolini, a far better equipped Italian army thrust its way towards Addis Ababa. Emperor Haile Selassie's impassioned plea in June 1936, shortly after the fall of Addis, for protection from the League of Nations had no effect—and the League's failure in this case, as well as its inability to protect China from Japan's conquest of much of the country, meant the end of the League and a reformulation of international organisation after WWII in the form of the United Nations.[1] But, at the start of the invasion, a young Kwame Nkrumah was in transit from Ghana headed towards the USA for university study—mainly financed by borrowed money—when he heard the news of the invasion of Africa's one historically independent country—and was outraged. It was a defining moment in a life devoted to African unity and strength.

Nevertheless, the Nkrumah that arrived in the United States had to live a very frugal student existence, washing dishes in greasy spoons in order to eke out his funds and coming to understand the location of a black person as a member of an under-class.[2] He attended a largely black institution, Lincoln University in Pennsylvania—which was in itself representative of a moment in US history of specialist provision for black education.[3] Its founders, John Miller Dickey and his wife Sarah Emlen Cresson, were liberal (and courageous) white people with religious backgrounds. Dickey was a member of the

American Colonization Society that had helped inspire people like Edward Blyden, whose work we discussed in Chapter One. Dickey was a strong supporter of the effort to settle Liberia with black migrants from the USA but he was also mindful of the need to educate black people who remained in the USA to a high level. Chartered as the Ashmun Institute in 1854, it had changed its name to Lincoln University in 1866, after the assassination of President Abraham Lincoln. Although it expanded its mission to be multi-ethnic and multinational, it continued to attract a majority black student body. Langston Hughes, the American poet, and Thurgood Marshall, the first black American Supreme Court judge, studied there; and, even before Nkrumah went up to Lincoln, so did Nnamdi Azikiwe, who would become the first President of Nigeria.

Nkrumah graduated from Lincoln in 1939 and took a degree in Theology before taking two Master's degrees at the University of Pennsylvania, including one in philosophy. He also lectured briefly at Lincoln and was elected President of the African Students Organization of the United States and Canada, thrusting himself into a wide range of contacts and influences and, indeed, mentors. Among these were C.L.R. James and Marcus Garvey. He met and had a long correspondence with James, the author among other works of *The Black Jacobins*, about the black slave revolt in Haiti that sought to create an independent state; and was influenced to an extent by James's form of Marxism and Trotskyism. But it was Garvey, whom Nkrumah never met, who inspired in him the idea of 'return' to Africa—basically continuing the thought that had led to the formation of Liberia as a state—but spreading its vision to encompass the entire hinterland of continental Africa, i.e. the idea of Africa as a home. The idea of black personality enunciated by Garvey, as described in Chapter One, helped inspire Nkrumah to his own philosophy of Consciencism, discussed below.[4] The Harlem Renaissance of the 1910s to 1930s had exemplified that idea of black personality, where, in New York, a huge explosion of black art and music occurred.[5] It was, as it were, an American expression of what Césaire and Senghor later called 'negritude' by, exemplifying the depth of black culture as an equal to that of European culture.

Having said that, much of the history of Garvey's influence on Nkrumah tends towards the exclusion of all others.[6] We have already mentioned C.L.R. James, but there are at least two other important influences: before he went up to Lincoln, Azikiwe was a profound influence upon young students in Gold Coast, Ghana, such as Nkrumah; Aikiwe's sense of pride and black nationalism was highly formative of the young Nkrumah, who met Azikiwe and was inspired by him to study at Lincoln, where he himself had been.[7] The other influence came much more towards the last dozen years before independence, and that was the thought and mobilising energy of the Caribbean activist and intellectual George Padmore.[8] Nkrumah joined him in organising the 1945 Pan-African Congress in Manchester, which was the decisive breakthrough in black debate that thenceforth urged decolonisation and combined black liberty with black nationalism and independence. Padmore gave an organised sense of what a pan-Africanism could look like, bringing figures as seminal as W.E.B. Du Bois and the young firebrands of the first generation of African state leadership, such as Nkrumah himself and Jomo Kenyatta of Kenya, to Manchester. With influences from the USA, from the Caribbean, from the UK, and from Africa itself, the word 'pan' was an encompassing one but, from the time of Manchester onwards, it meant the organised unity of independent African states, and the first objective was to achieve independence. If independence was a clear goal, unity was a diffuse one, with a sense of desirability hanging over it but no clear agreement or plan as to its structure.

But this meant two things. Firstly, independence was hard-won in many African countries and was achieved in different years with different levels of development, of—as we have seen—education, and national infrastructure. Making a country work was going to be hard. Making a continent cohere would be very much harder. Secondly, no matter what pan-African aspirations were held by the nationalist leaders, once back home, they had to campaign in the face of colonial impositions, suffer imprisonment, and at the same time somehow try to convince the population at large that the effort was worthwhile. There was no guarantee the project of liberation was universally shared or shared in the same way. Of course, this condition gave rise to the sense that a cohering philosophy was required in each country.

However, when not in prison or under other restrictions, there was no guarantee that crowds that had gathered to hear public speeches from the aspiring leaders agreed with all aspects of the visions or programmes being promulgated. Ayi Kwei Armah, in his bleak but plangent novel on Ghanaian corruption, includes a scene of ridicule against would-be leaders who spoke as if on high. Henry Bienen made the same observations about the reception of ideas, even within his own party, by Julius Nyerere.[9] In the face of slowness to move forward towards the vision together, the resort to authoritarianism became almost a norm.

Once back in Ghana, arriving in 1947 after his US education and after the 1945 Pan-African Congress in Manchester, Nkrumah was briefly arrested in 1948. After his release, he set about building himself a power base amongst cocoa farmers, trade unionists, and students—and even appealed to women, although without any specific feminist agenda—and formed the Convention People's Party (CPP), which rejected the colonial government's effort to fob off the clearly mounting call for the franchise; the British colonial authorities offering a limited property-based franchise of the sort rejected earlier in the USA by W.E.B. Du Bois. Nkrumah's stormy rejection of the compromise offer led him to organise strikes and civil disobedience—and led to his imprisonment again in 1950.[10] The interesting thing is the tactic of civil disobedience. Gandhi had obviously employed this in his campaign against British colonial rule. And Martin Luther King was to inaugurate an entire strategy based on civil disobedience from the Montgomery bus boycott, which began in December 1955, onwards. Nkrumah preceded King in this case, but both drew not only from Gandhi—King openly admitted his debt to Gandhi—but from one of Gandhi's intellectual mentors, Henry David Thoreau,[11] almost the quintessential American philosopher whom Nkrumah would have studied as he read for his Master's degree in philosophy at the University of Pennsylvania. His celebrated essay on civil disobedience was starkly simple in the framing of its argument:

> The authority of government, even such as I am willing to submit to—for I will cheerfully obey those who know and can do better than I, and in many things even those who neither know nor can do so well—is still an impure one: to be strictly just, it must have the sanction and consent of the governed. It can have no pure right over my person and property but what I concede to it. The progress from an

absolute to a limited monarchy, from a limited monarchy to a democracy, is a progress toward a true respect for the individual.[12]

The principle of the consent of the governed was used to good effect by Nkrumah's CPP followers and a wide range of the public in striking and civil disobedience as he began his three-year prison sentence. It did not take long for the British to concede the desirability of an election held under general franchise. Essentially, it was a concession based as much on the force of argument as the weight of disobedience. Even though Nkrumah remained imprisoned throughout the election, the CPP won by a landslide, taking 34 out of the 38 electable seats. Nkrumah was released, and the British Governor asked him to form a government. He was named Leader of Government Business, but this was changed in early 1952 to Prime Minister. He immediately requested independence. That took another five years to be granted but what it meant was that, although Ghana was the first black sub-Saharan country to attain independence from a colonial power in 1957, it had actually attained self-government in 1952.[13]

The 1960 Ghana constitution made Nkrumah President, Ghana a republic, and had a provision to cede sovereignty to a Union of African States. All seemed on course, as the initial years of independence saw much progress and development. Prospective civil servants and, from 1964, other students were required to take courses of 'ideological orientation'—although it was not fully defined what this ideology might be. It had elements of socialism and non-alignment but was essentially a humanism that proposed itself as African in origin. Nkrumah was overthrown by a military coup in 1966 but, even in exile afterwards, sought to articulate his beliefs and compose them into a philosophical unity. In one speech, he laid out his essential humanist principle:

> We know that traditional African society was founded on principles of egalitarianism. In its actual workings, however, it had various shortcomings. Its humanist impulse, nevertheless, is something that continues to urge us towards our all-African socialist reconstruction. We postulate each man to be an end in himself, not merely a means; and we accept the necessity of guaranteeing each man equal opportunities for his development.[14]

But its reference to African 'principles of egalitarianism' was not borne out by historical practice. For instance, the mighty Ashanti Empire was hierarchical, feudal, and slave-owning.[15] The idea of egalitarianism was a search for an ideational framework for a cooperative society—and for an African version of the socialist state. But certainly not fully in line with egalitarianism in Nkrumah's own time, Ghana became a one-party state in 1964, with Nkrumah declared President-for-Life. By then, the economy had started greatly to fluctuate and deteriorate, partly because of volatility in world cocoa prices—with the dissatisfaction of cocoa farmers with Nkrumah's response of effectively withholding income from them—and mismanagement with ambitious but poor economic planning.[16] Nkrumah had also, from as early as 1958, shown increasing signs of authoritarianism. He had declared strikes illegal as early as 1955, even though they had helped him defeat the British authorities. He began to arrest opponents and detain them without trial. The one-party state and his elevation to a lifetime Presidency finally all proved too much for his people to take. The military coup was widely popular in Ghana.

However, there is one particular work, written before his fall while he was still president and seeking to impose ideological training upon students and civil servants, that stands out from the others. He died in 1972, so he did not live long after his ouster. Some of his writing on class war and socialism—accomplished in exile in Guinea Conakry—is mechanistic, seeking to impose laws of history on a world seen increasingly in material terms. I once asked his son, Gamal, about these and their deterministic qualities of thought. He would not comment but did make a facial expression that seemed to be token recognition, at least, of what I was saying. I make this observation by way of contrast to Nkrumah's greatest intellectual legacy, his book on 'Consciencism'.[17] This is vibrantly written and humanistic, idealistic, and is a key part of an intellectual genealogy that began with the black American thinkers in Chapter One, but seeks to take this genealogy into the future.

Even here, however, the humanism which we shall discuss is linked with the materialism of his exile writings. Its foundation is materialism impregnated with egalitarianism and an ethical view of man. Having said that, the central theme is to do with an African personality and a consciousness of it. In this Nkrumah to an extent foreshadowed the work of philosopher Valentin Mudimbe, who later wrote of an African *gnosis* or knowledge, self-knowledge, that was yet in the process of becoming fully unveiled or discovered—the intellectual history of which included people like Senghor. In this process it was important that Africa did not invent its own, in Edward Said's term, 'orientalism', did not create its own exotic myth about itself.[18] Nkrumah was also a descendant of a genealogy of thought that had begun with the writing of Edward Wilmot Blyden, and was a crucial theme also in the work of Marcus Garvey; so, if a myth, it had begun some years before. But Blyden's thought was compelling in his circumstances of discrimination and denigration: "if you surrender your personality, you have nothing left to give to the world ... to give up your personality would be to give up the peculiar work and the peculiar glory to which we are called."[19]

What, however, was this personality? Blyden's sense of it was of something conciliatory, gentle and supple—an opposite of the white man's domineering traits. It was, in short, cooperative and egalitarian, and it is perhaps from Blyden's influence that Nkrumah insisted upon an inherent and historical egalitarianism in Africa, despite a huge array of vertical and hierarchical forms of social and political organisation throughout the continent, not least in the history and practices of the Ashanti people with their empire in what became Ghana. And, after attaining self-government, Nkrumah moved to drastically prune back the power of the chiefs, so that vertical obedience to them would not impede his vision for the new republic. In the Nkrumah view of African personality, this was something that had to be given institutionalised political expression to protect it from the "various shortcomings" of the past, and the baleful influences of colonialism, including Christianity.

For Nkrumah, this involved a nine-point programme:[20]

1. What is important is the thought rather than its written articulation.
2. In Africa, there are (i) a traditional way of life, (ii) Islamic tradition, and (iii) Christianity and Western culture used as parts of the colonial project.

3. In the traditional way of life, there were no sectional interests. These came with colonialism.

4. True independence requires a new and true harmony that can forge tradition, Islam and Christianity into a humanist ideology that speaks from the depth of African thought and culture, from African consciousness, and thus Nkrumah proposed 'consciencism'. Such an ideology would be the springboard for thoughtful development that would be meaningful in Africa.

5. The restoration of African egalitarianism requires socialism.

6. It must be a socialist response to the African environment and the living conditions within it.

7. Philosophical consciencism must fit the African personality.

8. The cardinal ethic of consciencism is to treat each man as an end and not as a means.

9. The enemies of this ethic, philosophy and ideology are colonialism, imperialism, disunity and lack of development.

Each of these statements is problematic. The ideas of humanism and egalitarianism were taken up by Kaunda, although he was deeply Christian; of a responsive socialism grounded in the African experience, by Nyerere; but treating each man as an end was corroded by the imposition of one-party states—the ends becoming party coherence and party-directed political and developmental policies. But three other key elements remained problematic. Firstly, as noted above, much African historical and cultural experience was hierarchical, feudal and therefore sectional; moreover, in a vast continent of some 2,000 languages, there was no starting point for unity. Secondly, if the thought is more important than the written script, what was the point of Nkrumah's writing, if not to capture and express something not easily expressible if left silent? Silence would not lead to development. But, with 2,000 languages, there are 2,000 modes of epistemological reasoning, or at least articulations of reason. As Kwame Gyekye wrote about the Akan language, widely spoken in Ghana, true understanding of Akan culture would depend on understanding the language.[21] Thirdly, although Blyden wrote his masterwork with a key theme on Islam and Africa, Islam's entry to sub-Saharan Africa was also one, hundreds of years before the advent of European exploitation, of slave trading, conquest, and sometimes forcible conversion to Islam. The religion became deeply embedded and has in many ways become 'Africanised', although differently in, for example, Senegal and Tanzania. The same might be said of Christianity as it partakes in a syncretic alliance and transformation in many parts of Africa today—with, all the same, sometimes strong links to American Pentecostalism, for instance.

Having said that, what remains special about this work by Nkrumah was its aspiration. Notwithstanding the degeneration of Ghana's economy, which he could not reverse—and which left problems that were only successfully addressed by one of his successors, Jerry Rawlings, many years later (see Chapter Five)—the political fate of Nkrumah, his being cast into exile despite being the father figure of African liberation and the desire for unity, makes this book of aspiration also somewhat heroic.

Despite its faulty arguments, for example in its historical referents, what was key was its refusal to accept a European 'orientalism' of Africa. The risk was an orientalism of his own. But the idea that the African personality must cohere within its own recognisable psyche, free of imposed conceptions from the West, while simultaneously the African continent in all its diverse parts should seek a political unity, was certainly a heroic aspiration. It continues to speak to an Africa deeply divided today, not least between Islamic and other claims of authenticity, but between states and within states. Nkrumah would have hated the comparison: a flawed and tragic hero along almost Shakespearian lines. But Julius Nyerere, who translated Shakespeare into Swahili, would have seen a grim but apt likeness.

Nyerere

Julius Nyerere, leader of Tanzania from independence in 1961 until 1985, was a man of letters, not unlike Angola's Agostinho Neto. He published both poetry and his own translations of Shakespeare into Swahili. The Shakespeare play most notably associated with Nyerere's output as a translator was *Julius Caesar*.[22] That play, of course, involved the assassination of Caesar, the debate on power versus the wider republican good, good and consent, rebellion and

53

ethical sanction for it. One could have almost applied it directly to Nkrumah. But it was published in 1963, just as Nyerere moved what was then called Tanganyika into becoming a one-party state. It had become self-governing under Nyerere in 1960, independent in 1961, a republic with Nyerere named as President in 1962 and, almost immediately after the institution of a one-party state, Tanganyika amalgamated with Zanzibar in 1964 to become Tanzania. In a very particular way, the amalgamation was accomplished as an exemplary step towards an eventual continental union of Africa. In other ways, it was much easier than continental union, insofar as Swahili was a language common to both territories. It also allowed a union of a predominantly Islamic territory, Zanzibar, and the mainland with its combination of African and Christian religions. It was almost like a laboratory test case of what Nkrumah later advocated in his work on Consciencism. It also allowed the territory as a whole to claim a written history because Swahili, with its Arabic influences, had a rich written literary tradition, which allowed from the start an alternative to European written histories.

Despite the sense of seeking an authorial 'independence' from the Western literary canon, Nyerere's work on Shakespeare was culturally important. It opened the possibility of cultural engagement when Shakespeare was removed from the school syllabus even in conservative neighbouring Kenya. Alamin Mazrui writes of how Kenyan President Daniel Arap Moi had him restored to the syllabus.[23] Although this was some years after Nyerere's translations, it shows how a fervent debate had grown up around literary authenticity. Even Alamin's namesake, Ali Mazrui, said that translations by themselves, unless fundamentally rewritten works that went far beyond mere translation, could not be considered Swahili for a school curriculum.[24] To a certain extent, Nyerere pre-empted even this sort of debate by inflexions of an almost ideological kind. As well as *Julius Caesar*, he translated *The Merchant of Venice* using the Swahili words, *Mabepari wa Venisi*, which may be rendered as 'the bourgeoisie of Venice', perhaps prefiguring a class analysis which he never really developed.

Nyerere would also have been aware of how groups throughout Eastern Africa, including Tanzania, had absorbed various Western influences such as big band and accordion music, not only for entertainment (and religious purposes, e.g. the Salvation Army) but for the specific purpose of satirising the white colonialists. The syncretic and adaptive nature of culture was apparent in a succession of these adaptations and movements.[25]

Unlike Nkrumah, Nyerere was able to complete his higher education (Economics and History) under a scholarship—at the University of Edinburgh. He went up in 1949 and became the first Tanzanian to complete a degree in Britain and only the second to do so at any university in the world outside Africa. The British approach to higher education for Africans differed considerably from that of the French and Portuguese, notwithstanding the creation of universities in Nigeria (Ibadan) and Uganda (Makerere)—but the emphasis was not at all on bringing African colonial subjects to study in Britain. Nyerere was treated kindly at Edinburgh and imbibed a Presbyterian Scottish sense of socialism as a duty. Like Kaunda in Zambia (see below), he was greatly influenced by the developments in social welfare thought in post-war Britain in the late 1940s and 1950s. Thomas Molony argues that exposure to key thinkers in British socialism profoundly affected his still developing ideas about the nature of the state and its relationship to citizens.[26]

What this meant was a sense that the state had an obligation to provide for its citizens in a socialistic manner. For Nyerere, this became much more important than authenticity in the literature syllabi of schools. As with Cabral, authenticity was by way of practice in production and the cultural organisation of production. However, unlike in the case of Cabral, he was prepared to enforce it rather than use mere encouragement. Cabral had taught his soldiers how to speak persuasively to the chiefs. But as with Nkrumah, Nyerere did not seek to go through the chiefs and traditional modes of social organisation—Nkrumah lessening quite significantly the power of the chiefs—but to do so through the new state under the single party. Thus, when Nyerere came to articulate the thoughtful details of his philosophy and policies from 1967 onwards, it was not simply the enunciation of a philosophy but that of a compulsory national project. And that was the point: ujamaa (literally: 'extended family') sounded very attractive to his British and other Western admirers[27]—they had, before the Arab-Israeli wars at least, lent the same admiration to the kibbutz movement in Israel, but the kibbutz movement was not compulsory. It was voluntary. *Ujamaa* was mandatory for those working the land. It was a socialist egalitarianism, as laid out in the Arusha Declaration (below). The policy was the end in itself, not the citizen as an end in himself. This was so because the practice of cooperative and communal farming was declared in Nyerere's philosophy to be 'African'. It became a state-led and directed 'African-ness', compulsory because it was deemed authentic. Authenticity was the end in itself.

Nyerere's 1967 Arusha Declaration embodied the directions in which he wished the country to go.[28] As a one-party state, Tanzania had no real choice but, as a national entity, to follow. What did the Arusha Declaration say? The objectives were stirring, with the state's role, mentioned in the last two paragraphs, being regarded as necessarily instrumental in ensuring these objectives are met.

(a) That all human beings are equal;
(b) That every individual has a right to dignity and respect;
(c) That every citizen is an integral part of the nation and has the right to take an equal part in Government at local, regional and national level;
(d) That every citizen has the right to freedom of expression, of movement, of religious belief and of association within the context of the law;
(e) That every individual has the right to receive from society protection of his life and of property held according to law;
(f) That every individual has the right to receive a just return for his labour;
(g) That all citizens together possess all the natural resources of the country in trust for their descendants;
(h) That in order to ensure economic justice the state must have effective control over the principal means of production; and
(i) That it is the responsibility of the state to intervene actively in the economic life of the nation so as to ensure the well-being of all citizens, and so as to prevent the exploitation of one person by another or one group by another, and so as to prevent the accumulation of wealth to an extent which is inconsistent with the existence of a classless society.

It is important to understand that the Arusha Declaration was one made in the name of Tanganyika African National Union (TANU), Tanzania's single party, it represents the party creed, described in fact as a 'faith', and it is the party that henceforth directed the state in ensuring the Declaration's objectives were met. Notwithstanding debate over the worthiness or otherwise of the programme enunciated by Arusha, the fact was that there were no checks and balances in ascertaining whether the party got it right, either in strategy or day-to-day application. No encouragement was given to any development of national expert civil society, and local civil society could not get in the way of party operatives. The party was meant to be one of workers and peasants, particularly peasants, but the party infrastructure and, indeed, its hierarchy revealed a chain of command rather than any flat-line equality of input. It was, to all intents and purposes, a Leninist party that saw itself as a mass organisation that subsumed all civil and civic organisations to itself, and government departments as being under it.

The Arusha Declaration nevertheless expressed a belief in democracy, but this could only be limited within a one-party state. It affirmed faith in socialism, but one that was peasant-based. Peasant agriculture was more important than industrial production. This had henceforth to be production within a centralised socialist system, notwithstanding earlier efforts by peasants in some regions to participate in the capitalist economy.[29] Above all, TANU and, through it, the government had to be honest and free of corruption. The main points of the Declaration on this were:

- All leaders had to be uninvolved in anything capitalist or feudal.
- They could not own shares in companies.
- They could not hold directorships in private companies.
- They could not receive more than one salary
- They could not own houses that they rented to others.

To this extent, society was to be made as flat-structured as possible, certainly in terms of proximity in terms of income possibilities between leaders and ordinary people. And, indeed, for the first years of Tanzania under Arusha, the income differentials nationally were smaller than in any other African country. It was this that, above all, engendered international support for *ujamaa*, even as the agricultural policies began to fail. And they failed because of the effort at 'scientific' relocation of entire rural and peasant communities to new locations that would purportedly be better for agricultural production. But this meant uprooting from traditional or culturally important, even merely sentimentally important, locations. It caused huge resentment on the part of many peasant communities and, consequently, a loss if not collapse in morale and support for the party's policies.

But the apparent honesty of the leadership, seemingly evidenced in a flat social structure where even elite public persons clearly did not live luxurious lives, continued to elicit support from outside Tanzania while, inside, support ebbed and, because Arusha had discouraged industrial development, no fall-back production could act as an economic cushion as agricultural production tanked. Increasingly, Tanzania had to rely on foreign aid from sympathetic governments. As early as the 1970s and 80s, this was increasingly from Scandinavian governments as others began to lose faith in Tanzanian policies.[30] But this was, in itself, antipathetic to the Arusha Declaration, which had devoted entire paragraphs to the desirability of not partaking of foreign aid.

And, as corruption did finally increase, not least because of the leakage possibilities of foreign aid, the party (renamed Chama Cha Mapinduzi in 1977) became less a vanguard with mass aspirations and more a power-occupying elite. Since the return of multiparty democracy in 1992, it has won every election, not least because of the power of incumbency but also because vested economic interests and party interests have coincided. Parliament, with a weak opposition, has not been any real check or balance.[31] A capitalist economy has now taken root, and industrial production has been strongly encouraged.

The writings of Nyerere have sought to explain and justify his policies, and, indeed, it has to be said that failures and slow development notwithstanding, until his death, he never lost the respect of the majority of his people. They believed his honesty and that he sought to be properly philosophical in a fatherly and guiding manner. *Mwalimu* (teacher), as he was called, evokes a reverence for someone above ordinary people, in this case at least because of his wisdom and not his wealth. Wisdom, even in its failed application, was revered more than the fact he held power. This is a considerable tribute to a noble aspiration, at least.

There is a difference between Nyerere's emphases and those of Nkrumah. Nyerere's vision was less to do with the 'African personality' so much as the African character in an organised setting, hoping that real or imagined communalisms from older times could sit easily within their impersonation by a tightly controlled party. That 'character' of the Tanzanian people protested the impositions of Nyerere's party, but recognised the impulse as thoughtful—even if wrong.

Obote

The aspiration, and prestige, in being seen as thoughtful was strong in many parts of Africa, and, as we shall see in the next chapter, if not thoughtful, then 'authentic'. But some over-reached themselves in seeking to deploy the image of thoughtfulness and quickly came to use it as a cover for authoritarianism. Milton Obote (who led the country initially from 1962 to 1971), of Uganda, next door to Tanzania, who was in power for a lesser time than Nyerere, left no residue of thoughtfulness, and certainly not in terms of anything that had national subscription and adherence in the time of his violent successor, Idi Amin, who deposed him in 1971. Those who opposed Amin did not do so based on Obote's thought. And, indeed, it was the thoughtful Nyerere who finally overthrew Amin in 1979 by force of arms. Family and brotherhood came to nothing in the face of the power politics of the region. After Amin's fall, Obote again held power from 1980 to 1985 but, by then, no longer even pretended to prioritise any political philosophy.

Unlike Nyerere and Kaunda, Obote did not stress an African communalism, Nor did he, like Nkrumah, stress the necessity and power of an African self-consciousness. The British Labour Party very much inspired him in its approach to the nationalisation of key public services and centres of production. His sense of the 'common man' was almost akin to the working-class hero of British left self-consciousness.

Uganda, like Nigeria, had posed the British colonisers questions that they addressed by applying their formulae for governing the

Indian Raj, and that was by way of incorporating kingship structures into their colonial public administration. Like Indian Maharajas and princes, Nigerian and Ugandan kings were awarded knighthoods and treated with dignities unknown in places like Tanzania and Zambia.[32] Universities, for instance, were founded in both Nigeria and Uganda. John Iliffe makes the basic distinction in his magisterial study of African systems of honour and dignity between kingship societies and those of a more horizontal form of organisation.[33] The British sought to exploit these kingship societies with their well-established chains of command. In the doctrine of 'divide and rule', it was important to have those who could actually rule—by virtue of long tradition and acceptance of their rule. The problem with Uganda was not just one but several kingship structures. This meant histories of rivalry, but it also meant societies with hierarchical and vertical lines of social and political organisation that meant Obote could not refer to an egalitarian African society and ethos. What he could do was to ally himself with one or other of the kingship communities—although the rivalry between the Buganda and the Acholi kingdoms would wrack Uganda for many long years[34]—and seek a modernity by way of the UK Labour Party mode of nationalisation of relatively large corporate endeavour. His 1970 'Common Man's Charter'[35] took a 60% share in all major private corporations and banks, but this fuelled rampant corruption, and his populist persecution of Indian businesses, as well as his outlawing of opposition parties, created a climate of uncertainty and great economic instability.[36] When Amin overthrew him, it was widely applauded in Uganda—notwithstanding the havoc Amin himself went on to create.

But he sought to share the credentials Nyerere and Kaunda built for themselves as humanist and thoughtfully egalitarian. He was reduced to nationalisation and plunder of that nationalisation.

Kaunda

We looked earlier at Kaunda in terms of his support for liberation in Southern Africa. But he also applied his thoughtfulness to the question of nationalism and national unity—seeking to establish both sets of moral principles. We have already seen in the previous chapter how white rebellion in neighbouring Rhodesia was a unifying factor for Zambia with its 72 ethnicities. This was not enough in itself to bring together a hugely disparate nation. The British, for instance, had made separate colonial arrangements with the Lozi people of southwestern Zambia[37] where—to this day—a residual sense of exceptionalism exists. There was also the danger that two of the largest groups, the Bemba to the north, and the Nyanja to the east, would overshadow many of the smaller ethnicities. And different groups had different historical and cultural practices of social organisation—the Bemba being a kingship society that practised feudalism and slavery, and the Nyanja having a more flat structure of organisation. So the task was to bring everybody into not only one nation, with one supervening national identity, but into one mode of political and social organisation.

Kaunda composed a social philosophy he called 'humanism'.[38] It was never 'philosophical' in the scientific sense of definitional acuity and in the sense of capacity for linguistic analysis that characterised much British philosophy at the time. Following formal rules of logic, such linguistic analysis was hegemonic in the methodologies of British academic philosophy in the 1960s. But the fundamental question about logical linguistic analysis in Zambia had to be, 'which language?' If English, the rules were there but largely alien to Zambian thought, indeed everyday thought in almost all Anglophonic jurisdictions, and certainly not present in Kaunda's writing. So, outside Zambia, Kaunda's work and writings were seen more as worthy sermons on necessary ethics in the face of white rebellion and nation-building than anything 'philosophical'.

After the 1980s began, with Zimbabwe now independent, the white threat from the south still existed in the form of Apartheid South Africa. Kaunda deemed it necessary to ensure all university students were exposed to humanism. He entrusted this task in 1980 to Lord John Hatch—who had called Kaunda a 'philosopher king'[39]— but Hatch was a senior journalist writing for organs like the *New Statesman* and a Labour Party grandee; though he had held visiting university posts and been involved in adult education, he was not fully an academic; and he could bring no academic methodology to his compulsory lectures. The students at the national University of

Zambia greatly resented this imposition. They also remembered the forced closure of the university in 1976, after student protests against the Kaunda regime and its seeming support for a dissident liberation party in Angola (also supported by the USA and South Africa) that opposed the newly independent regime of Neto. Angola's war of liberation had featured three major militarised political parties, but when one achieved government, the others launched a rebellion against it. The students were also protesting the imprisonment of several student leaders for some years; and the deportation of some expatriate faculty members who had sided with the students. For them, it had meant the end of free speech in Zambia, and the imposition of compulsory humanism seemed like the beginning of directed speech. And they also noted the irony that Kaunda was directing this imposition upon the very university he had been at such pains to create immediately after independence; the university had been a point of pride, as the British had built no such thing in Northern Rhodesia, nor encouraged higher education of any sort for anyone. But, above all, in strictly academic terms, if the courses in humanism had no philosophical method, what place did they have, the students asked, in a university? Hatch's career in Zambia did not last long, he left in 1982, and Kaunda gave up on this initiative.[40]

But was humanism simply worthy sermons? If there was to be, through humanism, a new African man, was he to be also a Christian man? This became a fundamental question in the contemplation of a thought that tried to have it both ways—Christianity being to this day the greatest colonial export to Zambia, so much so that Zambia became constitutionally a Christian nation in 1996. Certainly, as we saw earlier, Christianity and its 'turn the other cheek' ethos gave Kaunda ammunition in addition to Gandhian thought to offer a pacific response to Rhodesian attacks while at the same time enabling Kaunda to offer exile headquarters to liberation movements on the 'love your neighbour as yourself' principle of Christianity.

However, the consistent binding glue of Kaunda's thought was one of equality: resistance to the British and to the white south was in the name of equality; nation-building with so many disparate ethnicities and languages had to be in the name of equality; and the syncretic nature of humanism—so-called African communal ethics and thought, socialist thought influenced by British welfare state theorists such as Laski and Tawney, Gandhian thought, Christian ethics and belief—all meant that the ingredients of humanism were themselves equal.

It was not just British members of the left who admired Kaunda's work and stand in the region's international relations. The Chinese admired him too, and they waited till 1974, until just after a state visit by Kaunda to China, during which the Chinese said he had profoundly impressed Mao before they published their own philosophy of international relations which they called the Three World Theory—in which developing countries and China were regarded as the equal of the imperial worlds of the USA and the Soviet Union.[41]

Humanism was declared the national philosophy in 1973, but Zambia had already become a one-party state in 1972, and the increasing authoritarianism of Kaunda's regime—even against dissident Christian churches like the Lumpa[42]—was what helped engender the student protests at the University of Zambia in 1976. From 1973, with an almost simultaneous fall in the global prices of copper and the huge increase in petroleum costs as a result of Arab responses to war and defeats in the Middle East meant Zambia continued to exist as an increasingly indebted nation. Kaunda had no economic thought or policy with which to stem such developments. The 1968 partial nationalisation of key industries under the 'Mulungushi Economic Revolution' meant government ownership or substantial ownership and direction of key industrial production—which, in the face of international economic emergencies, it was not equipped to direct properly. The 1969 'Matero Economic Reforms', seeking to link economics with philosophy, simply meant an avoidance of economic and technocratic thought so that the coincidence of both a one-party state and a one-nation humanism meant that a philosophy that had no acuity or methodology was meant to guide the nation in an almost compulsory manner. Insofar as Kaunda was meant to exemplify the good humanist, international supporters applauded his efforts. White rebellion in the south could be blamed for many, if not most of, Zambia's economic woes. Insofar as Kaunda's single party became authoritarian, controlling and, inevitably, corrupt—as well as resisting technocratic inputs—humanism increasingly lost its appeal to the Zambian public.[43]

Having said all that, in a Christian nation, perhaps the Christian style of sermonising was a proper attempt to take things forward. For the most part Kaunda's books were written with clerical co-authors or editors.[44] It is here impossible to divorce thought with a colonial, missionary origin from the material and colonial cultural legacy. The *chitenge* or wrap skirt, now regarded as fully traditional and national, was introduced by missionaries as an attempt to ensure female modesty in their new congregations and their communities; *nshima* or maize meal, which became and is regarded as the national and traditional staple food, was introduced by colonial authorities as a food that could be easily cultivated to feed the work-force. In this sense, Zambia is a composite or syncretic nation—just as many of its Christian churches have now acquired syncretic qualities of their own drawn from animist and charismatic beliefs and practices—so it is perhaps understandable and forgivable that the national philosophy should also be a composite, lacking definitional and analytic qualities, but composed as a means to bind a young nation through hard times.

For Kaunda, the new African man was a free man in the face of racism, but he was also a Christian man in Africa and, insofar as his idea was that the important ingredient of an economy was its moral content, its humanistic content, he could say his thinking was as modern as that of Tawney—who also influenced Thabo Mbeki—who wrote of a moral economy in ways now made once again fashionable by acolytes of Polanyi. The idea of a moral economy was certainly inflected towards the desirability of having a socialist economy, but the basic idea of people like Tawney was that the economy was not an end in itself. The economy existed to serve people and this gave it an essential moral character.

But it is important all the same to point out some of the cultural and historical fallacies in Kaunda's thought, especially when it referenced a great African communal past. Kaunda's own Bemba people were hardly committed to equality within communal life. John Iliffe cites missionary correspondence from 1590 from what is now Zambia: "There are no poor among them, because all are so."[45] But that was not the historical communality to which Kaunda referred. Finally, he sought a national future but based on a nostalgia that looked to a mythical arcadia of long ago. But his legacy is that he did indeed create a nation in which there has never been civil war, and he did in his own way stand up to the white south, and he did continue—as the noted anthropologist Rene Dumont noted when Kaunda's guest—to eat simple foods like beans (with his *nshima*); while sporting accoutrements which Dumont did not notice, in his 'simple' safari suit (from Simpson's in Piccadilly), with his handkerchiefs which he waved to rhetorical effect (from Turnbull and Asser's in Jermyn Street), with the occasional glimpse of a Rolex watch on his wrist. These are minor enough faults in the lexicon of African leaders and their affectations, as we shall see in the next chapter, and it meant that Kaunda, even in his personal taste, was—as in his philosophy—a creature of composites and contradictions. But we cannot deny his legacy in nation-building and as an enemy of racism, and it cannot be divorced from his effort to do these things thoughtfully.

4

'BIG MEN'

THE LIMITATIONS IN THOUGHT OF MOBUTU AND BANDA

The sense of an 'African personality', something not contaminated or at least determined by European norms and expectations, was a common theme—in various ways—in the writings of Blyden, Garvey, and Nkrumah. It was related to the writings and practices of Nyerere and Kaunda. It was theorised and poeticised in the writing of Senghor. All of these were, in one way or another, intellectuals called upon to be leaders. As we have seen, the drift towards authoritarianism, however, was something that was a danger even to the most thoughtful of men. And in those perhaps thoughtful but not intellectual, in those given to authoritarianism and even atrocity from the beginning? Those who sought to use the 'authentic' as a cloak?

And what about those who did not care for authenticity at all, but cared very much to be authoritarian?

The term 'big man', derived from Henry Morton Stanley, the celebrity explorer in Victorian times. Then, the exotica—the 'orientalism'—presented in his lectures, delivered in venues like London's Royal Geographical Society, would attract queues that stretched around city blocks. Stanley was like a rock star when he gave his accounts of Africa. He let nothing stop him. He was called *Bula Mutari* by his porters, the smasher of rocks, because of his expedient when-

67

ever confronted by rapids in rivers he wished to navigate of simply blowing up the rocks with dynamite. The big man let nothing stop him. He had explosive power. Independence leaders might have looked to Africa's pre-colonial societies to inform their visions of "the new African man", but this cultural legacy of the imperial "big man" and his dominance was also a powerful one on the continent.

There were certainly big men in other 20th century jurisdictions: Papa Doc Duvalier in Haiti, Saddam Hussein in Iraq and Nicolae Ceauşescu in Romania come to mind. Someone like Indonesia's Suharto was a big man who produced unusual results of economic growth—but also substantial accompanying corruption. Even so, his industrialisation policy could be said to have uplifted Indonesia, not-withstanding many deaths, notably over 100,000 fatalities caused by his invasion of East Timor. The examples that concern us in this chapter left little behind them that could be said to have taken their countries forward. In the case of Zaire, there was elite accumulation that, all the same, was not ploughed back into the development of a vibrant, employment-creating formal and modern sector. Zaire was mal-governed or not governed at all, with no nationwide public administration, and with warlords and local barons also involved in their own accumulation and disregard for human values, human rights and human life.

The enactment and emulation of this, despite any cost to human values, human rights and human life, has been called, by the Cameroonian philosopher, Achille Mbembe, 'necropolitics', the use of 'necropower'—the exercise of rule through the physical elimination of opponents. Mbembe came to widespread attention as a post-colonial thinker—something he might have resented, despite his use of the term in his highly regarded 2001 book. But he used this book to refute a still lingeringly powerful Western notion that Africa was a dark continent of madness without any sense of centre. Disparate, inchoate, it was merely half-created. In political science, it was the impression created, inadvertently, by Aristide Zolberg, writing in the wake of the Congo crisis of the early 1960s, that Africa as a whole was still a heart of darkness. Western political science has taken decades to recover from that and, the Area Studies journals aside, Africa still features very little in the specialist disciplinary journals of political science. When it does, it is as the object in someone else's foreign policy or aid policy. But, insofar as crises like that in the Congo were real, and not just instances for the creation of un-interrogated impressions, Mbembe almost had to write that, within Africa, the advent and existence of the necropolis were tangible and powerful.

Mbembe certainly had major European intellectual influences, but he takes himself beyond them, using them as an entry point to something deeper and, indeed, more chilling. Indeed, in recent work, he writes about a huge history of complex intellectual genealogies and their miscegenations. He writes about struggle as needing to be contextualised by location and history, by defined subjectivities as well as objective conditions.[1] He developed Foucault's work on disciplining and punishing, on the inscription of discipline within state apparatuses of control, on biopower. To Foucault's work, he added a category that went well beyond the structural control of the citizen. With the deployment of new weapons, the death of citizens creates 'death worlds', and this is easier than mere disciplining. But, even more, the reduction of people to one point above death, conditions of life in abject poverty and fear of death creates a world of living dead. This is the necropolis.

But necropolitics has a particular signifier also—not an exclusive one, but the signifier nonetheless, of the carnivalesque. There is a performativity, ritualization and outward show of authenticity as a legitimiser of necropower. There is a certain creativity in the realm of abuse, a certain 'domain of drunkenness' with its lack of objective rationality, and a certain 'intimacy of tyranny' as dictators hand out rewards and medals to those who served them with vigour and belief in the dictator's self-creation as a ceremonial figure of power.[2] Necropolitics becomes another idea about how power should be presented and used, and African leaders who adhered to necropolitics did so consciously. Although Mbembe was writing on Cameroon, his observations and analysis apply very certainly, if not more grandly, to the case of Zaïre, today's Democratic Republic of Congo, in colonial days the Belgian Congo.

Mobutu

Before looking at the vexatious historical circumstances of the Belgian Congo and its trajectory through Zaire to the DRC, it is well to note that the response to necropower and its carnivalesque performance can be one of anarchy and impersonation, of vibrancy, but amidst chaos, because there is no reliable public administration apart from bribery and death.

The earliest occupants of Congo were pygmies, joined by migrations of Bantu people 2,000 years before Christ. These developed kingship societies, the most powerful of which came to be the Kongo kingdom in most of what is now DR Congo and parts of Angola and Gabon. It was a princess of Kongo who, in the 17th century, petitioned the Pope to send priests to teach her court how to write so that public administration, particularly diplomacy, could be conducted in a formal fashion. She hoped the Pope would help her people against the malevolent encroachment of European power—to limited avail (the Pope did seek briefly to limit the predations of powers such as Portugal). The written correspondence on this matter and a quite extensive relationship between the church and Kongo is still archived in the Vatican today.[3] After Henry Stanley's explorations and his reports on riches there, the malevolence was fully enacted, and the Congress of Berlin in early 1885 awarded Congo to Belgium—specifically to Belgian King Leopold II as a personal possession. He never set foot in the territory, but the brutality of his exploitation and ransack became appallingly legendary.[4] So much so that even opinion in other colonial powers thought it too much and, under international pressure, Leopold had to appoint an investigative committee in 1904. In 1908, the King was forced to hand over Congo to the Belgian state—not that the policy and practice of exploitation diminished at all. So that, as the wind of change began to sweep over the continent and independence began to be granted, Belgium moved to decolonise the Congo in 1960—despite a comprehensive lack of development in the majority of a huge territory that encompasses 2,345,409 square kilometres. This was matched by a lack of public administration, a lack of highly trained or educated personnel, and a lack of public health care.

Bloodshed and massacres almost immediately erupted. The United Nations sent peacekeepers in a huge but only partially successful effort to restore calm and protection. The UN Secretary-General, Dag Hammarskjöld, died in mysterious circumstances—many remain

convinced it was an assassination by one or other of the great powers—as his plane flew over Ndola in 1961, a Zambian city near the
Congolese border. A few months before him, the democratically
elected Prime Minister, Patrice Lumumba, was assassinated—again
with many convinced that a Western superpower plot was behind
both the coup that deposed him in 1960 and his death in January
1961. Too left-wing, too inclined to look favourably towards the
Soviet Union—these were all reasons advanced as to why the elected
leader of a potentially very rich country had to go. There was, however, no lack of doubt that the West supported the advent of a particular 'big man' who helped launch the coup, then stood in the
background, before launching a second coup in 1965, which brought
him to the forefront and to power. He stayed in power till 1997. His
name was Mobutu Sese Seko, born Joseph-Désiré Mobutu, but later
in 1972 presenting himself with the full panoply of an official name:
Mobutu Sese Seko Nkuku Ngbendu Wa Za Banga—The All-Powerful
Warrior who, because of His Endurance and Inflexible Will, goes
from Conquest to Conquest, leaving Fire and Scorched Earth in his
Wake. If that was the beginning of Big Man-ism, making a name like
Bula Mutari seem modest, it was also, as we shall see, part of the
beginning of his national drive towards Authenticity. But, first came
the attributes of necropolis.

Having begun himself the practice of coups, he absolutely discouraged others from following suit. For instance, in 1966, a former
prime minister and three ministers, including the Minister of
Defence, were executed by hanging in front of 50,000 people. This
was to set an example for others. "One had to strike through a spectacular example, and create the conditions of regime discipline.
When a chief takes a decision, he decides—period." In 1968, a former minister who had rebelled was captured and, while still alive, had
his eyes gouged out, his genitals ripped off, and his limbs cut off one
by one. Mobutu did move towards massive bribery, buying off real
or imagined opponents, but those not part of the political world were
not always treated with such kindness. The 1974 heavyweight boxing
bout between Muhammad Ali and George Foreman, hosted in
Kinshasa, was a spectacular public relations coup for Mobutu. But, to
ensure public order rather than mass robberies of visitors coming to

watch the fight, Mobutu sent another example of repercussions by the simple expedient of executing 200 prisoners held in the city's main prison—no matter what their crimes had been.[5] Kinshasa was immaculately behaved as a result, and television coverage, not to mention the famous film of the event, *When We Were Kings*, depicted what looked like a modern city with many white skyscrapers.

Away from the skyscrapers, the Mobutu family stole most of the country's wealth. Even the army which kept him in power was not reliably paid. National debt skyrocketed, and the country was regarded as essentially a kleptocracy. But it was a US ally in the Cold War Years and the source of a huge amount of mining wealth derived from ores and minerals of great strategic use to the West.

Mobutu was far from unintelligent. He was simply never given the opportunity for higher education. Schooled by Catholic priests, he wrote, under a pen name, for journals and later worked professionally as a journalist. He became a friend of Patrice Lumumba and was exposed to his left-wing views and aspirations for an independent country. He even became a member of Lumumba's staff and appeared in public as his aide. As such, even though still a young man, he seemed to have impressed US diplomats. Whether later US support for his coming to power emanated from these early impressions is not certain but, once in power, Mobutu sought to carve out not only a fortune—at the expense of his country—but to depict himself as a true man of Africa. His authenticity campaign revealed his thought on how physical symbols could accomplish this.

In 1971 he renamed the country Zaire. The name comes from Kongo and means 'the river that swallows all rivers'. This was the beginning of the pro-Africa cultural awareness campaign, or the authenticity campaign. All Africans had to forego any European names and adopt African ones. Priests faced imprisonment if they baptised infants with European names. Curiously, of course, Christian priests remained a fixture in the newly authentic Zaire. Indeed, at the end of nightly television broadcasts, the signoff image was of Mobutu descending from heaven as an angel on a cloud. By day he was seen in the newly authentic attire of a (finely tailored) Mao jacket, thick-framed glasses, a walking stick, and a leopard-skin hat. It post-dated the 1966 Bob Dylan song, 'Leopard-Skin Pill-Box Hat', but the scathing lyrics probably meant something to Mobutu's critics.

The tailored jacket was similar to Nehru's crossover Mughal-court-meets-Savile-Row highly successful effort to create an authentic costume for India—although it was probably also a deliberately created alternative and contrast to Gandhi's dhoti, often ridiculed by the British. Insofar as 'authentic' costume in many parts of the world adopted Western tailoring skills, they were more products of fusion than authenticity. Zambia's Kaunda, as we have noted, had his 'simple' safari suits purchased from Piccadilly. Only Tanzania's Nyerere wore genuinely simple cloth—but all these leaders wore trousers with their jackets, and the jackets owed to modern Chinese and Indian dress rather than anything historically or culturally African. Only Nkrumah took to wearing, from time to time, traditional Ghanaian robes. Kaunda copied this, again from time to time, even though Ghanaian dress had nothing at all to do with Zambian history or culture.

In Zaire, it was not just Mobutu. All men had to forego Western suits and ties and dress in Mao jackets. Despite these sartorial symbols, Mobutu's taste remained French—if his chartering of Concorde for shopping trips in Paris was anything to go by. But did the authenticity campaign go beyond an ideology of symbolism?

Certainly, critical commentary on his motivations, especially insofar as crediting any deep thought to them, has been sparse and unappreciative in English. There is, however, some appreciative work in French and some from Zaire itself, both suggesting a link to pan-African currents of the idealism at least of symbols and, to an extent, taking his thought seriously. Mobutu himself went on record to seek to explain his motivations behind authenticity.

"For us authenticity consists of becoming aware of our personality, of our own value, and basing our action on premises derived from national realities, so that this action is really our own from the outset," he declared.

"Among the most evil consequences of colonialism one must cite the mental alienation of the colonized peoples, the negation of their being and all their values... Authenticity as we see it leads us to the rediscovery of our dignity as Zairians, obliges us to be proud to belong to the Zairian nation, proud of our cultural achievements—in brief, proud of our personality."[6]

73

He had been increasingly practising authenticity without calling it that for several years. The theoretician of the new ideology was likely a prominent and intellectual member of Mobutu's party, Mabika Kalanda—educated at the Catholic University in Leuven and founder of l'Ecole Nationale d'Administration du Congo in 1960. He published a study in 1968 on the 'mental alienation' of the black man, the Congolese in particular. Insofar as he was the 'house intellectual', he at least represented a felt need for the dignity of thought. Whether Mobutu read him deeply is another question. We discuss his work below, but, for all the linkage to thinkers like Fanon with his decolonisation of the mind, for instance, there was a question mark over Mobutu's centralisation of power, without too much dialogue and consultation, seeming more in the image of Napoleon crowning himself at his coronation than the image of a wise and collaborative African leader. It certainly gave Mobutu a political framework that he used as part of his deployment of ruthlessness. Jean-Jacques Wondo Omanyundu looks back from the perspective of today's Democratic Republic of Congo to a time, influenced by Mabika Kalanda, where the sense of national consciousness was at least given a physical manifestation in things like public dress and the naming of oneself. He writes rhetorically, but with a sense of outrage that without Mobutu's symbolisms, DR Congo had become a nation of deficit and without cultural animation:[7] Whether, however, symbolism is itself cultural animation, let alone culture, is another question. Certainly, the symbolism informed a consciousness by its visibility.

For Mabika Kalanda towards the end of the 1960s, "the situation in which the Congo finds itself has its origin, beyond the confrontation of capitalist interests with ours, in the *double deficit*, that of *historical conscience*, on the one hand, and that of *national consciousness* on the other hand, deficits which characterize the relations between the elites and the Congolese people, and between them, with their nation and their State. The deficit of the historic conscience characterizes a weak will-to-live collective constitutive of the Nation while the deficit of the national conscience explains the evacuation, in the sphere of the State, of the imperatives of the general interest and justice as equity."[8]

Kabongo Malu, a commentator on Kalanda, wrote: "Historical conscience and national conscience are concepts of cultural awakening without which the people cannot exist with dignity and freedom. *Historical consciousness is the product of History:* it establishes *man who is master of his destiny and an actor in its history.* The man, master of his destiny collectively takes hold of reality, his living space and his environment, convinced that without him, nothing can be done. We are in culture as man is coming true! Thus, *the deficit of historical and national consciousness is a crisis of culture, therefore a crisis of man,* and its main characteristic is that it is global and radiates the whole being of man, all his achievements, all his social, political and economic structures, all religious and anthropological structures, subverting them. It is enough to realize this by observing the Congolese school and university, the Congolese police and army, the administration ... All these spaces of great consciousness produce false models! Because, in such a crisis, man loses all creativity!"[9] To this end, Frantz Fanon writes: "If culture is the manifestation of national consciousness, I will not hesitate to say...that national consciousness is the most elaborate form of culture".[10]

This is, as I said, rhetorical and declaratory. However, it rings of Cabral and his concern for culture, albeit as the true engine of productivity. It rings even more so of the work of Garvey and Nkrumah, though speaking more of a national culture than an African personality. But the two are elided together, as creativity of an individual nature becomes impossible without the vehicle of a national culture. It rings to an extent of Senghor and his views of negritude and culture as a deep consciousness, with the emphasis on depth. How deeply or shallowly Mobutu took his appreciation of such declaratory affirmation of thought already in circulation is the profound question. On the surface of rhetoric, we also have the sense of symbols that may be seen superficially. But they do not hide certain key difficulties. These are what symbols by themselves cannot address.

We've seen how the question of language and its role in national identity was being confronted from Tanzania to Zambia. Mobutu, too, had to consider this—though his challenge was the place of French rather than English. Senghor retained French as the official language of Senegal, although the country also recognised 11 other national languages—but this was out of a total of 36 languages. Zaire also retained French as the official language, with four other recognised national languages—but this was out of a total of 242 languages. The choice of languages becomes, to an extent, a hegemonic exercise, if not an exercise in at least relative marginalizations. In such a situation, how can thought be authentic for all, or at least expressed with authenticity (whose authenticity out of 242 modes of expression?), especially when even the symbols—such as public dress—are declared authentic while borrowing from other cultures and Western tailoring?

As a political project, therefore, Mobutu made use of the creation of officialised authenticity, overlaid with necropower and the insistence on the 'big man' as the form of government, executing opponents as if he were blasting rocks out of water—and directing state finances to himself, his family and acolytes. He let war and anarchy overtake huge parts of Zaire and had no care that such actual state economy as existed was allowed to degenerate—so that, today, despite years since the fall of Mobutu by armed struggle in 1997 (he died of cancer shortly after), the problems of the economy and public economic administration of the country remain deep and legion.[11] War continues to stalk the land.[12] And education, upon which the future of culture as a modern force in a globalised world depends, has fallen from reliance on state provision and has been effectively privatised by citizen and civic group organisation.[13] But this means a series of disparate, if heroic, efforts at education that means the formation of a national culture with uniform roots of composition and meaning will not again seem possible.

And, as for the problem of 242 languages, a smaller Big Man, with admittedly fewer indigenous languages—none of which he in any case spoke properly, even his native Chichewa—was settled not only by recourse to an official English but also to Latin and Greek as the languages of elite civilisation.

Hastings Banda

Hastings Banda was in many ways the odd man out at the 1945 Manchester Pan-African Congress—certainly by way of retrospect when his national policies were so out of kilter with those of his erstwhile Manchester fellows. Malawi, the colonial Nyasaland, was a very poor country with no mineral resources though one of great beauty. It may be because of the lack of resources that Banda, who led the country to independence in 1964, turned it into a one-party state in 1966, seeking a concentration of focus, albeit without great economic foundation. He ruled till 1994.

He became Prime Minister in the government that came with independence, making himself President in 1966. He chose the name 'Malawi' simply because he had seen a similar name on a French map. There was no attempt, even with his country's name, at authenticity.

He decided very consciously to enter a formal relationship with Apartheid South Africa. He accorded it full diplomatic relations, and the result was a very great deal of South African economic assistance. I recall being amazed time and again by what I saw during my visits in the first part of the 1980s. The new capital of Lilongwe, until 1975 a provincial centre, had been built and rebuilt into a modern urban city under modern town planning rubrics, with grids and coherent infrastructure. It was ringed by renewable plantations of eucalyptus trees that were designed to be harvested on a rotating basis for charcoal—so that everyday cooking in households would not deplete other natural resources. There were grain storage silos of a size I had not seen anywhere else in independent Africa. South Africa had set out to make the new capital a showpiece of what non-hostility could mean. And it was, for Pretoria, a breach in the wall of continental antagonism—something with at least modest symbolism, even if Malawi was one relatively small state.

Having said that, the countryside remained mired in under-development. My every movement was shadowed by a government 'minder', and I was very cognizant of the fact that, in a small country, up to 18,000 people had been killed by Banda, on the real or faulty assumption that they were or could be enemies of his state. Up to 5,000 of these were Jehovah's Witnesses, targeted not because they were enemies of anyone, but because of their prioritisation of 'God's Kingdom' over any requirement to salute the Malawian flag. Gerald Horne, in his study of Zimbabwe, but referring to a wider Africa, noted that the 'oppositional character' of the Witnesses,[14] refusing to bow in any literal sense to governments, let alone white governments or dictators demanding symbolic displays of obedience, saw them

persecuted everywhere—but nowhere with the ruthlessness this mil-
lennial sect found in Malawi. If they were victims in a necropolis,
more objectively political enemies were also hunted down. Orton
and his wife, (my university colleague) Vera Chirwa, were kidnapped
by Malawian agents from Zambia in 1981. Orton died, deaf and blind
because of harsh conditions and torture, in prison in 1993. His wife,
held separately in the same prison, was not released until early 1994.
In her very moving memoir, she forgives Banda, and the value she
invokes is in the name of Christianity.[15] As in Zambia, Christianity
remained a key and dominating colonial legacy.[16] Imprisoned as well
was the distinguished Malawian poet Jack Mapanje, who also wrote a
memoir about his imprisonment.[17] His most telling account, however, was in his book of poems, *Skipping Without Ropes*, in which the
title poem relates a defiance of his imagination:

> I will, I will skip without your rope
> Since you say I should not. I cannot
> Borrow your son's skipping rope to
> Exercise my limbs, I will skip without
>
> Your rope as you say even the lace
> I want will hang my neck until I die
> I will create my own rope, my own
> Hope and skip without rope[18]

Although, even years later, he still lamented the use of harshness in
the prisons of Malawi[19] and the use of the 'Young Pioneers'. Much
of the necropolitics of suppression and 'removal' was conducted by
this quasi-militia youth wing of Banda's party, the Young Pioneers,
who were greatly feared in Malawi. Mapanje wrote of them as part
of deadly concertos:

> When you've never lived under
> A despot concede, you do not know
> The deadly concertos of his dancing witches:
> The Women's League, Youth league,
> Young Pioneers who whipped
> up his support.[20]

And from these poems published in 2007, many years after his release
in 1991, it is clear he never forgave Hastings Banda.

Banda fell from power when the wave towards multi-party politics swept much of Africa in the early 1990s. Neighbouring Zambia's Kenneth Kaunda had to hold multiparty elections in 1991, and lost. Banda lost likewise in 1993. He had been made Life President in 1970, but his life ended in illness and dementia in 1997. What did he stand for? At this stage, we encounter an enigma.

Educated abroad, he qualified as a medical doctor in both the UK and the USA. In the US, he earned his MD at Meharry Medical College, a Tennessee institution that catered for black students in the south of the country. There is no evidence that, like Nkrumah, he imbibed the sense of black thought and black emancipation that was a hallmark of black intellectual life in the US at that time. He took his British qualifications at the University of Edinburgh and thereafter practised in the UK. While living in London, he became a member of the Labour Party. But there is no evidence of his having imbibed the Fabian brand of socialism that impressed Kenneth Kaunda. He went from there to Ghana in the early 1950s, but there is no evidence that Kwame Nkrumah's thought influenced him. He did campaign against white rule in his country, against the federation of what are now Zimbabwe, Zambia and Malawi (called the Federation of Rhodesia and Nyasaland, 1954–63). This earned him such a reputation that upon his belated return to the region in 1958, after 42 years away, he was acclaimed as a future leader and also briefly imprisoned.

He took the title, 'Ngwazi', the chief of chiefs, or the great lion, or the mighty conqueror—its having multiple though related meanings allowed him to escape the kind of vain panoply of names adopted by Mobutu. But he also established in 1981 the Kamuzu Academy (named after his own name, which was normally preceded by his European name of Hastings), which was designed to be an 'Eton of Africa'—where Greek and Latin were core compulsory subjects. In some ways this was his pet project—a Europe, or rather European standards, in Africa.

The pause for thought this evokes suggests, perhaps, that the realisation of an African Personality or African Authenticity presupposes a foundation from which one country's can develop. It could be a utopia, as imagined by people like Garvey. It could be in reality like Ghana, Zambia, and Zaire, which all had resources—mismanaged, squandered, or whatever, there was a base from which to leverage the new world or incubate the new person. When you have nothing there is perhaps, all talk of personality and culture aside, no material base for talk and thought. You escape into a necropolis simply to prove that you can be a small Big Man.

What, however, of those who did have the power of necropolis more than any others, those with the guns and the organisation and training to use them? What about the coup artists who brought military big men to power? Did any of these have thought, having the power to attempt at least to impose thought?

5

THE COUP 'ARTISTS' AND THE
NEW NATIONALISMS ON COMMAND

RAWLINGS AND SANKARA

Military coups have been a feature of life in ancient as well as modern states. Julius Caesar's crossing of the Rubicon River into Italy was the start of his coup against the Roman Republic. Napoleon ended the bloodshed and chaos of the French Revolution by launching a coup. When he exported the ideals of the French Revolution, as enshrined in constitutional as opposed to arbitrary forms, but did so by the conquest of much of Europe, his armies evoked both fear and admiration. The young philosopher, Hegel, fleeing his university city of Jena when it fell to Napoleon, remarked—as a tribute to Napoleon—that he had seen the future, and the future was on horseback.[1] The image of the 'man on horseback', the military ruler, has echoed down to this day[2]—in Latin America (the British went to war against an Argentinian military junta), in Europe itself (where Portugal, Spain and Greece were under military rule in the post-war years, and where there were coup attempts in France), and of course in Africa.

Coups came to independent Africa within the first decade of independence. Power was seized in Nigeria and in Ghana, the two leading lights of Anglophonic decolonisation in West Africa. Tanzania's Nyerere survived an army mutiny and Kaunda survived a coup attempt. Mobutu came to power in a coup, and one which seemed to reveal the involvement of foreign powers, through the barrel of a gun, in the affairs of Africa. The 1971 Idi Amin coup against Obote in Uganda gave rise to the image of the coup leader, not as a noble man on horseback, but as a buffoon. In fact, it was the 'peaceful' Nyerere who finally took the fight to Amin, invaded Uganda, and drove him from power in 1979. But the Uganda that Amin left behind was in chaos. I was part of the international 'clean-up' initiatives and saw with my own eyes how every aspect of public life and production had been destroyed or damaged. The image of Amin, not only as governmentally incompetent but as silly, vengeful and arbitrary—ruling through necropower but far more stupidly than Mobutu—generated a view of Africa that exceeded even the 'heart of darkness' impression that was gleaned from the bloody early days of Congo's independence. In this chapter, however, I seek to redeem Africa from this view, even in the case of military rulers—some of whom took their countries very far forward and in thoughtful manners.

I have previously offered a typology of African military dictatorship:[3]

1. Ruthless, military-originated, family-based kleptomania: Mobutu of Zaire (as discussed in the previous chapter).
2. Ridiculous-seeming military splendour: Amin of Uganda[4] and Jean-Bedel Bokassa of the briefly named Central African Empire.[5]
3. Ruthless military dictatorship crudely reliant on cultural manipulation as much as force of arms: Taylor of Liberia.[6]
4. Ruthless military dictatorship with, all the same, a technocratic base: Abacha of Nigeria.[7]
5. Technocratic military dictatorship with impulses towards the return of civilian democracy: Obasanjo of Nigeria in the 1970s.[8]
6. Idealistic military dictatorship involving younger officers: Rawlings of Ghana and Sankara of Burkina Faso.
7. Incompetent military dictatorship involving younger officers: Momoh of Sierra Leone.[9]

Given this book's concern for culture and thought, we should insert a note here about Charles Taylor's Liberia. The terrible second civil war of 1999 to 2003 saw him as President of the country, whereas in the first civil war of 1989 to 1996, he had been a rebel warlord backed initially by Libya. He was US-educated—in Massachusetts—and his New England accent never deserted him. However, the atrocities credited to him, were born of a war that could be described as the revenge of the hinterland upon the descendants of the black migrants of the American Colonization Society (see Chapter One). Samuel Doe had launched a military coup in 1980 that saw the elevation to power of groups long marginalised by the migrant settlers.[10] To maintain power, Doe performed a wide range of esoteric rituals and ceremonies that were also meant to render him invulnerable. But the violence of his rule, and the equal violence of the rebellions against it, were marked by such rituals and beliefs on all sides. They were, in Stephen Ellis's term, a mask of anarchy—as they became the refuge of those who no longer held faith in any formal structures or laws. They were also regarded as expressions of authenticity, so that even Taylor, with his own US background, was reputed to indulge in such rituals, including purportedly the consumption of human flesh—although there is no direct evidence of this. But the rituals were often a condensed, even hurried rendition of the rites of transition to adulthood—and thus the capacity to go to war and to be protected during war. What would normally take years was compressed sometimes into weeks and concentrated on formulae to achieve invulnerability in battle. It mandated what seemed grotesque behaviour in war and in the preparation for war. I make this note to indicate a dark side to 'authenticity', which emerges not from intellectual enquiry and expression, but in compressed times of dire emergency and the need for survival amidst escalating atrocity—raising questions as to authenticity in the face of what? Authenticity derived from what under what circumstances and for what purpose? And with what processes save a condensation and recreation of ritual, done thoughtlessly as well as perhaps thoughtfully? The Liberia struggle is a profound test of an implied judgement that authenticity is *ipso facto* good for the African personality.

However, having said that, the two military leaders discussed in this chapter—both very young men when they came to power—were concerned, like Cabral, with technocratic thought and policy as much as anything to do with an authentic African condition and personality, except insofar as these things helped take their countries into a self-directed and progressive future. They were often taken as emulators of the left heroes of their time: Rawlings of Gaddafi and Sankara of Che Guevara. Rawlings developed his thoughtfulness very much as he went along, being driven in the first instance by idealism almost alone. Sankara had, however, imbibed much by way of thought, as we shall see, during his military training in Madagascar. Both were very dashing. They wore aviator sunglasses. Jerry Rawlings, who led two military coups in Ghana, drove around potholed Accra in an MG sports car; Thomas Sankara, who came to power in a coup in Upper Volta (then renamed Burkina Faso), drove a motorbike and played electric guitar in a jazz-rock band called *Tout-à-Coup Jazz*. They also had backgrounds that were not fully African, insofar as Rawlings was himself half-Scottish, and Sankara's deepest exposure to Marxist thought was in Madagascar, the large off-shore African island (or mini-continent) that had been settled by Austronesians/Indonesians, later African migrants from what is now Mozambique, and then indentured Indian labour—with more recent waves of Chinese migration. There has been a long Hindu and Buddhist presence, as Indonesia in about 500 AD, when Indonesian canoes reached Madagascar, had strong influences of that type. It all made being 'African' in Madagascar necessarily an exercise in fusion and adaptation.

But Rawlings was wildly popular, at least with the Accra underclass during his youth. I myself recall smashing the axle of my Land Rover in the potholes of an Accra slum in 1981. It was between the two coups that Rawlings launched—discussed below—and my driver said he would try to get back to the government depot and seek to locate a spare axle. I was to stay and guard the Land Rover, for it would be cannibalised if left unattended. It was stiflingly hot, so, eventually, I took shelter in the barbershop next to the Land Rover. While having my hair cut in a totally original fashion (the only Chinese punk in Accra emerged eventually), I noticed a small photograph of Rawlings stuck to the mirror. I told the barber I recognised who he was. He replied, "ah, you see, he will come again." It seems everyone in the slum knew when and how the second coup would occur—the government, for whom I was consulting, certainly did not—and his second coming was eagerly awaited as a moment of salvation.

Jerry Rawlings

After the overthrow of Kwame Nkrumah by a coup in 1966, there was a civilian government in Ghana led by Dr Kofi Busia, which was itself overthrown in a coup in 1972 led by General Acheampong; he himself was overthrown in a coup led by General Akuffo in 1975. None of these governments succeeded in dealing with Ghana's worsening economic problems, all reluctant to devalue the *cedi*, the national currency, for fear of increasing the local cost of living and thus losing popularity—or at least public tolerance of their rule, as the Generals became increasingly perceived as corrupt. In May 1979, Jerry Rawlings, a young 31-year-old Flight Lieutenant, launched an unsuccessful coup and was imprisoned, facing the possibility of execution for treason. His popularity among other soldiers who sympathised with his wish to reform the government saw him broken out of jail, a larger coup was then instigated, and Rawlings finally came to power in June 1979, 18 days before his 32nd birthday. In what was termed 'house cleaning', Acheampong, Akuffo and other Generals were executed by firing squad.

Rawlings' first impulse was that reform had to be led by a civilian government and that it had been the senior soldiers who had led corruption. An election was held, and Hilla Limann became President in September 1979. Limann also proved ineffectual in dealing with the economic crisis and so was overthrown in the second coming of Rawlings on New Year's Eve, 31 December 1981, the date forecast to me by the slum barber in Accra. The coup was greeted rapturously, especially it seems by the 'market mamas', the female market vendors of Accra, attracted by Rawlings's good looks, charisma and youthful idealism. But Rawlings did not have any real idea how to run a country, let alone one mired by economic despond. On my visit earlier in 1981, it was not as degenerated as Uganda in the wake of Amin, but almost nothing worked properly, prices of everyday commodities were prohibitive, roads certainly had not been repaired, and the security of key civilian installations was lax to the point of non-existent. Trying to leave Ghana, I found that all flights into the airport had been delayed. I casually climbed the stairs to the control tower and, again casually, asked 'where's Air Nigeria?', as I was going on to Lagos. The reply, laconic as if this kind of intrusion happened all the time, was 'Air Nigeria is now three hours away'. No one turned to look at who was asking the question, and I casually walked back down the stairs to sweat it out in an airport terminal with no air conditioning and no water. But, before then, I had also driven out of Accra to sample opinions in the countryside. There was no doubt Rawlings was viewed in a popular light. But everyone was hoping honesty would solve the economic problems, and it would take more than that.

At that time, the other example of a charismatic young military leader was Libya's Colonel Gaddafi, who had come to power in 1969 at the age of 27. He ejected Western military bases, advocated a pan-Arabism, and sought to introduce an autonomous non-Western way of thinking about development in his 'Little Green Book'—styled after Mao's 'Little Red Book' in the Chinese Cultural Revolution. He ruthlessly crushed opposition in cities like Benghazi, and sought to introduce a form of government spearheaded, in theory at least, by local committees. These were meant to be devolved instances of local democracy, but they reported to Gaddafi's centralised apparatus of control and became, in effect, organs to monitor behaviour and spot incipient unrest. In Ghana, one of Rawlings' first efforts at a 'new' form of government, responsive to the will of the people, was the introduction of similar committees—which, as in Libya, were swiftly perceived as monitoring and control devices—and they quickly became organs seeking to instil support for radical economic policies that, all the same, could not overcome global economic conditions that militated against economic autonomy in Ghana, nor accumulated debt and mismanagement, nor the lack of resources such as Libyan oil. The Workers' Defence Committees and People's Defence Committees became deeply unpopular because of coercive policies like price controls—and the underpinning thought that local economic discipline and the end of corruption would solve all problems, regardless of structural factors and international prices. In other words, Rawlings was perhaps more thoughtful and serious about how to build Ghana than the term "African military leader" might often be assumed to imply; but, in another sense, he was not, in the earliest years of his rule, being thoughtful enough—he was limited to technical strategies for fixing technical problems, without a wider transformational vision.

An economic crisis developed with intensity and Rawlings was forced in 1983 to change tack. He realised he had no choice but to ensure liquidity flows into Ghana from the outside world. He turned to Ghanaian economist Professor Kwesi Botchwey, whom he had appointed as Minister of Finance in 1982. Botchwey had already established a reputation as an internationally respected economics thinker.[11] However, rivalries in the circle of Rawlings's advisers had ensured his initial marginalisation. Many of these advisers were intellectual devotees of Dependency Theory, whereby the world at large, including Africa, was underdeveloped deliberately to benefit metropolitan countries, aided and abetted by a *comprador* or collaborationist class in each country, permitted their local accumulation as they diverted resources towards hegemonic, metropolitan accumulation. It was a class theory of nation-states and their elites in global relationships, rather than a class theory of groups and their relationships within a single state. Latin American in its origins, it was the dominant paradigm among left-inclined and liberal development economists in the West in the 1980s. But this diagnosis—for it was that as much as a theory, for it could propose no way out of *dependencia* until the overthrow of the global system unless, as in the case of Gaddafi's Libya, huge local resources like oil could dictate at least some terms to the outside world. Until then, all internal efforts would be unsuccessful if they did not take into account the international context in which a country like Ghana sat.

In fact, Nkrumah had tried to carve a way forward. He pitted his idealism and speed against international conditions, hoping to move faster than volatilities in world markets; get an industrial base up and running before or in case raw commodity prices plummeted. Professor Reginald Green of the University of Sussex's pioneering Institute of Development Studies, himself a Ghana devotee much noted for wearing items of Ghanaian cloth about campus, was unimpressed by Nkrumah's efforts—and this as a member of an Institute famed for its recognition of world structural conditions and flows. He used terms such as "utterly implausible ventures", "ineffective or irrational implementation", "unselective and untested importation of large-scale mechanized techniques", "inadequate public sector management," and only finally "misuse of funds and incompetence in high places".[12]

It was clear by 1983 that the economy would only deteriorate further if left to idealism, local fixes, and a *dependencia* critique of the outside world. By this stage, it was rumoured Botchwey had begun giving private weekly tutorials to Rawlings in economics. Botchwey tutored Rawlings in the detailing of the world economic system and the movement of capital globally, removing the stigma from having to deal with an inescapably dominant system and suggesting that Rawlings could deal with it better than his predecessors. Certainly Rawlings threw his weight behind Botchwey, but the 1983 budget that Botchwey announced in April completely astounded and even dumbfounded all in Ghana and much of the outside development-financing world. The *cedi* was devalued radically. This had been the stumbling block for all previous governments. No one had wanted to give a true value to the currency as devaluation would mean higher prices for all imports. But it was impossible to conduct international transactions with an inflated currency. Rawlings could change tack so radically, firstly because he concluded he had no choice, and secondly—young and charismatic and idealistic as he was—he had the power of a big man, the young officers behind him, and the execution of older officers also behind him. Botchwey did what previous administrations, civilian as well as military, deemed politically impossible with this devaluation. He raised prices on a whole range of foodstuffs. He increased incentives for productivity.

It was simultaneously an austerity and productivity budget, but the austerity would eat away political capital significantly and immediately, and productivity could not happen overnight. Basically, the budget and the reforms paved the way for Ghana to begin meaningful negotiations with the World Bank and IMF. It also established (in the eyes of the IMF in particular) that Botchwey was a technocratic personage with whom negotiations were indeed possible, but that he and Rawlings had already put down a 'deposit' on the normal preconditions for structural adjustment, and thereby induced the IMF to adopt a more flexible line in its approach to Ghana. In his authoritative book on the entire process, Jeffrey Herbst did make the point that Rawlings simultaneously constructed durable political constituencies in the process. The hero of the 'market mamas' now relied upon the hitherto neglected agriculturalists and farmers.[13] The problems of the agricultural sector hitherto were described by Osei-Hwedie and Agyeman-Badu, who also noted the need for a power base upon which to construct durable reforms.[14]

Botchwey continued as Minister of Finance until 1995, by which time Rawlings had retired from the military and won two elections as a civilian President, so durability also owed to consistency at the top. But Rawlings's winning of elections, adjudged free and fair, was also a sign that, however controversial, his reforms had an effect. None has been keener to trumpet that than the IMF itself. Ghana was evidence that its structural adjustment programmes worked. In fact, the success owed to Botchwey and Rawlings, who judged the political environment precisely, were prepared to take huge risks nonetheless and, in Botchwey's case, made sufficient adjustments to ensure that the IMF 'textbook' could be applied in real difficult circumstances. To this day, the economic measures undertaken by Rawlings and Botchwey remain controversial. The *dependencia* school sees it as a capitulation to the institutional forces of global capitalism, and even those who admire the progress of Ghana understand that it can now never be a model for any kind of alternative model of development. The key point relevant to Nkrumah's efforts is that, deleterious or beneficial to the material living standards of Ghanaians, what was done negates the possibility of a Consciencism, an African personality of equality and settled pride, in the cut and thrust context of capital-intensive development and membership of a fully capitalist world order—which, in itself, contests and negates the full possibility of equality.

Even so, debate on the accomplishments of Ghana under Rawlings and Botchwey emphasises the new departure of the IMF in itself benefiting from dialogue and participation.[15] IMF literature concedes this.[16] There was almost a rush as to who could claim most credit for what did indeed turn Ghana's economy around. Rawlings's own office never stopped advertising Ghana's lead role in playing the IMF better, almost, than the IMF.[17] Even Rawlings' successor as president, John Kufour, from the opposition party that Rawlings faced during his civilian terms, did not seek any return to radical economic policy.[18] By then, the beginning of 2001, the Rawlings/Botchwey economic bubble had burst and stagnation had set in, but Kufour's reinvigoration of the economy was orthodox rather than radical, with incentivisation rather than state control being the instruments. He too received a very great deal of help from international donors and the IMF.

One thing remained consistent from the beginning of the time of Rawlings to today, and that is that Ghana still has a large underclass and cities like Accra still have slums. Awai and Paller make the point that the government does not really control or govern the slums. Informal networks, alliances and criminal bosses do.[19] Which leads me to muse that, should once again my Landrover break its axle in the slums, would plans afoot to overthrow the government be known there, but not in the high places?

Rawlings remains controversial in many ways—not least because he abandoned his original left-wing ideals. He is thus viewed by many as a turncoat. He is sometimes compared unfavourably to another young military leader, Thomas Sankara of Burkina Faso, who would not solicit help from the IMF. Sankara has been described as a proper theoretician, i.e. a thinker along Marxist or class lines, if not within his country itself, then in terms of his recognition of a global stratification and exploitation not unlike that of *dependencia*, whereas Rawlings by contrast had no qualities as a theoretician and, apparently, many personal faults.[20] It is absolutely true to say that, even in the civilian committees of his first troubled year as President, Rawlings was atheoretical. He emulated Gaddafi, but it was Gaddafi who was, in his own way, the theoretician or would-be theoretician. The thought that took Rawlings through his terms, and which brought Ghana into fiscal probity and economic stability, was technocratic. In the world of African political thought, there may yet be a place for that.

Thomas Sankara

If Rawlings transformed himself essentially into a hero of the 'right', insofar at least as economic orthodoxy was concerned, Thomas

Sankara remains the flag-bearing hero of the left—although it should be said he greatly admired the early example of Rawlings. Like Rawlings, he also came to power in a coup and, like that of Rawlings, it was one that wore idealism on its sleeve. It is very easy to hero-worship Sankara. His feminist credentials, for instance, make him a very modern thinker. But he was in his own way a Big Man, and he could enforce the reforms he introduced to a country without any of the resources Ghana possessed. The world was little concerned about Upper Volta as the country was called before the advent of Sankara. In fact it was a joke that the capital city, Ouagadougou, consisted of two roundabouts linked by a dusty road. It was under-developed and lacking any apparent sophistication.

What he did, while in power from 1983 to 1987, before his assassination, makes for a very impressive list. As well as renaming the country 'Burkina Faso', The Land of Upright People, he may be fairly credited for the following:

1. He moved to end reliance on foreign aid, and this included liquidity flows from the IMF.
2. He vaccinated 2.5 million children against meningitis, measles and yellow fever.
3. He planted 10 million trees in an attempt to hold back desertification.
4. He redistributed land from feudal land-owners to peasants, suspended rural poll taxes, and doubled national wheat production.
5. 350 schools were built on a self-help basis in villages.
6. He instigated a nationwide literacy programme.
7. He encouraged the widespread construction of village medical dispensaries.
8. He began an ambitious national rail and road programme as national linking infrastructure.
9. He curtailed the power of the traditional chiefs.
10. He outlawed female genital mutilation, forced marriage and polygamy, appointed women to high offices, and encouraged girls to stay in school even while pregnant. He encouraged women to enter the workforce.

The national results were profound. And there were knock-on effects in terms of the liberation of cultural expression. Ouagadougou is now a metropolis, no longer a dusty road with two roundabouts, and hosts the biennial Pan-African Film and Television Festival—the greatest such event in the continent. The problems of the country have now taken on different complexities, with an increasingly difficult and bitter war being fought against Islamic extremist insurgent groups, with several hundred deaths at the hands of such groups.[21] Although international attention is now being drawn towards this insurgency, the international admirers of Sankara's philosophy and accomplishments were drawn primarily to items one and ten on the list above: the self-reliance implicit in not being 'held hostage' to international finance and liquidity flows—to 'financial imperialism' as it were; and the feminism expressed in his liberation of women from demeaning practices. His collection of writings on this is probably today his most popular book.[22]

However, to achieve this and the other internal results, he had to become, in quite a short time, increasingly authoritarian. He banned the free press and trade unions. He established, not along the lines of Gaddafi's Libya or Rawlings Ghana, but Fidel Castro's Cuba, People's Revolutionary Tribunals, and Committees for the Defence of the Revolution—the first functioning as a kind of political court, but without guaranteed or transparent due processes. Many were executed. However, he did emulate Gaddafi to the extent of having an all-female motorbike-riding bodyguard corps.

He not only alienated the former colonial power, France, but his own neighbour, the staunchly Francophile Ivory Coast. But this meant that those who felt marginalised by him, e.g. such a middle class as existed, not to mention traditional chiefs who had lost their feudal rights, had access to support in their desire to reduce his power, or do away with him altogether. This was particularly true of the middle class, and Sankara was killed on 15 October 1987, in a coup that installed his colleague, the more French-leaning Blaise Compaoré, as president.

Sankara had a mixed formation. He was born in 1949 as a member of the disadvantaged Silmi-Mossi caste of the Mossi ethnic group. His father had fought for the French against the Nazis in World War II (as did people like Frantz Fanon) and been held prisoner-of-war. His father and mother wanted him to become a Catholic priest. This did not eventuate but, despite his Catholic upbringing, he also became familiar with the Qur'an. However, if priesthood was one way out of a disadvantaged caste, a military career was another. At age 19 he joined the army and a year later, in 1968, was selected for officer training in Madagascar. Both Upper Volta, as it still was, and Madagascar had been French colonies. Both had achieved independence in 1960. However, the old relations of cooperation within the colonial sphere had not disappeared—so officer training on Madagascar was not something extraordinary. However, 1968 was also the time of the 'Events of May' in Paris, where students and then workers rose up against the French government, and the protests had a huge intellectual ferment that included debates on the nature and meaning of Marxism in the world as it stood, and what it could mean in imagined worlds of the future.

While in Madagascar, Sankara witnessed two uprisings against President Tsiranana, the independence leader: one in 1971 involving the poverty-stricken south of the country, and one in 1972 led by students. Tsiranana survived both uprisings but was weakened. He himself had begun life as an idealistic communist student. He was French educated at the *École Normale* in Montpellier but, after his return to Madagascar, fell out with the communists there. He believed in a mixed economy, but never stopped describing himself as a socialist.[23] The country remained dependent on France even when the weakened Tsiranana handed power over to General Gabriel Ramanantsoa in 1972. Again, French-trained, Ramanantsoa began a political epoch in Madagascar where a civilian/military hybrid government tolerated a multi-party system, with the proviso that all parties were either communist or socialist.[24]

Witnessing all this before his return to Upper Volta in 1972, what were the intellectual currents emanating from the Paris Events of May 68 that Sankara caught in Madagascar? Were they the same currents that Fanon and Iran's Ali Shari'ati[25] imbibed when they were in Paris and part of Jean-Paul Sartre's circle? Certainly Sartre's contribution to debate on French Marxism was profound,[26] disrupting a purely material approach to left wing thought and instead granting a place not just to the forces of production in the inevitable progression of history, but also to the individual, and individual agency. This was captivating for young freedom fighters in Francophone Africa just as much as it was for students protesting on the streets of Paris.

The 'stages of history' view was not uniquely Marxist or neo-Marxist. Adam Smith had his own version of it.[27] Later, the development economist Walt Rostow, almost as a justifying underpin to his theory of capital creation and inputs, with trickle-down to the poorest, described what he saw as 'stages of development'.[28] However, the overall idea that history developed through stages can properly be credited to Hegel,[29] who inspired Marx. What Sartre then added to this mix was a sort of youthful idealism that stayed with him all his life. He believed that the decision to act—to rise up—could *trigger* the inevitable next stage of history. In this decision to act lay the foundation of human freedom. "The power to commit one's self in present action and to build a future; it generates a future which enables us to understand and to change the present."[30] History could be created by human agency and human urgency. It was not something that progressed through epochs by itself. It was not an automaticity—as was the sense of Fukuyama's idea of history realising its fulfilment, its apotheosis, through the triumph of Western liberalism;[31] or in the sense of material drivers having a predestined development—but through, as much as anything else, will-power and desire.

This was the spark for action and the call for it. It contrasted with the more material emphases of the other great guru of 1968 Paris, Louis Althusser.[32] And it provided a sense of action as being key to resolving the contradictions French thought concerned itself with, between the forces and relations of production.[33] Basically, this contradiction within capitalism when it faces a moment of crisis, and it addresses the crisis by introducing flexibility into its command of the production process, allows subjugated forces of production to rise. The idea, therefore, was to force the moments of crisis. Insofar as Madagascar was intellectually influenced by France, especially in its 1972 student uprising, these intellectual currents would have had a profound impact on the young Sankara. And this is not to mention Simone de Beauvoir's pioneering work on feminism which had such an impact on the formation of feminist thought throughout the rest of the twentieth century.[34]

Do we find traces of these influences in Sankara's own writings and speeches? On his return to Upper Volta, Sankara distinguished himself in the war with Mali in 1974 (which he opposed), then he became head of commando training, and in 1976 formed an alliance with Blaise Compaoré within the *Regroupement des officiers communistes*, the Group of Communist Officers, modelled loosely on Nasser's Free Officers Movement that led to his 1952 coup and revolution in Egypt.[35] By 1983, Sankara was President—in a coup organised by Blaise Compaoré. The coup was supported by Libya, then quarrelling with France over each other's intervention in the Chad civil war. But, in the 1984 words of Sankara, a debt was owed to the examples of global struggle, and struggle in France:

> Our revolution in Burkina Faso draws on the totality of man's experiences since the first breath of humanity. We wish to be the heirs of all the revolutions of the world, of all the liberation struggles of the peoples of the Third World. We draw the lessons of the American revolution. The French revolution taught us the rights of man. The great October revolution brought victory to the proletariat and made possible the realization of the Paris Commune's dreams of justice.

The sense of internationalism was not unlike that of Cabral, but in this case drew very much from the French experience, and this comment was drawn from a quite remarkable exchange between Sankara and French President François Mitterrand, who visited Burkina Faso in November 1986. At the formal reception, Sankara, then 36, spoke eloquently and boldly—but very politely and diplomatically. Mitterrand, in his reply, seemed condescending in his praise of the boldness of youth.[36] It was in some senses a tit for tat, rather than any indication that Mitterrand would sanction the assassination of his host a year later. Mitterrand always infuriated people with his *hauteur* and sense of *grandeur*. Mitterrand had indeed been most reluctant in 1983 to accept that Sankara should become President of Upper Volta—the latter's seeming Marxism and sense of independence would act against French interests, but this did not prevent him from visiting Burkina Faso and being hosted by Sankara. Mitterrand had been a complex character from the start—a distinguished resistance fighter against the Nazis, under the *nom de guerre* of Captain Monier (among others), who all the same incurred the enmity of Charles de Gaulle for wanting to do too much in his own way. But his complexity, which loomed over the French left for much of the post-war period, was taxing.[37] Regarded as a true intellectual, he seemed nevertheless to epitomise the limits in the application of intellectual possibilities— his personality and behaviour as a thinker-in-action, *l'homme engagé'*, not shirking the contradictions and betrayals that were unavoidable as a political figure, even when in Mitterrand's case they were often carefully planned, astounded even the most worldly in the French left. This was the Mitterrand whom Sankara addressed. And it was Sankara who attempted the greater diplomatic politesse.[38] He welcomed Mitterrand warmly, with consistent inflections that he recognised the older man's thought and the true spirit of France.

He accorded such praise and benefit of doubt to France that it seemed he was almost against the suspension or diminution of French aid, but wished to be able to apply his nation's own terms. He then indicated, almost in list form, a raft of French international perfidities, and also a raft of international causes that should be supported. Basically he gave Mitterrand a lecture on righteous international relations—but, throughout, made references to words and writings by Mitterrand himself, including about the difficult search for truth. For Sankara and Burkina Faso, truth would bring cooperation without domination. The speech, when read in the original French, carries inflections of this sort. It was the speech of an idealistic statesman, and it was Mitterrand who responded merely as grandee. It was almost as if it was Sankara who was the democrat as opposed to someone who had achieved power through a coup, and Mitterrand who was the intolerant authoritarian figure. However, the speech indicated that relations, even with the former colonial power, were not a simple binary, not a simple opposition, but a series of contradictions that should be truthfully navigated—with emphasis on the navigation. Sankara delivered the speech extemporaneously. Had Mitterrand been able to read a copy in advance, it would have been interesting to see what response he would have framed.

But this is to suggest that Sankara's writings could be viewed as complex pieces, and not just as rhetoric struggling towards a utopia.

It should also be noted that, although there are several books under his name, they are compilations and anthologies of his speeches and occasional writings.[39] He never developed his thought in any sustained written form. Certainly some of these pieces were wonderfully written or spoken. For instance, he addressed the General Assembly of the United Nations in October 1984. President Reagan's office, after it sighted an advance copy of Sankara's proposed speech, and after Sankara refused to remove or tone down its criticisms of the great powers, declined to have him received at the White House. He was also prevented from travelling to Atlanta to meet its mayor, Andrew Young, who had been Carter's Ambassador to the UN and was becoming increasingly involved in African issues. Restricted to New York, Sankara addressed the United Nations with his original speech, and also made a public appearance in Harlem, conscious of its role in awakening black thought in the USA through the Harlem Renaissance and its cultural impact. But, at the UN, Sankara not only criticised the great powers, he made it clear that Africa had a responsibility to itself. Even without the great powers, Africa was falling short of itself.

> Of course, we encourage aid that can help us to manage without aid, but in general the aid and assistance policies merely led us to become completely disorganized, to enslave ourselves, to shirk our responsibility in our economic, political and cultural areas.
>
> We have chosen a different path to achieve better results. We have chosen to establish new techniques. We have chosen to seek forms of organization that are better adapted to our civilization, abruptly and once and for all rejecting all kinds of outside diktats, so that we can create the conditions for a dignity in keeping with our ambitions.
>
> We refuse simple survival. We want to ease the pressures, to free our countryside from medieval stagnation or regression.[40]

Here the blame was squarely on Africa itself. He was against reliance on aid, but the blame was two fold — on aid itself, and on the reliance. He had rehearsed some of these themes in his speech in Harlem. His oratorical power, even when speaking in French before an American audience, was clear—as evidenced from the video footage of the event.[41]

Like Cabral, Sankara also went to Cuba—doing this both before and after his UN speech.[42] He was greatly celebrated there and had meetings with Fidel Castro. Unlike Cabral, Sankara did not attempt any lengthy and learned disquisition on class formation. He iterated the accomplishments of the Burkina Faso revolution. He did speak about a new personality among the people, but this was to do with a commitment to self-reliant effort, to a national consciousness. It was not a view of something particularly African that had to be developed—otherwise there could have been no intense solidarity between Cuba and Burkina Faso, and between Burkina Faso and the Non-Aligned Movement (NAM). Sankara had attended the highly successful Delhi summit of the NAM in 1983. The new national consciousness was part of an international consciousness of joint effort in the face of common problems caused by imperial powers and finance.

It is fair to say that Sankara did have an affection for at least the image and reputation of Che Guevara. But, again, it was Che's words on commitment and self-reliance which struck the chord in Sankara:

> Che Guevara taught us we could dare to have confidence in ourselves, confidence in our abilities. He instilled in us the conviction that struggle is our only recourse. He was a citizen of the free world that together we are in the process of building. That is why we say that Che Guevara is also African and Burkinabè.[43]

Insofar as Sankara was almost assiduous about cultivating a dashing image—his tailored military fatigues and pearl-handled pistol were ostentatious exceptions to a highly frugal personal lifestyle—he could be said to have emulated the image of Che. Having female bodyguards might have been abstracted from the Gaddafi playbook, but having them on motorbikes was a reminder that both he and Che were aficionados of motorbikes.[44] Sankara also demanded that all government leaders should lead frugal lifestyles, not unlike his own. In that sense, as in Nyerere's early Tanzania, there was some levelling of society.

This extended to the curtailing of the feudal rights of chiefs, as Nkrumah had also sought to do in Ghana. In fact, it was clear Sankara saw them as hinderances to the revolution, and not as redeemable features of African tradition. Given his own background as a member of a very low caste, and given also the regional history which had been dominated by Mali and its hierarchical kingship system, Sankara out of local conditions as much as ideology and principle demanded an egalitarianism, rather than suggesting it had been a defining feature of the past. Insofar as there was a defining feature, it had been the subjugation of women.

Here, Sankara's writings and speeches fill an entire volume, and it is probably this that more than anything else attracts to his legacy a large devotion today. As Sankara said, citing Chairman Mao's words, "Women hold up the other half of the sky." Certainly the emancipation of women in Burkina Faso overturned long centuries of female subjugation. More than Blyden, Du Bois, Cabral, Garvey, Nkrumah, Kaunda, Nyerere, and Rawlings—and certainly more than Mobutu and Banda—Sankara both wrote about the need for female freedom and then enacted it in Burkina Faso.

But was he a true theoretician, a true Marxist? Many claim so, but rely principally on his stand against imperial finance.[45] Sankara was definitely an opponent against the world financial system, its debt trap for emerging countries, and the way money was used to bind former colonies to their former masters. In this he was as much a nationalist who believed in independence as a Marxist. But like Cabral, Sankara used a pragmatic language of solidarity, expressing an idealism that could be widely understood and attract allies such as Cuba. But he was always at pains to list the concrete accomplishments of his revolution—not to theorise about them. He expressed a pan-Africanism but his emphasis was always on his own country.

Did he have a Marxism with French undertones? Was he as ruthless towards his enemies as Mitterrand? Although Mitterrand did not have them executed without sentiment as many of Sankara's perceived enemies of the revolution were. But was he finally like Sartre, a champion of human action as the instigator of all historical change? I think this was the case—but with a twist, as caught recently by Amber Murrey. Speaking about the title of her book on Sankara, *A Certain Amount of Madness*, she relates that "the title takes inspiration from Sankara's words during an interview with Jean-Philippe Rapp in 1985", and these words were:

> I would like to leave behind me the conviction that if we maintain a certain amount of caution and organization we deserve victory [but] You cannot carry out fundamental change without a certain amount of madness. In this case, it comes from nonconformity, the courage

to turn your back on the old formulas, the courage to invent the future. It took the madmen of yesterday for us to be able to act with extreme clarity today. I want to be one of those madmen. [...] We must dare to invent the future.'[46]

To invent the future is not to reinvent the past. Re-citing Sartre, we find each echoes the other: "The power to commit one's self in present action and to build a future; it generates a future which enables us to understand and to change the present."

Human action perhaps in an ambition to achieve the impossible. Looking at Upper Volta as it was, and what he did to it as he turned it into Burkina Faso in just three years, would look impossible in prospect. Thoughtful and daringly mad might, finally, be a truly appropriate and complimentary assessment. Achieved, as it was, through a military coup, it also cements the need to differentiate, as suggested at the chapter's beginning, our views of military governments.

6

THE LEGACY OF FANON

He was not African, grew up in the Caribbean as an acolyte of Aimé Césaire, fought for France in World War II and was decorated for his heroism, was educated in France taking both a medical degree and a PhD, and became a key figure in the struggle of Algeria against French colonial rule. He was wounded in that struggle. Although, as an Ambassador for the Algerian liberation forces he travelled to sub-Saharan Africa, to places such as Accra and Addis Ababa, he never lived long in them. He was part of the intellectual circle around Jean-Paul Sartre, and Sartre wrote the extensive and influential Preface to his most famous book, *The Wretched of the Earth*. Apart from this and his *Black Skin, White Masks*, he penned other titles that included three plays—only two of which survive—as well as essays on French and African politics, in addition to his psycho-analytic studies. His more academic psychological study of the Marabout of Sri Slimane in Algeria is lost.

Apart from Sartre and Marx in the sense that Sartre gave him, Fanon (1925–1961) was influenced by the French psychiatrist and philosopher, Lacan. His books were dictated, as opposed to written directly by himself, and were often edited by his French wife, Josie. *The Wretched of the Earth* was dictated while he was suffering from leukemia, the disease which was to kill him. He died in a US hospital, allowed there by a USA which had its own quarrels with De Gaulle's

101

France, against which Fanon quarrelled on the side of Algeria. His body was smuggled back into Algeria by the liberation movement, where it received a hero's burial. This complex and, in some ways contradictory, man has nonetheless become the great hero of African thought on political freedom. Ngũgĩ, in his *Decolonising the Mind*, said it was impossible to understand African writing without reading Fanon. And he had a huge impact on the black diaspora. The Black Panthers in the USA adopted him as their intellectual mentor, although it is far from clear they properly digested his complex writings that utilised studies in psychiatry, phenomenology and ontology. Ngũgĩ would have considered that Fanon shared his views on language that the use of the coloniser's tongue is in some ways a submission to colonisation, and he did at face value, except that Caribbean Creole, Fanon's 'indigenous' language, is a hybridity far removed from the condition of a language like Kikuyu. Fanon, who spoke and wrote perfect French, and was immensely well-read, nevertheless understood that in some ways it was a concession to the coloniser to understand his language so well. Nevertheless, what he came to write could not have been written in Creole. His writings went on to have an inspirational effect on South Africa's Steve Biko, and continue, through Biko's legacy, nominally at least to influence today's youthful 'Rhodes Must Fall' movements in South African universities.

The Black Panthers

Let us start with the Black Panthers. A very perceptive work on the group, set in the time when two of the leaders took exile in Africa, is by someone who lived in Algiers alongside people like Eldridge Cleaver.[1] Elaine Mokhtefi came to know both Cleaver and Algiers well. She was attracted to Algiers because at that time, shortly after Algeria's liberation from French colonialism in 1962, its capital was the mecca and exile refuge of several liberation groups. What was known as 'Third World' solidarity found its headquarters in Algiers— much as Lusaka, some years later, became an exile headquarters for Southern African liberation groups. Already by that time, internal fissures and quarrels within the new Algerian government meant an unease and caution for the inhabitants of Algiers but, for outsiders, the city seemed to have the lustre of everything Fanon fought for, and those who had read, or at least skimmed, Fanon saw the city both as the suitable site of exile and as a place of pilgrimage in Fanon's memory. One of these was Eldridge Cleaver of the Black Panthers. Strikingly handsome, tall and charismatic, his Afro, black leather jacket and intense gaze (when not wearing sunglasses) made him the poster-boy of US radicalism. He affected an intellectual and poetic sensibility and his book, *Soul on Ice*,[2] written while in prison in 1965, was a hugely popular memoir and series of short riffs off Fanon—not that most of his US readers would have appreciated the latter. Even so, *The Wretched of the* Earth, the Grove Press English translation[3] of Fanon's *Les Damnés de la Terre*[4] did sell huge numbers, but few read far past Sartre's long Preface and the early sections on violence. The case studies, on trauma in the book's second part, clearly written by a psychiatrist, attracted very little comment.

But what Mokhtefi points out is the immense naivety of the Panther group in exile around Cleaver—and the group's insularity. No one seemed inclined to discover Algeria and the wider Africa. Treated well and with facilities and support infrastructure provided by the Algerian Government, the group lived comfortably and as an American enclave. Ideological, philosophical and indeed thoughtful interventions, even commentaries, on world affairs were absent, and much time was taken up ruminating on and trying to influence the power struggles within the Panther movement back home. The inside story of the Panthers is without glamour and had an element of gangsterism, but the movement did have three major effects.

Firstly, in figures like Cleaver, black youth in the US had iconic role models who were both fashionable and attractively angry.

Secondly, the neighbourhood service programmes of the Panthers were often very successful in their care of poorer members of the black community. These were, in a very distinct way, pioneering and provided a model the echoes of which can be seen in the neighbourhood work of Hamas as it built up a community base from which to challenge Fatah in Palestine, and in the work of the 'civics', informal community self-help groups in the slums of South African cities like Cape Town. The combination of the Panthers' iconic imagery meant a fashion statement of authenticity (white men couldn't easily grow

Afros), a well-photographed posture of self-help with blacks uplifting blacks, and militancy with (again) well-photographed P.R. images of Panthers with shotguns and the occasional semi-automatic weapon conducting an impersonation of a neighbourhood military patrol. What words could not articulate, actions and imagery did.

Thirdly, notwithstanding the internal power struggles and the reluctance of Cleaver's group to integrate with the wider revolutionary currents in Algiers, the Middle East and wider Africa, other Panther figures did come to an African engagement. The key figure here is Stokely Carmichael, born in Trinidad, who became honorary 'Prime Minister' of the Black Panther Party. In terms of public recognition, this was much increased by his relationship with and subsequent marriage in 1968 to South African jazz singer, Miriam Makeba, internationally popular for what came to be called her 'click song' (so-called because US listeners couldn't read or pronounce the Xhosa title which utilised the different clicks in the Xhosa system of speech, each one as distinct as a different vowel sound in a European language). Makeba and the role of jazz, mentioned elsewhere in this book, played a distinct role not only in US civil rights but in the anti-Apartheid struggle in South Africa.

Makeba was briefly married from 1964 to 1966 to Hugh Masekela, the legendary South African trumpeter. The radical priest, Trevor Huddlestone, gave him his first trumpet,[5] although some accounts also say that Louis Armstrong later presented one of his own trumpets to him as a gesture of solidarity between the struggle for civil rights in the US and the struggle against Apartheid in South Africa.[6] The two legends are conflated in the memorial museum in Kliptown, to this day the most underdeveloped part of Soweto but where, in 1955, 3,000 delegates who had clandestinely made their way to the township signed the Freedom Charter which still underpins ANC declared values. The conflation suggests that Huddlestone, who was present at the Congress of the People that signed the Charter, carried Armstrong's trumpet to Masekela. This conflation is probably a confusion, but a visitor to Kliptown will be reminded from all the memorabilia and art work in its only hotel that jazz played a significant role in the South African struggle. Mandela was a huge jazz fan and was reputed to have skived off university classes to visit the Johannesburg black jazz clubs. Music formed a bridge between the black communities in the US and South Africa (and also Rhodesia, where the jazz 'classic' Skokiaan, was composed by August Musarurwa). It meant that Makeba had a ready audience in the civil rights groups in the US and she was hugely popular there both in her own right and in her collaborations with Harry Belafonte.[7]

Makeba later sang at the independence ceremonies of several African countries, including Kaunda's Zambia and Nyerere's Tanganyika, and she increasingly became a public enemy of Apartheid. This never left her. Even in 1977, she recorded a song written by Masekela called *Soweto Blues*, following the slaughter of protesters there the previous year. Makeba had met Mandela in 1955, and in the US also met Martin Luther King in 1962—but criticised King for his movement's willingness to hold investments in South Africa.[8] In so doing she linked the two struggles in a way that went beyond music. The world of capital could traduce any mere declaration of solidarity or identification. It was in the 1960s that she met Stokely Carmichael. By that time her South African passport had been revoked—a common tactic by the Apartheid regime against its opponents when they travelled outside the country.

Makeba and Carmichael married in 1968. Carmichael had been coming under hugely increased pressure and intimidation because of his work with the Panthers, including orchestrated harassment from the FBI, so in 1969 the couple moved to Guinea. This was Guinea Conakry, neighbouring but not the Guinea Bissau for which Cabral had fought; even so, it was noted for its refusal to fit into the French schema for its former colonies in West Africa and thus seemed a fitting destination for the radical couple. Makeba, by marrying Carmichael, had earned the excoriation of many in her white American following. Martin Luther King was one thing, the Black Panther leader quite another. Carmichael changed his name to Kwame Ture, inspired by Ghana's Kwame Nkrumah, who also befriended him. Ture had already come out strongly against the Vietnam war, and became a strong admirer of both Fidel Castro and Che Guevara. The latter had fought briefly in 1965 in Africa,[9] and Castro had sent the weapons he captured from the CIA invasion force that failed at the Bay of Pigs to the Algerian freedom fighters against

France. Castro would later accord Ture treatment for the cancer that finally killed him in 1998. He died in Guinea aged 57. But his sense of an international struggle had been well formed by his experiences and the allies he found. Even before then, he sought to apply the writings of Frantz Fanon to the situation in the USA. He went far beyond Eldridge Cleaver in his attempt to appreciate Fanon. Even so, what he gleaned from Fanon is problematic.

Carmichael reflected on the civil rights movement in the USA, which he deemed too ready to moderate its goals and strategies in order to maintain working alliances with the Democratic Party or at least key Democrats. Also, while not refuting non-violence as a tactic, he did not agree it could be the central guiding principle. He was Fanonian in that regard by virtue of Fanon being an antidote to Gandhi. But he also read Fanon as stipulating a very high bar for equality in cooperation. Cooperation, in this case with any section of the white establishment, liberal or not, necessarily involved a form of patronage, condescension or *noblesse oblige*. One was helping the other from the virtue of a higher position. There was, in such a circumstance, no complementary capacity, no overlap that was equally premised. This meant for Carmichael there had to be equal power, economically, socially and politically. Until that achievement there could be no meaningful cooperation with the white establishment. The goal of the black movement was to build up all power capacities in the black community until equality with the white community was established. This had to be achieved independently, i.e. in a form of separate development.

Ironically, this sounded like a form of Apartheid but volitional and purposeful from the black point of view. The black community had to be united in this and when unity had achieved power, then coalitions were possible. Otherwise, ideas of the black struggle being part of a class struggle across the race divide, of solidarity with the working class and trade union movement were illusory. As was any idea that friendliness and sentiment—by which he included mere moral solidarity from white well-wishers—could take the black cause forward. Thus a Black Power movement was inescapable and fully desirable; hence radicalism was the only way forward. He advanced the sense that he had been inspired by African independence movements and by Fanon.

The idea of anger and violence may be attributed to Fanon—but, as we shall see, there was more to Fanon than that. Fanon's ideas about equality did not demand separate development. And it seems Carmichael's views of African independence struggles were reductionist. Kaunda and Nyerere, for instance, did not have to resort to militarised violence or even sustained civic unrest—although other African leaders certainly had to do so, although not all made it their central or sole strategy. Mugabe and Cabral may have seemed to, but both made great use of support networks internationally by way of protracted lobbying of political sympathisers. Carmichael himself had to appeal to Castro, although Cuba could hardly be described as the white establishment. But that did mean there was whiteness and whiteness, and even Fanon relied on the work of white thinkers and publishers. But the idea of needing to be determining of one's own cause, of setting one's own direction, of having one's own goals, and of having one's own sense of when one had 'arrived'—these may fairly be attributed to Carmichael and as setting a standard of the foundation rationales for any liberation struggle.[10]

To an extent, Carmichael would have found Guinea Conakry as an example-in-action of his refusal to accept benevolence which all the same disguised the reality of a huge asymmetry in power. Guinea's refusal to subscribe to the Francophonic state system, with the economic benefits that came with it, were because it would not accept the political conditionalities that accompanied those benefits. However, the country's President, Sékou Touré (in office 1958–84), was autocratic and, while he claimed a democratic accomplishment based on a political equality of sorts with France externally, and a dampening of ethnic tensions internally, his claim resounds more with a project of equality external and internal, rather than one of democracy.[11] He was certainly favourably disposed towards Cuba, towards the goal of African unity (and continental liberty), and in many ways was the perfect host for someone like Carmichael. But neither Touré nor Carmichael investigated Fanon as deeply as Carmichael certainly would have wished to claim.

Fanon's was the intellect that inspired his generation internationally. Was it for his intellectual contribution or his intellectual charisma? He inspired, in South Africa, Steve Biko.

Steve Biko

Biko was only 30 when he was assassinated by being beaten to death by police in 1977. This meant his legacy came about as much by posthumous appreciation as any written legacy—which consisted in short articles and speeches, many from his student years. As his legend increased, his origins were often overlooked. Born of Xhosa descent in Eastern Cape and educated in Natal, he was immersed in environments with large black and Asian populations. For him, being black and fighting for black emancipation and equality meant an inclusion of all those not white. As for the whites, he viewed them with ambivalence—despite having many white friends and supporters, and white lovers. The first expression of this ambivalence was in the student politics of his era, where he felt the national student body was overly dominated by well-meaning white liberals who, all the same, did not know what it felt like to be within the lived reality of enduring discrimination. In 1968 he helped start a new student body which excluded whites, but did include Asians and people of colour. This was SASO, the South African Students' Organisation. This should be seen not only as a reaction to the white student body, NUSAS, the National Union of South African students, but also as an echo of the student movements of the time. 1968 was the year of the 'Paris events', the uprising of radical students, first in France and rapidly elsewhere. Even before then, the 1964–5 Berkeley Free Speech Movement showed what impact a form of academic civil disobedience and outspokenness could have (and what retribution it could bring as California Governor Ronald Reagan tear gassed the Berkeley campus from helicopters and sent in his 'Blue Meanie' riot police with shotguns—which they used).

There was support from the Berkeley students for community groups, including the Black Panthers. One of my longest-standing friends was shot by a 'Blue Meanie', but also helped lead a neighbourhood law office staffed by law students like himself who defended Panthers in the courts. Not being black, he grew his naturally dark and curly hair into an Afro so he could 'pass' as a light-skinned black man and thus gain the confidence of his clients as he defended them. The era was one of a miscegenation of movements that condensed on Paris in 1968, and then exploded outwards again.

The Apartheid government was at first supportive of SASO, seeing this only in South African terms and deeming it as able to be related to its national doctrine of separate development. There is thus some irony here as Biko went down the same path as Stokely Carmichael. In this, albeit with the inclusion of Asians and people of colour, Biko, like Carmichael, was probably more in the line of Marcus Garvey than Frantz Fanon.

Biko did claim to have been influenced by Fanon, but also by the Black Panthers. It is not clear how much of Fanon he had read, or whether he was channelling the Panther interpretation of Fanon. 'Black Consciousness', however, became the central principle and guiding philosophy of his new student organisation, and this certainly had an echo of Kwame Nkrumah's Consciencism. But it did draw from Fanon. Gordon and Parris argue that Fanon

> refutes Euromodern psychiatric formulations of the Black as innately diseased and, instead, reveals the socially generated phenomenon of anti-black racism as the root of the Black's perceived mental illness. This sociogenic analysis and decolonial method provides a critical foundation for Fanon's clinical and theoretical innovations. For Fanon, Black consciousness is the psychological manifestation of liberatory self-actualization; the psychic movement away from the reductive, racial designation of 'the black,' to the self-affirming identification of 'the Black,' an actional agent catalyzing revolutionary socio-political change.[12]

It meant that self-awareness was important in the sense of being aware of the self as beautiful. Otherwise, the true psychological impact of Apartheid was the conviction that one was inferior because ugly, therefore visibly unworthy. The 'black is beautiful' mantra was emanating from the USA at that time—jazz singers who worked with Miriam Makeba like Nina Simone had hit songs like *Young, Gifted and Black* (1969). This all was a continuation of what Ali Mazrui had called the Atlantic loop, where black influences crossed backwards and forwards, had an echo also of Césaire and Senghor's *negritude* of black cultural beauty and cultural equality (Biko claimed them among his influences), and an echo finally of US black Baptist and Pentecostal churches where all were equal before God—conspicuously different to the common Dutch Reformed and Lutheran church endorsements of Apartheid, where doctrine was preached that the black race was in its inferior position because cursed by God. The emergence from a self-belief in one's inferiority was an emergence from the trauma of self-denial as a person. In this, Biko channelled the Fanon who was the psychiatrist with a deep clinical as well as political concern for the trauma caused by oppression. Overall, however, all this places Biko as the recipient of several international currents of freedom and rebellion and self-emergence. It makes him the great cosmopolitan figure of the struggle against Apartheid.[13]

Biko's great admirer was Donald Woods, who wrote about him. The 1987 film directed by Richard Attenborough, *Cry Freedom*, is based on Woods' accounts of the life and thoughts of Biko. Woods did take care to cite Biko's own words often. On Biko's attitude to whites, Woods records that Biko said he was "not sneering at the (white) liberals and their involvement" in the anti-apartheid movement, but "one has to come to the painful conclusion that the (white) liberal is in fact appeasing his own conscience, or at best is eager to demonstrate his identification with the black people only insofar as it does not sever all ties with his relatives on his side of the colour line."[14] For Biko, solidarity had to be whole-souled. And indeed, white liberals, even in histories by white scholars, do not always emerge well, only a handful taking their solidarity beyond words.[15] Miriam Makeba felt this in the USA when she married Stokely Carmichael and promptly lost a huge portion of her white fan base.

Indeed, in 1992, two years after the release of Nelson Mandela, I accepted a visiting appointment at what was then the University of Natal. One night I was invited to a very private party held in an enclosed courtyard around an ornamental pool. Late in the evening my host said to me: "Well, if a bomb went off now, all the white resistance in Durban would go up in smoke." I realised only then it was a reunion where people finally felt safe to meet, so I stammered, "but, apart from me, there are only 30 people in this courtyard…". They were, it transpired, white members of the ANC armed wing and allied underground. My host said: "Yes, of all the white people in Durban, these alone took the risks that the black resistance took."

Biko became too dangerous in his advocacies for the Apartheid Government to stomach. In some ways it is ironic that consciousness of Biko's death having been an assassination came about only because of the fearless investigative journalism of the young reporter, Helen Zille[16]—herself fallen on recent political bad times for carelessly revealing the internal ambivalences and limitations of white liberalism.[17]

If Biko was the product of his times, international currents, internal contradictions and ambivalences, and a determination to lead a way forward based on 'Black Consciousness', much but not all of this derives from Fanon. His anger against whites is said to be Fanonian— but does this sort of view tend to reduce Fanon only to a trope? Fanon is reduced to anger and violence? This is the right place therefore to examine Fanon himself.

Frantz Fanon

There has been a long genealogy of writing that associates Fanon with violence.[18] It is difficult to avoid using Fanon as a springboard to interpret generalised, almost universal, conditions. Even when not discussing him in the context of violence, but in the context of trauma associated with violence—both in the suffering and the decision to perpetuate it—one is drawn, as I was, to using him in contexts he had not envisaged; in the case of my writing in the context of an Islamic suicide bomber.[19] Having said that, there is now a genuine literature, albeit of a specialist sort,[20] that deals with the psychological and psychiatric aspects of his writing—and this writing on his part was extensive.[21] Even here, however, his writings, which were very largely within an Algerian and Algerian diaspora context, have been used to more generalised and wider effect.[22]

Insofar as there has been some emphasis on Fanon's approach to psychology and psychological conditions, they seem less drawn from the second part of The *Wretched of the Earth*, with its clinical case studies, and more from his other great book, *Black Skin, White Masks*,[23] which was first written as a draft for Fanon's doctoral thesis—and was less 'medical' than perhaps was required. To an extent, a psychological system has had to be re-inserted into this work to render it clinical. This does not diminish its power as a critique of the psychological condition forced upon the colonised and the oppressed. But both violence and psychology must be seen in the overall context of his life and formation. Here the best full-length account is by David Macey, and this amounts to a proper 640-page intellectual history, dealing with his Caribbean, French and Algerian years.[24]

Each of these epochs left a mark on him. I wish to deal here with some of the lessons gleaned from them, and indicate also some primary French influences, which included psychoanalytic and psychophilosophical influences—and which featured the Preface of Sartre to *The Wretched of the Earth* which certainly played its part in establishing Fanon as the Apostle of Violence. Starting with the issue of violence, we turn to the appreciation of Achille Mbembe—able to read Fanon in the original French and able also to apply a series of almost Cartesian distinctions to the otherwise generalised term, 'violence', and therefore express certain nuances.

Mbembe, the master of thought on the violence of the necropolis, gives a granular view of violence as propounded by Fanon. It is worthwhile to remember firstly that the violence wreaked upon Algeria, and particularly the Algerian resistance, by the French Government was a total suppression, a total war. This was caught in the searing 1966 film made by Gillo Pontecorvo, *The Battle of Algiers*.[25] The strategy behind this total war was devised by French General André Beaufre, and it was later the template used by Apartheid South Africa to wage war against the surrounding 'frontline states'—including Zambia which hosted the exiled ANC. The South Africans even named it 'Total Strategy'.[26] In Algeria, although also fine-grained—psychological as well as military—the net result was a total violence. Against this, the response in violence could not be the reply of a liberation necropolis that was a replica of the colonial necropolis. Mbembe proposes that Fanon has embedded in his writing a philosophical treatment of violence as follows:

For Fanon, there was something of a *duty* to revolt, to rise up. The violence of the French was not only physical, it was clinical. By that, Fanon meant it was determined to reduce the Algerian as a subject incapable of response—incapable of struggle and, indeed, incapable of violence. Basically the Algerian was rendered incapable of equality, a sub-subject, In this sense, violence was an expression of subjectivity and hence equality.

It is this that Stokely Carmichael took as a foundation for his refusal to cooperate with the white political establishment until equality was achieved. However, what Fanon meant was that the very decision to struggle, and the act of struggle, was already a clinical freedom—even if the road to political freedom was destined to be harsh and long.

But colonial violence began with greater capacity for force. Emancipatory violence responded from the underdog's position. What was at stake was the assertion of a French identity, a French ontology. The rebel asserted, against all odds, his and her own ontology and insisted that each identity and each ontology was capable of the same bleeding and death of the body. Against a necropolis with genocidal qualities, there was a response that was not genocidal but certainly bloody.

Genocide is a system. It is possible to commence it with the genocide of social organisation, so that the encampment of a French civic system, public administration and political modality upon Algeria was also an entanglement and strangulation of the sense of social self previously held by the Algerians. Because the Algerian was enmeshed therefore in a system, one capable for instance of pinpointing its targets, the response in violence was not at first systematic. In fact it appeared quite random. A woman leaving a bomb in a basket under a table in a public place could choose any public place, any table. It was violence as something 'phenomenal', i.e. using the language of the French existential philosophers, many of whom—including Sartre—supported the Algerian cause in a France torn asunder by the polarisation of views on this subject, it was a 'phenomenology of violence', and we shall look at this below.

Where the violence of emancipation began to acquire its own system, it was a system of mercy. The Pontecorvo film opens with the harrowing execution by guillotine of an Algerian resistance leader. Interrogation was often by torture—especially as the resistance instructed its fighters, if captured, to maintain silence for 24 hours. Then, they were free both to talk and also have some relief from torture. This made French torture even more savage.[27] Twenty-four hours was enough time for the resistance to regroup. However, the Algerian resistance as a rule disdained the torture and execution of its French military prisoners, and even gave those wounded hospital care. The hospital and psychological care given to Algerians who suffered in the war, including to women who had been raped, was also a feature of a developing system of liberation. So, to one ontology an ontology with some similar but other quite distinguishing features was developed. For Fanon, one ontology in its violence sought to dominate, the other in its violence sought finally a dimension of humanity.

In the account of Mbembe, "Fanon gave the escape from the 'great night' several different names: 'liberation', 'rebirth', 'restitution', 'substitution', 'resurgence', 'emergence', and 'absolute disorder', or 'walking constantly at night and in the day', 'making a new man stand up', 'finding something else', a new subject emerging whole out of the 'cement which had been mixed with blood and anger.'"[28] If this sounded finally poetic, and the idea of a new subject idealistic, it was also an admission that the project of liberation is inescapably messy. So, to the granularity of distinctions comes contaminations—but the direction of travel, even if sometimes confused, is to a freedom not envisaged by the project of colonisation and the violence of its enforcement.

Certainly Mbembe's account of Fanon is better granulated than Sartre's sometimes crude and themselves poetic attempts at evocation. In his Preface to *The Wretched of the Earth*, Sartre used these words: "By this mad fury, by this bitterness and spleen, by their ever-present desire to kill us, by the permanent tensing of powerful muscles which are afraid to relax, they have become men."[29] Perhaps it was because Sartre, for all his gifts, was himself a physical wimp, or he was seeking to evoke a powerful image among those who thought in terms of laboured archetypes, but the idea of a 'native' with coiled black muscles wanting to kill white men without thought but only bitterness is directly antithetical to Fanon's idea that emancipatory violence, while often confused, is nevertheless thoughtful or attempting a condition of thought. Through this thought it is seeking a condition also of equivalence. I said earlier that violence was an expression of equality; however, it sought equivalence. The distinction becomes clear when looking at an oratorio that Fanon found highly meaningful, and which was composed by Aimé Césaire, the co-founder with Senghor of *negritude*. This works off Hegel's master–slave dialectic, where the master recognises himself as a master precisely because he has a slave, something both Césaire and Fanon also found meaningful.

The oratorio is entitled *Et les chiens se taisaient* (And the dogs were silent), first published in 1961 in Sartre and Simone de Beauvoir's journal, *Les Temps Modernes*. It is about a slave revolt in Martinique, and one slave who killed his master is sentenced to death. He gives his last explanation to his mother. The slaves are about to storm the master's house. He is the first to enter.

> The master's bedroom was open. The master's bedroom was brightly lit
> and the master was there, very calm... and our men halted... it was the master.
> I went in. It's you, he said to me very quietly. It was me, it was indeed me,
> I told him, me, the good slave, the faithful slave, the slavish slave,
> and suddenly his eyes were like two frightened roaches on a rainy day...
> I struck a blow and blood flowed: that is the only baptism I can remember today.[30]

There are three things to be said about this passage. The first is that, when death was struck, it was struck almost gratuitously. It was simply just. There was no reflection or angst as to whether it was just. The killer is almost stunned by his lack of remorse and the automaticity of it all. The second is that Fanon, in citing this passage, along with Césaire, meant to say something about Hegel's master–slave dialectic. The third is that Fanon meant to say something about equivalence, and he makes this point clear towards the end of *White Skin, Black Masks*.

On the first point, Fanon had encountered this sense of the gratuitous, the numbed lack of reflection or guilt, before. His first sojourn in Algeria had been as a French civil servant with the duties of a psychiatrist and psychological assessor. Two teenage Algerian boys, 13 and 14, had killed a French boy. Fanon was assigned to assess their degree of criminal responsibility. They explained they were not old enough to kill an adult. No one but this boy, or another their age, would go with them into the hills where the killing took place. They were all friends, which is why they could kill him. The French boy had not personally offended them, there was no direct reason to kill him, but they regretted nothing, could explain nothing, and were prepared to accept the penalty. The boy was there. They killed him. He was dead. It was, as it were, a perfect set of unconscious if unconscionable phenomena.[31] It was, in terms associated with Sartre and the existentialists, phenomenological. For Fanon, the quest for a moral ontology was one thing. The path towards that quest was itself acts of violence that were phenomenological—without reflective or moral dimension. Whether or not this meant a sublimation of trauma would only emerge in the aftermath, when freedom was won. Fanon didn't express this, but the cost of freedom might have been seen in the authoritarian tendency of the post-liberation government, where all things were controlled—perhaps to prevent the trauma of struggle spilling over into the moment of victory, the moment of political, if not psychological, victory.

As for the second point, the oratorio also expresses something about Hegel's master–slave dialectic. The master recognises himself as a master because he has a slave, but the slave recognises himself as a slave because he has a master. There is here a mutual recognition and each needs the other in order to recognise himself. Each, by existing, reciprocates the other.[32]

Fanon, however, argues against this. He says that the master recognises not the slave, but the slave's value, i.e. the service and work of the slave. The slave cannot make himself otherwise recognised.[33] There is no equivalence.

This is where Césaire's oratorio is powerful. It demolishes the idea of reciprocity as symmetrical within the master–slave relationship. The slave bursts into the master's bedroom. Momentarily the master is reassured, for it is the 'good slave, the faithful slave, the slavish slave', but suddenly a realisation seizes the master and his eyes become 'like two frightened roaches on a rainy day'. The reciprocity the master at least had always assumed was no longer there. In killing him, the slave kills the master. Without masters there are no slaves, as Fanon argued. When there are no masters or slaves there is a state of equality. However, in the act of killing, in the assumption of power to do so, the slave acquires equivalence.

In his work, Fanon frequently cited Lacan. It seems to be the case that Lacan influenced Fanon on how to think one's way, and act one's way towards a full subjectivity. Fanon revealed himself as a student of psychology throughout *Black Skin, White Masks*. As well as Lacan, he mentions Freud and Jung and includes a section on Adler.[34] But it is to Lacan that he is most indebted. This has engendered almost an industry from what is now a Lacan 'industry'. So that, even the child's exclamation that Fanon recounts, "Look, a Negro!", is dissected both in terms of the subjectivity of the child and that of the 'Negro' who overhears him.[35] But, more pointedly, in terms of our discussion, Lacan's work "provides an instructive example of how Fanon's theorizations of colonial oppression might be supplemented by means of Lacanian social theory especially in respect of how the colonized are positioned as 'non-subjects' relative to the master-signifier of whiteness."[36] The recovery of self as subject begins with the recognition that one has been subordinated to the status of non-subject. But the perhaps most insightful, if controversial Lacanian intervention may be that by Françoise Vergès, and this is to do with the creation of subjectivity. Vergès referred this directly to Fanon himself.

Vergès speculated on the need to create alterities to what we see of ourselves in the mirror—basically to overcome what we see. Fanon had a special complaint that Martinique and the French Caribbean territories in the Antilles had never risen up. They were somehow supine. To create someone who was not an Antillean when he looked in the mirror, Fanon created himself into his new subjectivity of an Algerian. As an Algerian, he not only rose up but he, Fanon, played a special role in that uprising.[37] This is an ingenious reading, perhaps also fanciful, but its import lies in the need to create subjectivity and, thence, equivalence and equality with the would-be masters of the universe.

As it was, Fanon soon came to the realisation that the uprising was not just Algerian, but African. To become self-liberated by becoming part of a greater project of liberation applies, perhaps to Fanon personally, but applies far more pertinently to the project of liberation itself. It too grows, and its international subjectivity is not the same as its component national subjectivities. Two things occurred in 1960: Fanon travelled as the ambassador of the Algerian resistance to a conference in the Congo; the second was the publication of Sartre's great work, *Critique of Dialectical Reason*.[38]

Congolese Prime Minister Patrice Lumumba had convened a pan-African conference in Leopoldville (today's Kinshasa) but, by September 1960 when it began, Lumumba's position was already under severe threat. The recently independent Congo was in turmoil, secession and rebellion were in the air. Crowds, incited by Belgian and CIA sources, were in the streets calling for Lumumba's downfall. Foreign powers felt their investments in Congo's mining industry might be jeopardised by the socialist-inclining Lumumba. Nevertheless, Lumumba bravely came to give the closing speech of the conference: "It is not Africa itself that the Colonialists are interested in, but the wealth of Africa; and everything they do in Africa is determined by what is best for their own financial interests, at the expense of the African people. They will stop at nothing to get hold of that wealth."[39] Lumumba was assassinated in January 1961 but Fanon, who had heard the speech as Lumumba delivered it, was profoundly impressed by its bravery and by the realisation that the Algerian struggle was one part of a world-wide struggle—certainly an Africa-wide struggle.

Although Sartre's *Critique of Dialectical Reason* appeared only a year ahead of Fanon's *The Wretched of the Earth*, the two men had conversed frequently and at length in the years leading up to the publication of the two books, and Fanon would have known Sartre's argument.[40] Sartre had written, in any case, as early as 1946, that struggle was the ultimate truth, implying that struggle also formed thereby a universal truth.[41] As something universal struggle consisted in a 'colossal mass'. Sartre wrote his epic work at the height of the Algerian war and was highly conscious of it as a backdrop to his thought. In this new work, Sartre set out the basic categories for the theory of history that he believed was necessary for post-war Marxism. Sartre's formal aim was to establish the dialectical intelligibility of history itself, as what he called 'a totalisation without totaliser'. In short, that 'colossal mass' of unified protest and unified uprising would itself be the agent of history without prioritising the need for an individual leader. To be part of this mass was to achieve one's true agency as a participant in history. This, probably far more than a Lacanian search for one's alterity, probably propelled Fanon forward as such a participant—not just in the Algerian struggle but, towards the end of his life, the African struggle.

One might forgive Sartre's 'tensing of powerful muscles' moment in the light of his more profound sense of history—in which the 'colossal mass' had thought. For without thought, agency and there-fore history is impossible.

Sartre's premise in his work was that a negative project of history seeks to destroy what exists. But it is simultaneously positive, in that it seeks to create something new, to open up to something that does not yet exist. It is a leap into the future, and it is the leap that is transformative. For Fanon, it was the leap away from slavery and the transformation into freedom. To be a free creature of the world, but learning therefore from all the world. The Fanon who imbibed many influences went on, posthumously, profoundly to be a great influence in all the world.

7

THE OLD LIBERATIONIST

ROBERT MUGABE

It is impossible to leave Robert Mugabe out of this book as he did so much in the name of liberation and authenticity, and—perhaps more than any other African independence leader—prided himself on his self-declared intellectualism. I have been writing about him and Zimbabwe for decades, having been involved in the birth of the country in 1980[1] and in training parts of the new government. After the period leading to independence, I published four further titles directly related to him and Zimbabwean politics,[2] and a further four titles in which, among others, Zimbabwe was a significant case example.[3] In part, these were an attempt to balance a picture of great negativity towards Mugabe and his regime on the part of other authors and scholars.[4] There have been other efforts at objectivity, telling both sides of his story,[5] but by and large he has been portrayed as a thoughtless and ruthless pariah. Yet Mugabe had a far more intellectual sense of African destiny than his critics would acknowledge.

In Zimbabwe itself, the works of local scholars and intellectuals have sought to theorise not so much the style of Mugabe's government, but the direction of the country's politics as seen through the lens of International Political Economy, with a strong *dependencia* orientation,[6] and partaking in an intellectual genealogy associated with the Egyptian thinker, Samir Amin (discussed in Chapter Ten of this book), one against economic imperialism and also against Euro-centrism.[7] In that sense, even when critical of Mugabe and his hegemonic party—which lived off the reputation (and fruits) of liberation disproportionately, heavily dominating thought on Zimbabwe's future—these observers provided a sophisticated backdrop to an intellectual impulse that Mugabe himself never really articulated.

There is now new African writing, from both inside and outside Zimbabwe, that offers reassessments of Mugabe and his achievements, good and bad.[8] And, certainly, outside Zimbabwe itself, Mugabe's is a name not gainsaid. Away from the lived experience of economically depleted Zimbabwe, his nationalist project involving land redistribution has struck at least a populist, if not genuinely popular, chord. At Nelson Mandela's state memorial service towards the end of 2013, in a huge stadium on the outskirts of Johannesburg, South African President Jacob Zuma was booed and hissed by the crowd, but Mugabe's appearance was marked by a huge ovation.[9]

Because of a very long relationship with the country, this chapter captures instances of my personal experience as well as my research. It partly draws from my earlier works on Mugabe and from my lengthy obituary of him in the *Guardian*.[10] The picture that emerges is of a division: first there was Mugabe the freedom fighter, whose ghost was cheered by black South Africans as recently as 2013; this Mugabe was engaged with and driven by ideas about Zimbabwe's liberation. Then there was Mugabe the ruler, more preoccupied with performing authenticity in order to keep his grip on the country. At times this was simply a matter of crushing opposition, with no attempt at intellectualism; but there was some vestige of ideology in Mugabe's most famous and most controversial policy: land reform, meaning land seizure and nationalisation. The sound-bites spoke of land almost in sentimental terms, and those in themselves were not sufficient to pass as a thoughtful and thoughtfully articulated foundation for authenticity. Nevertheless, we can trace his attachment to land seizures back to the vision he developed in his youth, of Zimbabwe and Africa coming into their rightful inheritance. And Mugabe always viewed *himself* as a thinker.

We might say that, over the course of his reign, Mugabe increasingly drew on his own unshakeable confidence in himself as an intellectual, in place of any real attempt at considered thought. We will see, for instance, that he looked down on the less well educated Morgan Tsvangirai, even as his own ill-considered policies were running Zimbabwe into the ground. The collector of several master's degrees, Mugabe was a man who judged his fellows by their familiarity with the texts of pan-Africanism, even while pursuing bitter and divisive policies. So, in what follows, I have developed my comments on, if not his political thought, then the context of his thought, and its fading over time in favour of a fixation on power and revenge. For an intellectual man, certainly as he viewed himself to be, no articulated thought was left behind by the old liberationist.

* * *

It was while serving a ten-year prison sentence handed down by the colonial authorities, from 1964, that Mugabe 'arrived' as a nationalist of note. A university of the cells was established by the prisoners and Mugabe, who had been a teacher in Ghana in the early 1960s, was one of the lecturers. While incarcerated, he collected several degrees in subjects such as Law and Politics by distance education, from universities in South Africa, as well as the London School of Economics and the School of Oriental and African Studies. He emerged as the leader of the imprisoned nationalist movement. His prison seniority placed him in a position to contest the formal overall leadership of the party after his release in 1974 into a Rhodesia still mired in racial discrimination and increasing conflict.

He took exile in Zambia, but President Kenneth Kaunda considered Mugabe—who was vehemently opposed to any compromise with Rhodesia on the part of the other Southern African states—a risk to his delicate tight-rope walking between a pacific image and the hosting of rebel groups. Kaunda had him arrested. Revenge tastes sweeter as it becomes more petty. After Zimbabwe's independence in 1980, the presidents of the frontline states would be honoured with streets named after them in the capital, Harare: Kaunda's street was the dusty industrial transit road beside the increasingly derelict railway station. It still bears his name, and the railway station services still meagre traffic.

Kaunda had in any case realised that arresting Mugabe was an embarrassing action for a president who sought, however carefully, to be a patron of liberation; the Zambians likely facilitated Mugabe's 'escape' from their custody a little later in 1974. Mugabe resumed his nationalist activities in Mozambique but, once there, President Samora Machel also briefly arrested him. This was, it was said, for Mugabe's own safety, to protect him from the Zimbabwean guerrilla leaders already there, but it was clear that Machel shared Kaunda's unease about Mugabe and that, although Mugabe was now seen as the pre-eminent nationalist leader, this had not yet translated into a leadership of the armed element of the liberation struggle. On his release, he successfully out-manoeuvred the guerrilla leaders with the help of one of their number, Rex Nhongo (known later as Solomon Mujuru), who became Mugabe's leading military strategist.

It was during his time in Mozambique that Mugabe developed a crypto-Marxist worldview, seeing black liberation as a critical stage among the inevitable progression points of history. Mozambique was a Lusophonic country, recently liberated from Portuguese rule. As we saw in Chapter Two, the revolution in Portugal saw its own intellectual ferment, with a range of French communist and left-wing views.[11] These were in tandem with and often intersected with left thought on development, liberation and history. Variants of this inflected almost all left thought at the time: Wallerstein's sense of economic movement from peripheralism to semi-peripheralism as an almost essential epochal step towards the possibility of assertion against the metropole that sought to order the world beneath it as parts of its own periphery, is such a variant.[12]

As for African thought on these questions, quite apart from an acceptance of *dependencia* in intellectual circles in Africa, not least as represented by groups such as CODESRIA (Centre for the Development of Economic and Social Research in Africa, established in 1973 and based in Senegal, with its founding [1973–75] Executive Secretary as Samir Amin) with its pan-African sense of intellectual unity and its essential opposition to both economic and intellectual imperialism, and with its strong presence not only in Dakar but in locations such as Dar es Salaam and Harare, we have ingredients of thought for a generally post-independence school of African political economy and philosophy. Zimbabwe was late coming to independence because of white minority intransigence, liberation struggle and emerging thought occupied the same epoch.

THE OLD LIBERATIONIST: ROBERT MUGABE

This is not to say that Mugabe was affiliated or even consciously committed to *dependencia*, but its thought was infused not only with a neo-Marxism but with an idealism that a new dawn was sweeping Africa—and these two ingredients were fused by a sense of historical inevitability, as we saw in Sankara's political awakening in Madagascar at the time of May 68. Willpower and desire could be enough to set the events of that struggle in motion, and the desire to be free, to be equal, to be an equal part of history, was something common to almost all neo-Marxist inflected liberation struggles of the 1970s and into the 1980s.

Mugabe could be said to have inherited and to have become an actor in such a dynamic historically based idealism—not just a sense of history that progressed through material stages such as from feudalism to capitalism to socialism, but from subjugation and repression, through liberation, to full autochthonous expressionism.

* * *

Mugabe did not instigate the armed movement for liberation—but he did capture it from those who had, skilfully and ruthlessly sidelining the rebel leaders in Mozambique. In 1977 he was formally elected president of the Zimbabwe African National Union. He subjected the military leaders to party rule and the nationalist struggle to his pan-Africanism. Young people in Rhodesia flocked to fight under his leadership, training in Mozambique and Tanzania and then being sent back to fight across the border.

Not that the Chinese training was always helpful. The Chinese had no sense of the Rhodesian terrain, and no real knowledge of the response times of the white Rhodesian army. A huge number of early guerrilla operations inside the country were used almost as experiments—the young soldiers used as cannon fodder—to find out the hard way what could or could not be done.

It is part of the mythology created by Mugabe that his guerrillas won independence and majority rule for Zimbabwe, forcing the white Rhodesian forces to capitulate. His fighters did force a stalemate, and they inflicted much more damage on white interests and self-assurance than the rival forces of Joshua Nkomo's Zambia-based Zimbabwe African People's Union. The two rival armies, ZANU and

ZAPU, were made up of differing ethnicities from opposite ends of the country—Shona in Mugabe's east and Ndebele in Nkomo's west of the country. A long history of rivalry existed between the two peoples. In addition, Nkomo had begun his own nationalist struggle as an urban trade unionist and became Soviet-affiliated, whereas Mugabe's Chinese support reinforced his sense of a peasant-based uprising. Though at times barely on even speaking terms, the two men joined forces politically to secure independence, entering into negotiations with the Rhodesian Prime Minister, Ian Smith, in 1979. It was with some initial reluctance. There is the famous story that Tanzania's President Nyerere, seeking to establish a cooperative front between the two, saw them separately in Dar es Salaam. Nkomo went into Nyerere's office first. When it was Mugabe's turn, he point-blank refused to sit in the same chair that had been offered to Nkomo. In addition to the differences mentioned above, the two men simply did not share any sense of chemistry.

Complex talks among all the warring factions, supported by Julius Nyerere, Kenneth Kaunda, Samora Machel, the new British Prime Minister Margaret Thatcher, her foreign secretary Lord Carrington, the Commonwealth secretary-general and even Apartheid South Africa, led to the transformation of Rhodesia into Zimbabwe. The South Africans had concluded a negotiated independence was better than a military victory for the guerrillas, as that would inspire their own restless population. The negotiations, first in Lusaka and then at Lancaster House in London, both in the second half of 1979, led to an uneasy agreement. The truce that resulted was followed by elections at the end of February 1980, which Mugabe won by a landslide. I had been in the country throughout the months of the truce and election. The result stunned not only the British, but everyone in what became Zimbabwe and, indeed, had a stunning effect throughout Africa. Mugabe's national address of reconciliation between black and white mollified almost everyone. The tone of his address surprised everyone. Softly spoken, it looked beyond the end of war to a national sense of cooperation. It was statesmanlike in the sense that Mugabe realised that only a full end to black/white conflict would allow progress towards the fruits of liberation. Given the savagery of the war, and given the remaining stubbornness of Apartheid on his southern borders, it was a landmark speech in the discourse of opposition—black against white, white against black—which had characterised the region and much of the continent.

But the idealism of Mugabe's guerrilla war, and of his position as the leader to bring together all of Zimbabwe, would soon fade. He would remain in power from 1980 almost until his death, winning every election, increasingly through rigging and voter intimidation. This quest for validation never deserted him. I attended every Zimbabwean election, except the one of 1985, and it seemed almost as his need for validation, and a personalisation of himself as Zimbabwe, grew. When he suspected a rebellion among disaffected veterans of Nkomo's ZAPU army, he instigated slaughters in Nkomo's heartlands from 1982 to 1987; tens of thousands of civilians were killed.

Mugabe easily won the 1985 elections but in 1990 faced opposition from his former liberation colleague Edgar Tekere. Mugabe engaged in a series of intimidatory tactics that flawed an election that he would have won anyway. It set a tone of "democracy if there is no serious opposition". It almost seemed to echo the concerns of what we described as the 'big men' of other African countries, seeking not to be challenged. There seemed no irony when, in 1991, the Commonwealth, at the end of its summit of heads of government in Zimbabwe, released the Harare Declaration on Human Rights (covering all member states). I was there for its public unveiling, seated just below the podium and there was not the slightest sign of embarrassment in Mugabe's facial features or body language. And, on a visit to China in 1992, Mugabe lectured the Chinese on the desirability and harmlessness of opposition parties.

* * *

In 1992 the land question—which Carrington had refused to include in the independence negotiations—arose once more: belief in the need for redistribution of land from white farmers to the black majority, by force if necessary. Mugabe considered ownership of land as both an economic nationalism, to complete the achievement of political nationhood, and also as an ownership in Marxist terms of the means of production. But he also inflected a spiritual and romantic quality into the essence of land. Even by the late 1990s, two-thirds of the arable land of Zimbabwe was in white ownership, acquired in the first instance by seizure and legislation in which black voices had played no part—although it should be said that many titles had changed hands over the years of independence, all sanctioned by the laws of an independent country. As late as 2005, when I debated Carrington at a meeting in Cambridge, he, having then lost none of his forcefulness, declared emphatically that there was nothing he could have done at the Lancaster House negotiations in 1979 about the land issue without its jeopardising the political peace process and the independence that came from it. Even so, some issues cannot be swept forever under the carpet.

Mugabe had insisted at Lancaster House that most of the landowning settlers were of British origin, and so could not be seen to have any legitimate claim to the land, if independence were to be recognised as just and legitimate. The cause of reclaiming this land has iconic, declared spiritual, and agricultural attributes and became, for Mugabe and his followers, an emblem of an authentic and completed national project. Mugabe had held an intellectual vision of black culture as having a place within history, of needing to have its historical moment, and that human agency could initiate this moment. It would represent the achievement of the black personality as independent of colonial forces in the modern world.

Scholars such as Terence Ranger[13] and David Lan[14] saw the importance of land as a spiritual foundation for rising against white domination in Zimbabwe including white domination of the ownership of land—although Norma Kriger cautioned that land, even with its spiritual and thus cultural attributes represented, could only be part of a multi-faceted story in Zimbabwe alongside other equally important elements such as political and economic aspirations.[15] And Billy Mukamuri made the strong point of how access to the actual spirits of the land could be misused by charlatans and opportunists, impersonators, as much as used by authentic interlocutors, shamans, who with great training and ceremony could interface with the spirit world.[16] In short, albeit with careful analysis, land in Zimbabwe could be seen as a central animation for rebellion, as part of a declaration of the authenticity that required to be emancipated, along with political emancipation—or, as Mugabe would have it, as the unfinished part of political emancipation.

1992 saw drought sweep Zimbabwe and questions of productivity of the land were swiftly caught up in those to do with ownership of it. A Land Acquisition Act was passed, but not enforced. There has been some argument made that the reason the international community was not keen on land reform in 1992 was to avoid scaring off the white negotiators in talks in South Africa to end apartheid, but there is no real evidence of this. In 1992, when I spent much of that year in South Africa, talks between the ANC and the National Party were mired in an entire series of difficulties about political representation, and not about economic issues. Had a gradual, phased and compensated programme of land nationalisation been given international backing and negotiated in Zimbabwe at this time, what was to come might not have been so disastrous. Instead, Mugabe forced the question of land rights, transforming Zimbabwe's fortunes, its self-sufficiency, and its international image—never mind its capacity as a modern state. From 2000 onwards, the Zimbabwean state began a programme of compulsory land acquisition for redistribution.

Mugabe continued, as he had done during the independence negotiations, to present nationalisation and redistribution of white-owned land as a question of liberation, and presumably continued to be motivated by his belief in this, but we cannot consider the seizures to be the implementation of an ideological vision. For one thing, the land seizures were, in one way or another, a political programme, even if it appealed to spiritual and authentic, almost pastoral motifs. Notwithstanding non-material factors, the timing of the seizures was primarily political and occasioned by a rising challenge by opposition leader, Morgan Tsvangirai and his new Movement for Democratic Change (MDC) party. The land seizures began a week after Tsvangirai defeated Mugabe in a referendum Mugabe had launched that would have increased presidential powers. Whether or not Mugabe also believed it was to set in play an apotheosis of African history, completing a history of struggle, the political drive was inescapable.

And, perhaps more damning, it is hard to believe that Mugabe was acting out an idea of Zimbabwe with the land seizures when it was so clear that he had no actual vision concerning them. He set about seizures without any planning to do with the uses, productivity and economic foundations of land. It lacked technocratic skill, foresight or even interest. The economy collapsed as a result and has not recovered two decades later. Indeed, the removal of the foundations of the Zimbabwean economy, productivity of land, not just owner-ship, has meant an economy that merely continues to worsen. There was none of the (even if eventual) technocratic appreciation and work of someone like Jerry Rawlings who came to power also in the 1980s. Rawlings demonstrated that, even without deep philosophical thought, technocratic thought was a critical key to success. In Zimbabwe land reform had become a little-thought-out end in itself, and as the economy slowly but markedly deteriorated from 1997—the beginning of the downturn of Zimbabwe—freedom itself was increasingly curtailed by Mugabe, in his determination to cling to power against growing discontent.

* * *

Mugabe's increasingly authoritarian demeanour, and the cost of par-ticipating in the wars in the Democratic Republic of Congo—by which, all the same, Mugabe guaranteed the continued support of his generals by allowing them to loot the mineral resources there—prompted the creation of the Movement for Democratic Change (the MDC) led by Morgan Tsvangirai, in 1999. It became immediately apparent that the new opposition party had national support, based on dissatisfaction among the general public with Mugabe. And against all Mugabe's expectations, it defeated him in a referendum in early 2000 which he had called over constitutional issues, including an amendment to give the presidency even more power. This was the referendum that was swiftly followed by the launch of land seizures, seemingly a knee-jerk attempt to regain authenticity by appealing to liberation—the source of Mugabe's heroism and legitimacy as a ruler—as an ongoing struggle for which he was still needed. Pro-Mugabe war veterans were unleashed to begin the seizure of white-owned farms, and administrative and financial chaos descended. Zimbabwe's export economy was, however, heavily dependent on commercial crops. My green beans and flowers from my London supermarket were grown in Zimbabwe. But the strawberries had been grown in Zambia. Once Zimbabwe lost international markets, even close neighbours were poised to take Zimbabwe's place.

What Mugabe never seemed to realise was that the agricultural economy of his country was based, not on a romanticised sense of peasant ownership and peasant production but on an aggressive and highly modern agriculture industry that sold food and tobacco on the highly competitive international markets. So what was required in any land nationalisation programme was a comprehensive outreach to do with commercial agricultural education, and state assurance of continuing agri-industrial inputs such as fertilisers, materials for dam maintenance, and equipment to access underground water tables— not to mention financial planning capacity at micro-level.

There was one bit of thought left to be squeezed out of the old freedom fighter, in his 70s by the turn of the century. In the face of Western sanctions and economic meltdown after 2000, Mugabe did develop one kind of rescue vision: his Look East policy, meant to take in a number of East Asian countries, but centred on looking to China.[17] It was enunciated in 2003 but was long a background policy. As we have seen, China was involved from the very beginning of Zimbabwe's militarised struggle for freedom, providing equipment but also training in bases in Mozambique and Tanzania. The bond was more than military. Once, in February 1980, when I was acting as Commonwealth liaison with officers of Colonel level in the various armed forces who were meant to be observing a ceasefire, I met two of Mugabe's officers. They, seeing I was Chinese, immediately smiled and pulled chopsticks from their webbing. Then offered to cook for me. "Your people helped us when no one else would."

Even so, the Government of Zimbabwe was slow in appreciating Chinese needs and requirements in the relationship between the two countries. Like the land reforms, Mugabe's last idea turned out not to have enough thought behind it. Look East couldn't save Zimbabwe in the absence of technocratic skill and comprehension, perhaps even honesty. Transparency and accountability in funds made available became a deeper and deeper concern for the Chinese Government. And the laziness and ignorance of Zimbabwean officialdom was apparent when, in the period shortly after Mugabe's announcement of his Look East policy, a visiting Chinese business delegation was greeted with signs written in Korean.[18] To this day, China remains publicly supportive of Zimbabwe, but will commit no budgetary support, no balance-of-payments support, and no significant financial input to help engineer debt relief. Monies made available have almost entirely been programme and project-based. This is because, however generous and longstanding China's support of Zimbabwe has been, it will not fund a government, let alone make up shortfalls in government accounts, without fiscal discipline. Mugabe instigated a nationalism and authenticity that he hoped would be without cost, including the cost involved in honesty and economic rigour; and in making the long-term commitment to productivity even with short-term pains.

I have been involved in China/Africa relations for many years, and have negotiated in Beijing with a high-level African delegation led by the Deputy Chair of the African Union.[19] What struck me over the years was how, from a low base, Chinese research on Africa has improved. There is less 'money for solidarity' now, and more investment for long term gains. Research that includes political risk analysis as well as economic projections is the new normal in Beijing. Has African research kept up? Yes, although not in Zimbabwe. Angola has done very well in advancing new negotiating techniques in its meetings with the Chinese.[20] But it is the Ethiopians who have the finest appreciation of a range of Chinese strategies, strengths, weaknesses and hesitations. This has been evident in the work of cross-over academics and senior officials like Fantu Cheru,[21] and the work of cross-over academics and government ministers like Arkebe Oqubay.[22]

By contrast, opposition leader Morgan Tsvangirai was spending the 2000s precisely trying to position himself as a leader of ideas, principle, and thoughtfulness. I had long conversations with him during this period. I published, first as a *samizdat* book for the 2005 elections[23] and later in regular editions,[24] a book of interviews with him. In these interviews, Tsvangirai clearly sought to present his intellectual credentials. Tsvangirai's response to this was, in a sense, to play Mugabe at his own game: to play up his authenticity as a suitable leader for Zimbabwe, appealing to the currency of ideas. It is noteworthy that, although Mugabe's rule seemed neither principled nor thoughtful by the early twenty-first century, Tsvangirai sought to oppose him at least in part on intellectual grounds. Mugabe had been resorting increasingly to violence and highly sophisticated vote-rigging. The MDC was suffering repression, heavy-handed police action and paramilitary violence. Notwithstanding any effort by Tsvangirai to project himself as thoughtful. He was charged with treason, very much as part of a campaign of psychological undermining of any appearance of oppositional coherence. Tsvangirai was acquitted but began making mistakes—relying increasingly on a 'kitchen cabinet', leaving others feeling marginalised, the result being that the MDC split.

Tsvangirai was facing an extremely unequal playing field, and part of this was because his adversary made it clear he looked down on him intellectually, describing him of no account because of lack of formal academic formation. Tsvangirai sought to redress this perception through his collaboration with me. The aim of the book, distributed in the first instance to election observers, was to do with (in the vocabulary of Mediation Studies) 'facilitation'. In this case, to level the playing field by presenting an intellectual profile of yourself that is equivalent at least to the public thought of Mugabe. An equal playing field is the aim. For Tsvangirai that field included thought on what it meant to be a citizen of Africa, as well as a citizen of Zimbabwe. He too claimed a wider African consciousness to indicate that Mugabe's consciousness had shrunk to one only of local physical ownership.

But, as a result of all the harassment and the MDC split, all popular wisdom and political punditry suggested that Tsvangirai would lose the 2008 presidential and parliamentary elections, and Mugabe was supremely confident. But the ruination of the country had been such that the voters were about to insist on change. I was in Zimbabwe for the elections and, on election night, my polling had Tsvangirai and the MDC with 56% of the vote. South African Broadcasting had it at 52%. But Mugabe and his party found ways to manipulate the results, ultimately resulting in a laboriously negotiated and fragile power-sharing agreement: Mugabe remained president, while Tsvangirai was made prime minister and given the task of getting Zimbabwe out of the economic mess that Mugabe had caused. I was again in Zimbabwe at that time—and the sense of appalling anti-climax was profound.

The Tsvangirai 'victory'—finally denied him—spoke to voter frustration with hyper-inflation and the sense of failed promises despite what was claimed would be a completed nationalisation. But Tsvangirai's charisma, promising a new start—and the essential failure of the Mugabe campaign to unbalance him psychologically and diminish his intellectual stature—spoke to the electorate as emanating from a person of substance.

Not even in the aftermath of this electoral shock, did Mugabe seek to compensate for the lack of initial thought surrounding his land seizures by developing either an agronomic programme or any detailed ideological, philosophical, cultural or ethical rationale that went beyond sound-bites and declarations. As we shall note, for Mugabe's successors, retention of power and its privileges even today in the post-Tsvangirai and post-Mugabe era has a priority over any serious attempt to uplift the majority. Nevertheless, and even though Tsvangirai did, as part of the power-sharing coalition, manage to stabilise the economy to some extent, it was still Mugabe who prevailed in the 2013 elections. Voter fear of political destabilisation and unrest made Mugabe seem an unsatisfactory but 'safe' option.

At this point, Mugabe's leadership of the country disintegrated. He became increasingly preoccupied with internal ZANU-PF power struggles, rather than urgent issues of national government, such as poverty, national non-productivity, and the inequity that had swept the country in terms of an oligarchic class of ruling party supporters, many of whom had achieved their fortunes by corruption—often in tandem with acquisition of the best farmlands after the land seizures that began in 2000. Obsessed with the possibility of plots against him, Mugabe purged the party of even his most prized lieutenants. Joice Mujuru, his vice president, a war heroine and the widow of Solomon Mujuru—who died in mysterious circumstances in 2011—was purged in December 2014. In the midst of economic meltdown—for Mugabe produced no real economic plans after the Tsvangirai premiership—public unrest was growing. He no longer seemed a safe option of any sort. Demands for economic justice were turning into a critique of an old man in his 90s with no new ideas.

* * *

Mugabe clung on to power, and neutralised his other vice president Emmerson Mnangagwa—a celebrated veteran—to make way for his wife, Grace, to succeed him. The economy continued its slide into disaster. When the generals deposed Mugabe in November 2017, it was a move against mismanagement, and the prospect of more of the same from Grace. Mugabe fell from power after weeks of political tension and intense behind-the-scenes plotting for pole-position in the race to be his successor—presumed up to that time to be a succession following his eventual death. He could scarcely believe he had lost power. The senior military leadership who arrested him, detaining him in a most polite house arrest, went out of their way to deny they were conducting a coup—and, even though it in fact was; it was the politest of coups.

There is a persistent rumour that General Constantino Chiwenga, while visiting China, with a plot swirling against both him and Mnangagwa on the part of Robert and Grace Mugabe, was given a tacit approval from the Chinese—Zimbabwe's benefactors—that they would not object to the coup that then did follow.[25] Chiwenga acted even before his plane landed back in Zimbabwe, having his troops deployed at the airport to prevent his being arrested. Then the coup rolled forwards.

It was an ignominious downfall for someone who had risen so high from nothing. But, in his wake, mismanagement continued unabated. It was a change in personnel at the top certainly but, even with Mugabe's slow motion and grudging resignation, it was still his party, Zimbabwe African National Union—Patriotic Front (ZANU-PF), in power and there was no rolling back of his policies despite public relations rhetoric of a new start and a re-engagement with the world as a reformed state. Certainly the mantra of 'Open For Business', much bruted abroad, seemed momentarily like a new start but was intended—perhaps without choice—to act as a cover for Business As Usual.

Emmerson Mnangagwa, the new president, basically conceded he had inherited an economically degenerated country—politely not saying so directly, but implicitly laying the blame at the door of the post-2000 Mugabe years. But his government did not perform much better, lacking the tools to do so after so many decades of Mugabe's destructive rule. Take the Look East policy: Chiwenga who became Vice President would have known when he allegedly went to the Chinese that they had grown uneasy about an ally that could not repay its debts and would not learn how. But that kind of knowledge in the round is very different from acquiring the detailed knowledge of how to act differently. In a way, looking to China for investment as opposed to aid, as opposed to bailouts, meant a technocratic level of expertise the Zimbabweans, still within the inheritance of Robert Mugabe's policies, have not yet been able to accomplish—and certainly not without diluting it with corruption.

The question has been raised as to whether Mnangagwa and Chiwenga are still captive to a 'Mugabe-ism'. There is, however, no such thing. Despite the apparent and cultivated brilliance of Mugabe, and his enthusiasm for political ideas early on in his nationalist career, there is no intellectual legacy, no sustainable evidence of technocratic thought, only late evidence of a neo-Marxist thought, and a deep rumination to do with the resentments that racism causes and a desire for an evening-out of history at whatever the cost.

Counting the cost falls to President Mnangagwa. But he is surrounded, not by thinkers—who would they be, when Mugabe did not cultivate thinkers during his near-forty-year reign?—but by oligarchs who assume the roles of both key supporters and of interest groups. Many of the elite are not only oligarchs but military personnel. They are the ones who wield the barrel of the gun. There is to be no dispossession of them if Mnangagwa is to survive. He has secured the services of a technocratic Minister of Finance, Mthuli Ncube, who views the restoration of Zimbabwe's fortunes as requiring the formalisation and stabilisation of the economy—notwithstanding the survival of the bulk of the non-oligarchic population by informal means, and the acquisition of wealth by the oligarchic class again by informal means, i.e. corruption. In economic management also there is no appropriate thought.

Mugabe was the liberation leader—with the curious deaths of other contenders for that title—but he was never a liberation fighter. He never carried a gun in battle and, despite his emphasis on land reform, his own un-callused hands betrayed the fact that he had not spent years hoeing fields. Others fought and risked death, and others worked the least productive areas of Zimbabwe that had been left by the white settlers who had acquired the most fertile lands. Indeed, far from being a peasant hero championing the nobility of the simple farmer, there was his scathing disdain of all rivals, dead or alive, friend or foe, particularly in intellectual terms. This scorn was not to his credit, but all the same he insisted, not always successfully, on at least a notion of African destiny.

Apart from a neo-Marxist sense about the international economy, Mugabe expressed on more than one occasion the sense of how much racial discrimination could mark someone so that it is never able to be forgotten. In Mugabe's leadership we have a driving force for struggle in the Marxist sense of a final and irreversible inevitability of triumph, and a restitution for racial discrimination suffered at the hands of those who owned land. As I remarked in my obituary at the time of his death, he would, in some ways, have made a better professor than a president; but, as a president, he clung to power far too long. His rule has left behind a ruthlessly dominant political party but also the economic mire into which he had submerged Zimbabwe, particularly from the land seizures of 2000 onwards. He achieved liberation in the name of authenticity and created a tragedy that lives on through the successor regime.

In the Mnangagwa era, what used to be the opposition MDC led by Morgan Tsvangirai has splintered into quarrelling fiefdoms—and democracy has itself become a profitable business as foreign funds pour into the support of 'democrats' who, all the same oppose each other as much as they oppose the government. There is no centralising ethos within opposition policies. As with the government, there are many quite glossy soundbites. The absence of thought, even fitful thought, is the legacy of Mugabe—who purported to think much while thinking at key junctures too little.

8

THE MORAL AFRICAN AND THE
AFRICAN RENAISSANCE

THABO MBEKI

Nelson Mandela was famously imprisoned for 27 years and, even more famously, forgave his captors and inaugurated a national policy of forgiveness. There were huge elements of moral force to be sure, but also calculation and pragmatism. He was not a pacifist. He had trained as a saboteur in Ethiopia,[1] just as his successor, Thabo Mbeki, trained in Moscow.[2] Today, we would call that training in terrorism. But his dignified and defiant speech at his treason trial, his continuous politeness to his prison guards, and the moral *grandeur* of his post-prison speeches, from immediately after his release, made it seem as if an ethical giant had stepped onto the world stage at a moment of historical change and would govern that change. Western governments, both out of admiration but also seeking to keep the 'new' South Africa 'onside', led the praise. In part, this was also out of guilt—not having done very much to have him released throughout those 27 years.

Those who did, such as a Group of Commonwealth Eminent Persons visiting Pretoria in 1986, led by Australia's Malcolm Fraser and Nigeria's Olusegun Obasanjo—both former national leaders—who had, therefore, to be received with (frosty) politeness—nevertheless had their pleas for a new path forward, including the release of Nelson Mandela, rejected by the simple demonstration of South African warplanes bombing Lusaka.[3] But none of the great Western powers attempted so much—the US Government still had Mandela on a terrorist watch-list as late as 2008.[4]

How Mandela remained a force within the ANC, even from his prison on Robben Island, was recounted to me in 2007 by a fellow inmate, Mosiuoa (Terror) Lekota, a prominent ANC activist who later resigned from the ANC to campaign against Jacob Zuma.[5] Our planes were delayed, and we were for some hours stranded in Italy. Bottles of wine liberated his tongue. By the same token, they may have exaggerated his stories, but I recount them here as indicative of Mandela's determination to oppose Apartheid—even from prison—and not simply be bravely long-suffering as depicted in films like *Invictus*.[6]

- The organisation of the cells: Prisoners on Robben Island were held in isolated blocks precisely so they could not share strategies of defiance or disobedience. One block was not meant to be able to communicate with another. According to Lekota, that all the shower rooms of the different blocks shared the same plumbing and water egress systems. Accordingly, using stones that they had been breaking down each day in their hard labour regimes, they would tap out morse code messages on the outflow pipes to one another.
- The transmission of messages to the outside world: Mandela's instructions to all the prisoners to be at all times unfailingly polite and courteous to the guards finally began to make some of them feel guilty. A small number began offering to carry messages to the outside world whenever they went into the mainland. There, the messages would be picked up by ANC operatives. These could not be detailed communications of any complex operational kind for the liberation fighters, but they were enough to maintain links and to craft overall directions for the resistance. People such as Sydney Mufamadi, later Mandela's youngest minister, acted as part of the liaison chain between internal ANC groups and the external wing in locations like Lusaka.[7] In this way, the organisation as a whole remained coherent.
- Debates on the shape of the new South Africa: Mandela was also a key participant in the lectures and debates of the informal 'univer-

sity' established by the inmates. There was much debate on what they would do to change the country when Apartheid was finally defeated. Govan Mbeki, the father of Thabo and Moletsi, argued for a state-led socialist economy, a centrally planned regime that would ensure equity and equality. Mandela himself understood the dislocation that would be caused if the great capitalist corporations had to leave, close down, or be nationalised, and so argued for a mixed economy with guaranteed provision for the poor.

A lot of this sense of building on a lack of jeopardy, basically a sense of caution combined with a sense of care—not to have people enter freedom with less than what they had before, thus the need for stability in transition—informed the (in)famous Brenthurst 'fireside chats' at the Oppenheimer estate as it became clear Mandela was a person with whom the international and large national corporations would have to treat. At these meetings, leaders of the corporations persuaded Mandela of the need for precisely a mixed economy and stability, and undertook to assist and cooperate in the transition to a more equitable South Africa[8]—even though these were by and large the very corporations that had to one extent or another supported Apartheid or not used their pivotal financial positions to undermine or seriously ameliorate it.[9] By this stage, Mandela had been contemplating a third option between those debated on Robben Island, and that was to go immediately for across-the-board social and economic justice, raising up the lowest socio-economic groups—primarily those who have been subjugated by racial discrimination—borrowing the necessary finance from the donor community, the World Bank and the IMF. This would have had an immediate effect but left South Africa in long-term debt and risk long-term stability.[10] So, for better or worse, Mandela adopted the Brenthurst formula.

Mandela was not always the finest strategic negotiator. In 1992, two years after his release from prison but still midway in the negotiations with the National Party of the Apartheid Government, I spent some time in KwaZulu-Natal—looking on in horror as the ANC negotiators made one mistake after another,[11] and also at the mounting violence in the KwaZulu hills of Zulu militants against ANC communities.[12]

Nevertheless, the ANC recovered its advantages, not least because of Cyril Ramaphosa's skills as a negotiator, and South Africa was able to move onto the triumphant elections of 1994 and, finally, to majority rule.[13] But the South Africa that had achieved this was also the South Africa of very lengthy discrimination and bloodshed.[14] Mandela and Desmond Tutu's idea of forgiveness as an ethos, as well as a pragmatic device to build a bridge away from the past, the 'rainbow bridge' into the future, was a stroke of brilliant engineering that astounded the world.

The Truth and Reconciliation Commission,[15] a pioneer of what is now called 'transitional justice', with emphasis then more on the transition than justice proper—conceived largely by Desmond Tutu as a fast-track but Christian mode of forgiveness, but strongly politically driven by Mandela as the footpath, if not highway, for mass traffic to his rainbow bridge, it attained huge credibility both for allowing Apartheid criminal and victim to come face to face—so that forgiveness and 'healing' were not abstract qualities—and for the participation of people like the distinguished jurisprudential scholar and lawyer, Albie Sachs. The process was one of admission of guilt in a formal and public court-like setting; as far as possible, guilt was also admitted in the presence of the victims or their kin; admission of guilt led to forgiveness from guilt. People walked out relieved of guilt and the nation incrementally relieved from vengeance. The photos of Sachs immediately after the assassination attempt against him, howling in pain while lying in the street, raising his arm to appeal for help without fully realising the arm had been blown off, became a testament to the horror perpetuated by the Apartheid regime. Sachs's subsequent forgiveness of the would-be assassin, even inviting him to dinner and, on the lecture circuit, for years regaling his audiences with the story of himself meeting Henry, the assassin, was both a healing for Sachs to be sure but also a huge public relations success for the TRC.[16] And, while Tutu may have viewed the process as emanating from a Christian impulse and value, it was also seen by him and by many as the beginnings of modern *ubuntu*.

Ubuntu is a deeply problematic (Nguni language) term, not so much in its direct translation, which refers to a humanism within a community context (each needs the other, each recognises him/herself as an individual because there are others—what the Chinese would recognise in Confucian philosophy as reciprocity and the obligation implicit in reciprocity), but because it is a term of traditional ethical philosophy which has no written body of work to do with its explication, elaboration, interrogation and its capacity for philosophical problematisation. There has been recently, especially in the wake of the TRC, a welter of works that purport to express the traditional ethos but which in fact create the ethos into a modernism applicable to a complex South Africa.[17]

This was necessary in the sense that the new South Africa needed a value system that predated white settlerdom, and which then overcame the vicissitudes of that white settlerdom, allowing a fresh start based both on thought and the action of forgiveness. *Ubuntu*, because never formalised in its early history into a system of moral philosophy, became a generalised ethos in the process both of creating a moral public space and of itself being created into a political morality. It was well expressed as a 'relational model of public discourse'.[18] It was in this discourse that Mandela proved himself to be a master.

All this meant that for better or worse—certainly for better in the short run—South Africa became an improvised nation.[19] This is not meant necessarily as a criticism. It was in very many well-applauded respects a brilliantly improvised nation. It is hard to imagine a more seamless transition—even if it is now more than possible to ponder the deep morass of today's South Africa with its contradictions and not fully reconciled relationship with the past.[20]

But, if this was Mandela's true though not complete legacy, a magnificent improvisation, but one professing a moral core, it still leaves him a giant among men. Mandela's vision for a democratic South Africa has been extremely well documented, and little of value can be added by rehearsing it here. Instead, we will turn our attention to an equally vital, yet overlooked political leader and thinker. The actual running of the country—Mandela had not learned to be president of a complex state while spending 27 years in prison—was left to the technocratic mind and thought of Vice President Thabo Mbeki.

* * *

Technocratic policy was Mbeki's. But it is in the complexity of his thought—*ubuntu*, rainbow bridges, diasporic black literature, socialist and social-democratic political and economic philosophy, thought on the US policy of affirmative action, that makes him fascinating—more so in fact than Mandela—and his ideas of renaissance made him the last great pan-Africanist, something many South Africans to this day do not appreciate or understand.

Mbeki played an important role in the negotiations that led, slowly, to the end of Apartheid. In exile rather than in prison, he rose in the ranks of the external ANC. At first, the South African government was confident it could set its own terms for any amelioration of institutionalised and legalised racism but was prepared to explore options and certainly the limits of the ANC. In 1984, utilising Track Two or unofficial diplomacy, it sanctioned a two-person delegation to Lusaka to explore negotiations with the ANC. The two were H.W. van der Merwe and Piet Muller. Van der Merwe had been trying to establish the possibility of negotiations before, had met Mbeki and indeed had been allowed to visit Mandela in prison, so Mandela himself understood what was underway. Van der Merwe's efforts were approved by President Kaunda of Zambia. As a key international leader of the ANC, Mbeki was constantly visiting Lusaka and so would also have been apprised of such initiatives. He met with van der Merwe and Muller when the two arrived in Lusaka towards the end of 1984.[21] The results were positive enough for Track Two to continue as the preferred methodology; several other such meetings led, for instance, to a delegation of South African businessmen meeting ANC leaders in Dakar, Senegal, in 1987.[22] Throughout, Pretoria kept up a twin-track strategy—waving an olive branch of readiness for largely secret incremental negotiations, together with the deployment of its military might. Its 'Total Strategy', modelled on the French suppression of rebellion in Algeria in the 1950s, destabilised and weakened many of the 'frontline states' in Southern Africa as a means of discouraging them from supporting the ANC beyond limited points.[23] It was only with the defeat of South African forces by the Cuban military in Southern Angola, at the Battle of Cuito Cuanavale in 1988, that Total Strategy collapsed, and the ruling National Party in South Africa changed its leadership to explore more fundamentally serious negotiations.[24] These involved Kenneth Kaunda and F.W. de Klerk meeting on Zambian soil in 1989, but they also involved Thabo Mbeki. From 1987 to 1990, but especially after Cuito Cuanavale in 1988, secret talks involving senior members of the

South African Government and the ANC were held in Somerset, UK, with Thabo Mbeki taking the lead from the ANC side.[25]

So that the Mbeki who returned to South Africa following the release of Nelson Mandela was also the Mbeki who had led the ANC in exile, albeit with such steers as Mandela could smuggle out to him while remaining essentially ignorant of the complex international campaigns and low-intensity armed struggle the ANC was fielding. After release in 1990, Mandela would have depended on Mbeki for much more than simply providing the technocratic input to his moral vision. He would have needed Mbeki to introduce him to most of the exiled ANC that had grown up over 27 years.

Mbeki was, as we shall see again, highly respectful of the authority age and years of commitment confer. He was a diligent Number Two, but ruthless in his sidelining of possible competitors for the succession to Mandela. Some of this is described in William Gumede's biography[26]—which earned him the wrath of much of the ANC[27]—but it is clear, despite more laudatory even if occasionally critical biographies,[28] that Mbeki was not only a technocratic but a political animal. He would not have survived the sometimes vicious politics of the ANC in exile, not just in Lusaka[29] but around the world, if he had not been such.

And he was a worldly man. He was born in 1942 and left South Africa aged 20. So, when he returned after Mandela's release in 1990, he had been outside South Africa from 1962 to 1990, or a total of 28 years. In short, he had lived outside South Africa for longer than he had lived in it.[30] To all intents and purposes, he was a stranger to his own country. And so, in effect was Mandela, having been imprisoned and isolated from its everyday dynamics for 27 years. Both men had a lot to catch up on. But, whereas Mandela had a very small circumference of space, Mbeki had roamed the world and imbibed very many influences. As a young student in the UK, at the University of Sussex, he had led campaigns seeking (in the end successfully) to persuade the British Government to lobby against death sentences in the 1964 Rivonia treason trial, where his father, Govan, faced capital punishment alongside Mandela. It was a huge relief to him and also a confirmation, at a very young age, of his organisational and diplomatic capacities.

Events in Southern Africa were beginning to develop rapidly. In 1965, Ian Smith made his white-minority Unilateral Declaration of Independence in Rhodesia, and Mbeki saw at first hand the inept response of a Great Britain that was itself suffering economic malaise and debt. It was also in 1965 that he began his Master's degree at Sussex. He was a Development Economics student at the very moment that Development Economics and Development Studies began as serious disciplines in Britain and from there spread out to the wider world. It was at Sussex in 1966 that Dudley Seers and Hans Singer established what swiftly became the world-famous Institute of Development Studies (IDS). Its early emphases were on book-length, data-driven, individual country case studies, studies often financed by the International Labour Organization (ILO), but with almost all such studies back-dropped by an analysis of the structural nature of the world economy. This was less directly Marxist and more owing, through Singer who collaborated with him, the work of Raul Prebisch, who was often associated with the *dependencia* school, but who also stressed the nature of flexibility, and thus comparative advantage, gained by developed countries through advanced industrialisation.[31]

This is not the place to debate what is known as the Singer-Prebisch Theory,[32] but it is to say that Mbeki was tutored in the complexities of the inequalities of the world. These were not simply and baldly stated in declaratory and almost abstract theory but could be analysed, measured, and to some degree at least subjected to strategic amelioration. From 1969 to 1970, Mbeki studied in Moscow, where he was also trained as a saboteur. In the 1970s, by now having assumed a prominent place within the exiled ANC, especially at first as a youth spokesman, he made several trips to the USA to rally support for the anti-Apartheid cause. To all of these influences, *ubuntu* was added as a very late-comer. To a certain extent, these many influences on him cannot be disaggregated, but their combination, impacting him in a very condensed period, makes Mbkei often seem overly complex and lacking in a single ideology.

In addition, there were his boyhood influences from his father, Govan, and Govan's own admiration for both Marx and Gandhi. As recounted earlier, portraits of these two men sat on the family mantlepiece. Gandhi inspired Du Bois, Kaunda, and Martin Luther King.

Even the young Barack Obama, when he first became a Senator, hung a portrait of Gandhi in his office. The nature of Gandhi's disregard, indeed condescension, for black Africans during his time in South Africa is now well known. The Mbekis would have known this as well. But Gandhi took on and defeated the British Empire, and so was an inspiration. He was not African, but he was not white. But he was also noted for his careful, incremental strategies of resistance—that resistance could not be blind but had to be plotted and planned.[33] Development had to be planned too. This sense of preparation and planning had a huge impact on the young Thabo Mbeki.

And the planning had to have a moral purpose and dimension. The work of the British social-democratic thinker and intellectual progenitor of the welfare state, R.H. Tawney, who lived from 1880 to 1962, was also a huge influence—as he still was in the Britain of the 1960s.[34] His was an early advocacy of a moral economy being inextricably linked to economic policy in general. The former had to be the latter's purpose. An example that could be interpreted in Tawney-an terms was the US undertaking of Affirmative Action under Presidents Kennedy in 1961 and Johnson in 1965. It became a matter of law that what the British later called Positive Discrimination should be part of the fabric of economic and, thence, social life and upliftment. Affirmative Action was something that began at the same time as Martin Luther King's civil rights campaign swung into high gear. All of these things happened while Mbeki was in his student years. Affirmative Action had its later echo in Mbeki's own policies of Black Economic Empowerment, discussed below.

Mbeki was Mandela's vice president from 1994 to 1999 and then president from 1999 to 2008. How he applied all his influences can be divided into three sections.

1. Economy
2. *Ubuntu* in international policy
3. The African Renaissance.

Before delving into these, it is well to remember that Mbeki and South Africa faced four key problems:

Firstly, the Apartheid model of public administration was extremely pedantic and step-driven. There was little flexibility in its procedures and thresholds for moving from one step to another. While this worked, often very well, in ensuring a high standard of living for a minority population, its lack of speed and flexibility meant it was highly unprepared for dealing with a sudden majority expecting and demanding uplift.

Secondly, there was a felt need to appoint ANC cadres to senior governmental and civil service positions. Not all were well qualified. The ANC ranks were replete with lawyers and political scientists, trained in foreign universities, but not with experts in new technology or bureaucrats fluent in the language of process. The new appointments followed existing public administrative protocols—the key change was a black person in charge—but no one in the ANC Government knew how to adjust or upgrade these protocols and their procedures.

Thirdly, at a grassroots level, the need for economic uplift meant the entry of a workforce and new firms into an environment that demanded competitive and entrepreneurial skills, but these, with high-level financial, investment and banking skills, had been suppressed to an alarming degree by Apartheid.

Fourthly, the ANC entered government, and this was even more the case when Mbeki succeeded Mandela at the very moment electronic communications and means of communication were making their first wave of impact felt in the world. The immense slowness of the new government to appreciate this, invest in it, and to train all its civil servants in it, hampers public administration to this day. For a long time it was a joke in academic circles that downloading a complex file sent from a computer in Durban to one in Johannesburg took so long that a memory stick carried by a homing pigeon would arrive more quickly. My friends and I tested this theory and, yes, the pigeon arrived first. When I explained this to a senior minister in 2010, she had no idea what I was talking about. 'File', 'download speeds' and 'bandwidth': were alien terms to her even though she was well-educated and associated with a science portfolio. Until recently, and this is anecdotal evidence (but from a Cabinet Minister), the majority of the Cabinet could not work their own emails. We surmised it was as if, exhausted from the effort, all history and learning had stopped with liberation.

So, with these difficulties in mind, any revolution in provision, uplift, and the encouragement of a formal economy of new firms, new jobs, and new opportunities, without always access to new skills and new procedures, was bound to be simultaneously visionary and plodding.

The Economy

To be fair, to even begin to achieve the goals of Mandela and the ANC within a mixed, not centrally planned and socialist economy demanded constant growth. The Mbeki years of 1999 to 2008 saw an average national growth rate of 4.5%, not enough to meet the goals of national social provision, but better than any achieved since. However, the key programmes advanced in the Mbeki years saw economic growth concentrated in the middle class. This did mean the lower middle class rose higher so, to that extent, there was upliftment and, to an extent, security of income and personal planning horizons. The bulk of those in the shanty, urban subsistence and lower end informal sector were not uplifted. Education, including higher education, expanded dramatically and impressively, but not always in the scientific and technological sectors.[35] Mbeki had vision but not always the qualified personnel to execute it.

There were two key programmes that Mbeki, working with Trevor Manuel, his senior planning minister, pushed forward. Both sat alongside and within the overarching RDP (Reconstruction and Development Programme) introduced by Mandela in 1994. The RDP was a comprehensive series of development goals agreed by the government and key stakeholders such as the trade unions. Subsequent progress has often used these goals as foundational categories for measurement. Actual detailed planning to attain them was contained in programmes with Mbeki's stamp on them.

The most well-known may have indeed been inspired by US Affirmative Action. That began in the 1960s when Mbeki was a student. The much more modest British Positive Action push under the 2010 Equality Act came after Mbeki's tenure in high office. So Mbeki and Manuel had to gear a civil rights principle to a South African context—without a commensurate national crash programme of business training—to increase black participation in the economy. The goal was to stimulate and create black-owned firms. They would in turn create black employment. It was not the creation of jobs in the first instance—although many parts of the civil service and local administrations did show signs of bloating. The programmes were called Black Economic Empowerment (BBE) from 2003, and then Broad-Based Black Economic Empowerment (BBBEE), from 2007. The second was a modification of the first, intended to widen the range of beneficiaries.

The fundamental idea was that, in the tendering process, powerful corporations and government departments would, all other things being equal, favour or prefer firms with a majority black ownership and workforce. Such firms' contribution did begin to contribute to overall GDP, but not in any way that distorted the importance of the contribution of larger and longer-established private corporations and large public enterprises. The problem was often shoddy work as new providers struggled to gear up to new demands and new volumes of business. The construction of low cost but modern housing units, a key promise of the ANC, saw BEE and BBBEE firms awarded many contracts—with variable results. Sometimes this was due not just to problems of coming up to speed, but making profit with least input. The second problem of noticeable dimensions was the award of contracts—particularly by municipalities, by a process of insider trading in the tendering process (alerting providers as to the level of tender from their competitors)—to friends, cronies, or ANC party members. This last category soon led to membership of the ANC being a route towards upwards financial mobility. It also led to corruption as providers paid 'commissions' to key municipal, then provincial, then national authorities. Having said that, these programmes did change the face of service and business provision in South Africa, but only to a ceiling, as the plethora of new firms were not geared by way of training, or indeed municipal and governmental demand, to provide hi-tech services. In this way, the modesty of the success of these programmes reflected the paucity of understanding of the new hi-tech world on the part of the ANC national leadership.

The second key programme was Growth, Employment and Redistribution (GEAR), adopted in 1996 while Mbeki was Vice

President. However, it should be seen as his effort to realise Mandela's decision to go for a mixed economy with growth ensuring provision and safety nets for the poor. It was, two years into the Mandela Government, an actual economic strategy—the first. But what it had to do, in line with the Brenthurst fireside agreements, was to encourage the large corporations to create wealth. It was essentially neoliberal and not unlike what Tony Blair attempted in the UK from 1997 onwards. It was in antithesis to what Govan Mbeki, his father, sought. It was something Mandela had accepted as the only plausible way forward without great disruption. But it had its own logic which, to Mbeki too, appeared inescapable. It would benefit the poorest by the simple process of 'trickle down' and was, in that respect, basically a textbook rendition of the principles and strategy articulated by Walt Rostow. A key difference was the encouragement, both explicit and widely implicit, that the large corporations would do well to take on black executives in senior positions. This went right up to executive board level and to boards of trustees. It has been called 'pepper potting', black grains among the white, but it did change at least the cosmetic face of South African capitalism and created a new class of black oligarchs, the current President of South Africa, Cyril Ramaphosa arguably being one.

Whatever the relative merits of neoliberalism and greater socialism, what it meant was that the two strategies, GEAR and BBBEE, were designed for different socio-economic impacts and the participation of different socio-economic groups.[36] Together, it is arguable that all this has resulted in a different and possibly improved South Africa—although the comparative measure was the denial of meaningful participation and reward under Apartheid—but it has led to a marked stratification of society. Whether it also means class formation is another question in the midst of so much unevenness in modes of production. It does mean that strata and/or classes coalesce within the ANC, which acts as a patron of available strategies, appointments, preferments and corresponding corruption, failure to renew itself, and cabalism. If the ANC were dynamic, technocratic, and not increasingly as with ZANU-PF in Zimbabwe, a state within a state, all might be well. But the degeneration of the ANC into a platform for power and, increasingly, wealth, has also paralleled a deterioration of South Africa and its provision of services and benefits to the poor, as public utilities and parastatals fail, and private corporations under-perform.

In some key respects, away from the moral glamour, these do act as part of the legacies of Mandela and Mbeki.

Ubuntu in International Policy

If there is no animating and overarching *ubuntu* in economic policy, the philosophy becoming known—certainly known as important—to Mbeki late in his career, it can be seen in his foreign policy within Africa. To this extent, the philosophy features in an applied, if sometimes murky, pan-Africanism conducted at the highest levels. The origins of *ubuntu*, a linking of 'oneself as another', a sense of fusion between individual and community so that what works for one's own benefit only really works if the community of which one is a part also benefits. It is a concept present in both Zulu and Xhosa languages, speaking to a universal bond. Archbishop Tutu used it as an ethical explanation for the Truth and Reconciliation Commission, but it was a concept that proved difficult to actualise in international politics.

The core example resides in Mbeki's mediation after the 2008 Zimbabwean elections which, after some months of intensive negotiations brokered by Mbeki and his team, agreed an imperfect but guardedly functional Mugabe/Tsvangirai coalition. Mbeki would try the same formula in 2009, after the end of his Presidency, in the terrible civil war of Sudan and Darfur—there without even short-duration success. But he had actually trialled his formula in the Democratic Republic of Congo in 2005, brokering a complex power-sharing between Kabila's central government and the outlying 25 provinces. Under the Mbeki formula, they enjoyed a form of semi-autonomy—which may have been the only thing possible in the case of DRC, but also prolonged the wait for any kind of centralised efficacy in government and public administration in a vast country. And it did not prevent war in southeastern DRC—which continues to this day with estimates of a fatality rate of 2 million, accusations of genocide, and certainly of gendercide, where rape is used as a deliberate weapon of war. Mbeki used many of the same team members for all three of these mediations so, to an extent, they were working a formula with basic strategic and tactical principles. Whether there were also philosophical principles is considered below.

The immediate precursor to the 2008 elections in Zimbabwe were the 2007 elections in Kenya. The extent and brutality of the violence that erupted after the results were announced there—with many considering the results manipulated—was such that the international community was widely alarmed. The African Union dispatched former UN Secretary-General Kofi Annan to mediate the situation and negotiate a way through. Annan promptly emptied Nairobi of all other mediatory missions and personnel. Conflict mediation is now an industry and, while sometimes very useful, also provides disputants with the fig-leaf of being seen to be talking with one or another of such groups while continuing the violence. The classic tactic would have both sides talking to different, and rival, mediatory groups. Annan claimed the mandate and authority of the African Union. Both the contending parties, if successful, would seek to continue membership of Kenya in the African Union. It was something supranational enough to be supervening in the morass of mediators. And he was not above playing upon the image that he, as an African, was better suited to the task than non-African mediators.

The outcome of the very swift—just a single month—of negotiations, with Annan prepared to use threats as much as persuasion (and indeed indictments, that were ultimately unsuccessful, before the International Criminal Court, were part of his armoury), was a coalition government. A Prime Ministership was extra-constitutionally created. The person whom many thought was the rightful winner of the Presidency was given the new Prime Ministership, while the person viewed by many as the loser became President.[37] Stability and the guarantee of a seat at the high table was finally sufficient to persuade the antagonists to enter a form of cooperation. It was in many ways a sheer pragmatism that Annan pulled off. He did it with verve, inducement, threat, and authority. Finally the way forward was not so much a unity but an inclusiveness. Could inclusiveness be seen as an ethos in its own right?

Mbeki's mediation after the 2008 Zimbabwean elections took many months longer than Annan's in Kenya. Appointed by the

Southern African Development Community, the regional body, he sought to reach an agreement entirely through persuasion and patience, with neither threats nor timelines for agreement with guillotine deadlines. Mugabe would have been used to these, having had them inflicted on him by Lord Carrington in the Lancaster House peace talks in 1979.[38] But in 2008, Mugabe had his military behind him and, to that extent, control of any guillotine.

As we have seen, ZANU-PF had entered the 2008 elections with confidence, as if oblivious to the resentment caused by massive hyperinflation, caused in turn by the collapse of the agricultural export sector upon which the country depended. Money was printed as if it had value in itself, without the need for underpinning productivity, until the inflation estimates were in the millions per cent. The shock on election night, as the results started coming in, was plain. As previously mentioned, extrapolating from them alongside my own polling during the campaign, I had Morgan Tsvangirai winning the Presidential elections with 56% of the vote.[39] South African Broadcasting predicted on its television broadcasts a win by Tsvangirai with 52%. Counting and the announcement of results abruptly stopped. When it recommenced, it took several weeks before the full results appeared. Tsvangirai, it was announced, had won the majority of votes but not enough to avoid a runoff. It was apparent that much manipulation had in the meantime been applied to the count. I have described some of the factors that had to have been involved in making the final published figures seem plausible.[40] They form a template for what must now be factored into computer programmes to manipulate electoral results. In 2008 Zimbabwe, they may indeed have appeared finally arithmetically plausible, but given the protracted count and the circumstances in Zimbabwe, few considered they passed the test of political credibility. Violence immediately broke out as the runoff round began, instigated with brutality by ZANU-PF militants, Tsvangirai withdrew in protest, and the runoff elections were declared for Mugabe. Even Southern Africa was alarmed at the circumstances of Mugabe's victory—and thus Mbeki was dispatched as SADC mediator.

Here again, as in Kenya, but after protracted haggling, the result was a coalition with Mugabe, having polled below Tsvangirai even after the protracted count, as President and Tsvangirai as again an extra-constitutional Prime Minister. There was extended haggling over the share of Cabinet posts among the major parties, with ZANU-PF retaining the defence and security portfolios, but conceding the finance portfolio to Tsvangirai's MDC—probably to an extent gladly as, having caused a huge financial decline, someone else could be blamed if the situation was not reversed. So, even in a power-sharing coalition, the forces of coercion remained with Mugabe. But the questions to be asked include three groups of simple ones:

1. Did the coalition reflect the will of the Zimbabwean people? In short, was the value and principle of democracy uppermost?
2. Did the extemporaneous invention of a post of Prime Minister respect the Zimbabwean constitution? It was not provided for in the constitution, so what was the value of constitutional rule, and where was the principle of constitutional rule?
3. If two typically fundamental principles were relegated, circumvented, or laid aside, what principle guided their replacement by a pragmatic power share? Was it just pragmatism, as seemed to be the case with Kofi Annan in Kenya? Or was inclusivity seen by Mbeki as a more important, supervening principle than the other principles mentioned? Was inclusivity meant to save people's lives from violent political struggle and did that become the cardinal principle?

I suggest that Mbeki deliberately drew upon the ethos of *ubuntu* in his work—not so much in the meetings among the teams of negotiators fielded by all stake-holding and rival parties, but in his own face-to-face meetings with Mugabe. These were private meetings, but with close aides in attendance, so the evidence is anecdotal—to an extent circumstantial and even conjectural—gleaned from Mbeki team members who were disinclined to give deep detail. However, it is suggestive of the direction of discussion in engagements that were committed to a certain politesse. It was a politesse grounded in modes of traditional respect—Mbeki was addressing an older man, a senior liberation figure who had won success before he had. Age and seniority were key here, and Mugabe knew how to deploy the implicit restraints of this politesse upon others—even if they were leaders of a more powerful country.

Nkosana Moyo, once a minister in a Mugabe Cabinet, and himself an occasional minority presidential candidate running on a techno-cratic (as opposed to properly political) platform, described to me—gleaned from sources close to Mugabe—that Mugabe would acknowl-edge, but end, Mbeki's representations with the words, "I have heard you". This represented neither an agreement nor disagreement, and sometimes indicated an inclination to think things over, but Mbeki knew at that point there was nothing more he should say.[41] In part, this helps explain the length of time negotiations took. It was waiting for the old man's ruminations to be completed. It was of course also a psychological ploy to keep people waiting until all arrived at the default expectation that progress depended on Mugabe alone. Mbeki was well aware of the carnivalesque manifestations of Mugabe's gov-ernment that had led to meltdown and to sufficient electoral irregu-larity for Mbeki to be involved in the first place, but he was prepared to play the game of traditional back and forth, utilising his own posi-tion as leader of Zimbabwe's immediate neighbour.

Here language and the behavioural expectations encoded in lan-guage become of great importance. Unlike the case of Annan and Kenya, where Annan's native language of Akan was far removed from the Kikuyu and Luo spoken by the two major antagonists in the elec-toral battle there—geographically the whole width of the continent away—the more proximate and intimate interactions and linguistic intersections of Southern Africa allowed for different languages with similar encoded forms of correct behaviour. This is where to speak of *ubuntu* as itself representing an African ethos is limiting. It may be said to be one linguistic subscription to an ethos, among others. For instance, in the Shona of Zimbabwe and the Tsonga in South Africa, the interlocking of 'friendship' and 'helping each other to live' allows for a conviviality that becomes expected behaviour. Chekero and Morreira conducted a study that:

> explores forms of mutuality and conviviality between Shona migrants from Zimbabwe and Tsonga-speaking South Africans living in Giyani, South Africa. To analyse these forms of mutuality, we draw on Southern African concepts rather than more conventional develop-ment or migration theory. We explore ways in which the Shona concept of *hushamwari* (translated as 'friendship') and the commensu-

rate xiTsonga category of *kuhanyisana* ('to help each other to live') allow for conviviality. Employing the concept of *hushamwari* enables us to move beyond binaries of kinship versus friendship relations and examine the ways in which people create reciprocal friendships that are a little "like kin." We argue that the cross-cutting forms of collective personhood that underlie both Shona and Tsonga ways of being make it possible to form social bonds across national lines, such that mutuality can be made between people even where the wider social context remains antagonistic to "foreigners."[42]

If that suggests an intersection between language and behaviour, a closer examination of aspects of Shona, Mugabe's own language group, uncovers something closely analogous to the *ubuntu* ethos. Magosvongwe wrote:

> Dependence on philosophies that are antithetical to one's existential conditions, expectations, and worldviews, has often blighted many participants' destinies. In examining the land developments in post-2000 Zimbabwe, this article defines and discusses Shona philosophy of *Unhu/Hunhu* and Shona onomastics [the origins of naming], both rooted in the land and its traditions. *Unhu*, the philosophy of social engineering born out of experience and struggle, encapsulates distilled wisdom, provides the benchmark of ethical conduct. In Shona traditional philosophy, the logic of being *munhu*/human being is labyrinthine with *Unhu*/ethics/morals/attitude to other people and life, rooted in belongingness with the land/*ivhu*/*dhaga*/soil. The essence of munhu is thus premised on both outward physical form and ethics, beliefs, values, and aesthetics as determined by society within its given geophysical land. *Unhu*, therefore, is expected to subtly influence responses to experiences and phenomena. Shona Unhu that informs the present article admits that persons are persons through other persons.[43]

The seeming closeness of words, *unhu* (Shona) and *ubuntu* (Nguni) is not the point. Shona and Nguni peoples are historically different. While there may well be crossovers in certain words, what is important here is the expectation of a crossover ethic. And Mbeki would certainly have played the 'we are both the products of struggle and liberation' card to Mugabe, seeking mutual respect between Mbeki and Mugabe—but also indicating that the process and product of struggle meant an interpersonality even with the opposition. The experience of fighting for land was, in fact, reinforcement of this idea since all were children of the soil. In this sense, the concept of inclusivity was not the cardinal virtue, except insofar as inclusivity provided an overarching context for mutuality. If looked at through this (admittedly) sympathetic lens, then the Mbeki mediation with its compromise coalition government was founded on a value more prescient to the Zimbabwean situation than democracy and constitutionalism alone.

The idea of language and its importance had in fact occurred to Mbeki before, again in a firefight over Zimbabwe, and it became an entry-point to his perorations on an African Renaissance.

The African Renaissance

This firefight occurred in 2003 at a specially called Commonwealth summit, in the Nigerian capital of Abuja to consider the continued suspension of Zimbabwe from Commonwealth membership. The suspension had occurred as a result of the land invasions and farm seizures. As British prime minister, Tony Blair was determined to keep Zimbabwe out of membership, and Mbeki travelled to Abuja wanting Zimbabwe back in. The two respected each other as senior international players, but Mbeki was sure he could depend on pan-African support from the Commonwealth membership. Blair knew that was Mbeki's assumption and worked to increase the number of his own allies and decrease Mbeki's. It was a classical, if cynical, diplomatic tactical play. But what it meant was, in a Commonwealth with Caribbean nations inhabited by an African diaspora, such nations were a key part of the variables in accumulating numbers of allies. Mbeki assumed he could count on all the African states in the Commonwealth and also, out of pan-African solidarity, all the Caribbean states. He did not even think of the non-white states of the Asia and the South Pacific. So Mbeki didn't 'work' them. Blair, by adroit diplomacy, captured all of them and also Ghana and Kenya.[44] Mbeki, defeated, was furious—but he had been beaten as much because he had made assumptions based on black solidarity as much because Blair had worked hard to ensure a diminution of possible allies for him. Mbeki stormed back to South Africa and penned one of his articles for the newsletter of the ANC to explain in grand terms what this setback represented in terms of Africa in the world.[45]

These ANC newsletters were a regular publication and always featured an article by Mbeki as President of the ANC as well as President of South Africa. No one could understand them. They were the penmanship of a learned and well-travelled professor. His reference points were not always African and seldom South African. In the case of his post-Abuja article, they were American and Kenyan. The American was Henry Kissinger, whose words Mbeki slightly distorted to mean that Western powers were intent on using human rights to subjugate African agency. This was a little rich, given that the South African constitution agreed after the end of Apartheid was arguably the world's richest in terms of human rights and equalities. But the interesting part of his writing was about the Kenyan novelist, Ngũgĩ wa Thiong'o, and his very influential book, *Decolonising the Mind*, in which Ngũgĩ wrote about the need both for himself thenceforth to write in Kikuyu, his own language, and to be aware that the formation of thought and its linguistic expression is a key to understanding the continuing work of the colonial project. To speak like a European is to think like a European.[46] To speak one's own language is to think one's own thoughts.

Mbeki didn't enter any disquisition on linguistic theory, nor did he query the process of linguistic evolution and adaptation to 'new worlds'. Is modern Kikuyu the same as pre-colonial Kikuyu? Nevertheless, Mbeki would have been aware of the power of language. The 1976 uprisings of students and other young people in Soweto were precisely against the imposition of Afrikaans as a universal medium of instruction. It was regarded, even though very many South Africans spoke at least some of it, as the language of domination. People were not against the language as such, but against the officialisation of the language for the upbringing of children. It was regarded as a means to achieve a formation of thought. So, both from Ngũgĩ and Soweto, Mbeki took the idea—while writing to the ANC in English—that modes of dominance went far beyond the political and economic. The denial of equality and prosperity was caused by the political and economic but the denial of authenticity by thought and language was the root of a host of Africa's problems. Africa literally had no voice with which to stand up to the world. His idea of an African Renaissance was very much a flowering of something authentic that could indeed stand up to the world.

It was a pan-African hope on Mbeki's part. He meant all of Africa. But given the 2,000 languages in the continent, he couldn't confine himself only to questions of linguistic determinants of thought. His renaissance had two key aspects: the first was that it was in fact a pan-Blackness. In other ANC newsletters his articles cited black US and Caribbean poets, 'Negro spirituals' (notwithstanding the fact that these 'spirituals' offered a particular celebration and affirmation of Christianity), and included North Africa alongside Sub-Saharan Africa as part of his quest for a path towards authenticity. He noted, archly, in the face of European restrictions on African migration to 'Fortress Europe', that the Carthaginian General, Hannibal (from today's Tunisia), once almost conquered Rome—probably utilising black as well as Arab troops, and certainly African elephants as the 'heavy cavalry' that decimated Roman army after Roman army. (Of course, Franco also used African troops as he conquered 20th century Spain in the name of fascism.) However, the basic assumption and sentiment of Mbeki's work was not unlike those of earlier thinkers: that there was a cultural congruity and common personality.[47]

There has been much academic writing on Mbeki's ideas of renaissance and its antecedents.[48] Probably the most even-handed, and critical, essay was by Itumeleng Mekoa—who all the same gave a pithy description of Mbeki's African Renaissance idea.[49]

The African renaissance concept was first articulated by Cheikh Anta Diop in a series of essays beginning in 1946, which are collected in his book *Towards the African Renaissance: Essays in Culture and Development, 1946–1960*.[50] The concept was further popularized by former South African President Thabo Mbeki ... heralding the beginning of the African renaissance, the same desire that drove the European renaissance. However, Mbeki"s articulation of the renaissance seemed to be in the tradition of early pan-African philosophers like Dr W.E.B Du Bois, Kwame Nkrumah, Julius Nyerere and many other African legends. Hence, the argument of this article is that no one can talk of an African renaissance without any reference to pan-Africanism and Black consciousness because they too stand in the tradition of African renewal or consciousness. Therefore, the African renaissance of Thabo Mbeki is preceded by these African philosophies of renewal. The term African renaissance was never used to refer to pan-Africanism and Black Consciousness, even though, in some sense, they were renaissance philosophies. They represented a peak of renaissance in

African philosophy. It is also important to make a distinction between African renaissance and European renaissance. They too emerged at different periods, contexts and with different objectives. African renaissance philosophy emerged as a political philosophy of liberation of the African people. European renaissance emerged as a counter-discourse to supernatural knowledge. Though it began innocently as a philosophy of rationalism, and self-determination, its universalism made it a political instrument of subjugation. Instead of building self-determination on the indigenous people, it suppressed them, and left a legacy of non-beings. This state of being was only restored by African renaissance philosophies.

The author goes on to argue that Mbeki's thought was insufficient to deliver an actual Renaissance. Whether anyone's could have, is a key question. But the key reference here is to Cheikh Anta Diop, inspired by Aimé Césaire, but for many years from the 1960s leader of the Senegalese opposition against Senghor. Paris-educated, like Senghor, to a high level, he was involved not only in the quest for a unifying culture but was a scientist, working in the *Collège de France* in nuclear physics. He was also a noted Egyptologist, and so, if anyone qualified to be a Renaissance Man in the European mould, it was he. Diop argued that there was a shared cultural continuity across African peoples. This shared continuity was more important than the varied development of different ethnic groups with their sometimes radically different languages and cultures. He sought, as his mission, to rebuild the African personality from a strictly scientific, socio-historical per-spective—but this was, in the face of so much diversity, a temptation towards forcing a point and a temptation towards a declaratory pseudo-science.[51] In a way it was as romantic an effort as Senghor's cultural *negritude*. Even so, Diop's intellectual inspiration was so important that, despite the cleavages in Senegalese politics, the nation's main university is now named after him.

Mbeki never acknowledged Diop as the continent's progenitor of thought on an African Renaissance. It is not certain he even knew about Diop—the Francophonic and Anglophonic formations of differ-ent parts of Africa being so different, making the quest for authentic-ity separate exercises. But, without being able to complete the Diop mission, i.e. providing a plausible and not simply romantic scientific foundation for original and now transcendent commonality, and thus genealogical and foundational unity within a contemporary pan-Africanism, the project remains aspirational but declaratory and rhetorical, and the idea of a Renaissance begs the question 'of what?'

Mbeki's other newsletter articles drew on the work of British thinkers like the moral economist Tawney, and even the English poet, Walter de la Mare (now forgotten on almost every literary curriculum in Britain itself), so to a large extent the reference to Ngũgĩ was exceptional—a one-off. And Ngũgĩ's work is itself unfinished. Curiously, it is within South Africa today, but through the work of a Zimbabwean scholar, Sabelo Ndlovu-Gatsheni, that Ngũgĩ's project might be brought to fruition.[52] For it is one thing to say that language reflects and in turn determines thought, it is another quite more complex thing to elaborate the epistemological structures and, above all, epistemological transitions involved, not only in the expression of thought and its intended meaning, but what happens in a multilingual world as meaning gets translated from one language to another. Diop, Ngũgĩ, Mbeki, and Ndlovu-Gatsheni himself were or are multilingual. Can one be 'authentic' within a world in flux and in which, in any or many languages, new definitions and inflexions are constantly required? Even so, the work of Ndlovu-Gatsheni represents the best serious and extended effort to give answers to such questions.

There is the added set of requirements articulated by the Ghanaian scholar Kwame Gyekye and his study of thought and its expression in the Akan language. There is a place finally, Gyekye wrote, for 'sagely knowledge', traditional thought and values as traditionally expressed. But to understand the nuances, and not just the bald and superficial meaning of that thought, one needs to speak and understand Akan.[53] And, for good measure, probably also to appreciate the socio-historical and cultural context of the lived tradition and how sage-liness was valued, and according to what value system of high and low regard.

Finally, it may come down to a project-in-progress being prosecuted with the goal of creating something new and meaningful in today's world, but based as far as possible in an appreciation of the past and, above all, an imagination of the past. Past and future collide or coalesce in European culture too. After all, Shakespeare had never heard of Freud's Oedipus Complex when he wrote Hamlet, but it is today impossible to read Hamlet without that almost prescriptive lens determining our appreciation. For Mbeki to be even involved in a project of both reclamation and assertion, and to do so through essays as well as efforts at programme, is something that sits well in terms of a retrospective appreciation of him. And, of course, there is the point that should be made, but is not often made in South Africa, as Steve Biko was never a member of the ANC and thus not consecrated in official ANC history as an intellectual forbear, but Biko's crusade for black consciousness, his inspiration by Frantz Fanon (see Chapter Six), has clear unacknowledged echoes in Mbeki's work. His assassination in 1977 (uncovered as a police assassination by Helen Zille, then a young crusading journalist—whose own political career has recently fallen on controversial hard times) removed from South African activism and thought a rising voice, inspirational to today's South African students who, all the same, repudiate the legacy of Mbeki.[54]

That legacy has certainly been mired in the economic crisis that now besets South Africa. The ANC is seen by many to have failed.[55] Its economic policies are certainly heavily criticised, Mbeki's GEAR and BBBEE not having led to any promised land, but certainly Mbeki's moral economy, and Mandela's dream of the new moral person—not the new African personality—have also become somewhat mired as the end of first quarter of the 21st century draws inexorably closer and with it, 41 years of freedom.

But, all South African and pan-African thought and aspiration aside, Mbeki's African Renaissance also must, as pointed out in the work of the Cameroonian scholar also now working in South Africa, Achille Mbembe, be part of the wider project of freeing Africa to be part of a freer world, a world undistorted by the vicissitudes and exploitations of capitalism and imperial outreach. Finally, all reason and renaissance must partake in a world of humanity.[56]

9

THE RESPONSIBILITY TO BE FREE

THE UNTAPPED POTENTIAL OF A NEW PAN-AFRICANISM

In this chapter we look at the agenda that lies ahead for African political thought. We do so by first looping back to the foundational idea of African unity, of a working and operationalised pan-Africa. In retrospect the idea that an enacted nationalism—i.e. the successful creation of an independent working state, one able to bring greater benefits to people who were now citizens than they received as subjects of colonialism—could be combined with a subsuming of all such new states being rushed into existence in a condensed space of time, and with different colonial legacies of functioning infrastructure, with a pan-nationalism, a pan-Africa, a United States of Africa, was bold but fanciful.

Instead, an Organisation of African Unity (OAU) was established in 1963 and was itself a compromise among the different blocs of new states that had emerged in Africa. What was labelled the Casablanca Group sought a political unity; the Monrovia and Brazzaville Groups sought only economic unity. Neither was in fact possible, both because the very young states had difficulty in their internal political unities and because almost all began life with great economic aspirations but uneven resources and planning structures. Even if economic unity meant only a common market for trade, the transport of goods from country to country in a vast continent of underdeveloped com-munications networks was often impossible. As Themon Djaksam pointed out, however, the very aspiration behind the OAU derived from the founding fathers of pan-Africanism discussed in this book. It was an effort to operationalise their dream.[1]

The OAU was, as Zdenek Cervenka said, in one of the early full-length studies of the organisation, an "unfinished quest for unity".[2] It certainly established a Charter with common principles for the con-tinent, although these were generally, if nobly, worded. It provided high-level liaison in an Assembly of Heads of State and Government, a Council of Ministers, and an effort at a common direction in specific areas by way of specialised commissions. Of these, the Defence Com-mission and the OAU Liberation Committee were probably the most important in an Africa that saw a series of civil wars and which was still not fully liberated from minority white rule. But OAU interven-tion could not prevent bloodshed in the Congo and the death of Lumumba; nor did it bring an early end to the war in Nigeria, which was prosecuted to its bitter end with the surrender of the secessionist state of Biafra. The OAU played little effective role in ending white rule in Rhodesia, nor in ending Apartheid in South Africa. And its economic role, as envisaged by the Monrovia and Brazzaville Groups, was better handled by the UN Economic Commission for Africa[3]— also headquartered, alongside the OAU, in Addis Ababa, Ethiopia, the oldest independent country in Sub-Saharan Africa.

Indeed, by 1980 it was clear that economic cooperation across a vast continent would be impossible without foundational steps. Those were agreed in the Lagos Plan of Action of that year to be the creation and strengthening of regional zones of cooperation. This was also meant to be in cooperation with the UN Economic Commission for Africa.[4] Groups like the Economic Community of West African States (ECOWAS) and what is now the Southern African Development Community (SADC) were meant to be the seeds of cooperation, each developing its spheres of impact and influence until overlap and inte-gration of the zones became possible. The problem was that, in both ECOWAS and SADC, hegemons became apparent—members who were simply more economically resourced than the others. Nigeria in ECOWAS and, later, South Africa in SADC, meant an asymmetry in what was meant to be equitable cooperation. The tip-toeing, some-times leaden-footed, not to commit too much to a regional economic grouping where one member could more easily assume the role of hegemon than the others, has bedevilled efforts to develop the East African Community—with Tanzania and Kenya at a clearly distrustful arm's length of each other.[5]

However, the clearest dissatisfaction with the OAU was its inability to protect African citizens from arbitrary violence. The Chinese-derived principle of non-interference, first enunciated by Premier Zhou Enlai at the 1955 Bandung Conference,[6] meant that sovereignty was not only a space of independent rule, it could be a space of atrocity without any expectation of interference, let alone external intervention of any military sort. The OAU was disbanded in 2002, a decision taken in 1999, with the ceremonial winding up presided over by that year's OAU Chairman, Thabo Mbeki, the proselytiser of African Renaissance and cultural unity. But it was immediately replaced by the African Union (AU), and the chief difference was a greatly enhanced commitment to security. Non-interference was replaced by the somewhat unwieldy term of non-indifference, which, all the same, was shorthand for possible military intervention in the affairs of others.[7]

This meant an array of new institutional mechanisms but, above all, it sought to internalise among member states an agreed set of norms for the application of violence. Agreeing on such things at a high level is one thing; ensuring poorly trained, ill-disciplined and unreliably paid soldiers observe them is something else entirely. The advent of a new generation of insurrectionary groups also meant there was no way these groups could be forced to observe norms of 'civilised war' in their incursions and rebellions. But what the new norms and institutions chiefly meant was that recognised member governments of the AU were obliged to honour them. They were not meant to be atrocious towards their own citizens and others—even towards insurrectionary groups. This clearly was problematic in an environment both of power-plays and often undisciplined militaries but, to be fair, the AU has had some limited success in peacekeeping and peace-making in Darfur, and to a lesser extent in Somalia—although both required UN Security Council support or endorsement, and both were controversial in their execution—sufficiently to suggest the need for new military strategic thought and provision. But even the desirability of action in Darfur and Somalia was the effect of new thought that one could not stand by. To an extent, 'non-indifference', in its application in Darfur and Somalia, was an African forerunner of the Responsibility to Protect (R2P) doctrine that began gaining adherence within the United Nations from 2005. African collective and institutional thought was therefore a leader, although not widely recognised as such since the actual efforts to protect, as we shall see below, were far from fully successful.

* * *

Darfur and Somalia—along with Mali, discussed below—were the greatest challenges to the AU mobilisation of security resources and, above all, guarantees. Rebellion in Darfur in the new millennium was met by the Sudanese Government deployment of militias that created wanton destruction and death. This alarmed the world and gave rise to a wave of celebrity campaigns against both the government and China, which was seen as supportive of both the government and its savage repression of rebellion. Without this, it is doubtful the Sudanese Government would have allowed external intervention. Despite the new AU doctrine of 'non-indifference', the AU was reluctant to intervene with peacekeepers unilaterally. Sending soldiers into a sovereign, even if turbulent, territory could be easily categorised as a form of aggression and invasion. On top of the Western posture of being scandalised, it took much diplomatic pressure, including from the UN Security Council, before Sudan agreed to an AU peacekeeping presence. This came in 2004 with the deployment of AMIS (AU Mission in Sudan).

UN Security Council Resolution 1564 of 2004 was the pre-eminent authorisation and not just a decision within the AU. The peacekeepers were to be allowed to use force—but were hardly equipped to do so. The first contingent of soldiers amounted to only 150, as a bodyguard for observers. By 2005 the numbers had grown to 7,000. It was clear, however, that AMIS had no real capacity in its numbers, let alone its deployment capacity. Despite being authorised to use force, it never mounted a large offensive against either rebels or government-sponsored militias. It was replaced in 2007, under UN Security Council Resolution 1769, by UNAMID (UN/ AU Hybrid Operation in Darfur). The reinforcement of AU troops by non-African contingents was a relief, though scarcely a break-through. Soldiers from as far away as Indonesia and Pakistan joined UNAMID, although its commander remained an African general, with one exception who was from Pakistan. UNAMID is still in operation, although drawn down from the height of its strength of about 20,000 soldiers and 6,000 police personnel.

I was able to have access to different levels of AMIS and UNAMID. The key feature is that Darfur is a huge territory—between the sizes of Germany and Texas, i.e. 493,180 square kilometres. That alone would swallow up 20,000 soldiers. However, the second key feature was the lack of transport and communications infrastructure throughout the vast territory. The peacekeepers were largely denied access to such rail lines that existed, which were reserved for Sudanese government and military use alone.[8] So that, once deployed—often with difficulty—UNAMID soldiers were a pin-prick presence that lacked mobility. One ZamBat (Zambian Battalion) soldier complained privately to me that they were effec-tively "sitting ducks. We build camp, try to fortify it. Then we wait for the militias or rebels to attack us. We can't move out to attack them or prevent them from attacking us." His opinion was that their presence was symbolic. "No one sent us here to be able actually to do something." The price of this symbolism included their casualty and fatality figures, as well as continued civilian deaths.[9] This was, in effect, a damning indictment of worthy thought that was not backed up by strategic thought or logistical capacity.

I was able to speak privately at reasonable length to UNAMID commander, Nigerian Major General Martin Luther Agwai, in post from 2008–9, but who also commanded the last year of AMIS. "What do you need?" I asked. He replied immediately: "Helicopters. I need helicopters. I am able to rent two." "You have two helicopters for a place bigger than Germany?" "They're not even mine. I have to rent them. Oh, they're of no use at all for peacekeeping, let alone peace-making. I use them to attend the funerals of my fallen soldiers in the different salients."[10]

Other aspects of our conversation must remain confidential, but I took the issue of the helicopters to senior personnel in the UK Ministry of Defence. "We do not have enough helicopters for ourselves," came the world-weary response. Nothing daunted, I accepted an invitation to Beijing, where I was able to put my request to officials from the Ministry of Foreign Affairs, and separately to senior figures in the People's Liberation Army. "To make it a viable peacekeeping operation, they need 100 helicopters." "We do have 100 helicopters, but it is unlikely they will be sent to Darfur." The Chinese did increase their own peacekeeping ground soldiers, using this as a step to counter the criticism they had received from Western quarters for seeming to support President Bashir of Sudan.[11]

The point, however, is that peacekeeping is not simply about soldiers. It is about their armaments as insurgent and rebel forces can now often have greater firepower. But, above all, it is about their deployment and mobility and command of terrain. Without that, peacekeeping—let alone peace-making where antagonistic forces have their heads forcibly rubbed together towards some kind of negotiation—can remain fatally symbolic. It was not UNAMID that reduced the terrors in Darfur. Huge international diplomatic pressure, and finally, the gradual decision of the Chinese[12] to apply leverage against Bashir, did that.[13] And the need for mobility and command of terrain was a lesson not learned the right way in Somalia, as discussed below. The way the French did it in Mali points to a lesson for thought on African peacekeeping. There is also the question of unintended consequences. Insofar as UNAMID played some role in stabilising Darfur sufficiently for refugee protection to be mounted, and camps for displaced persons protected by peacekeeping soldiers to be built and often fully equipped in terms of hospitals, the laborious transit of valuable medical equipment to these camps opened opportunities for bandit gangs—who promptly declared themselves rebel groups, making peace negotiations both over-populated by delegations with no real bona fides in the quest for peace or any just settlement, and creating populations of the 'displaced' who sought medical help not normally available in their home territories. Darfur became, under peacekeeping and diplomacy, a humanitarian industry. It should be said that this was an unintended but huge consequence of thought that was incomplete in the stages that ran from principle to execution. The humanitarian industry side of things at least did not happen with the ongoing AU intervention in Somalia. Perhaps quite the opposite.

This intervention, again made legally acceptable by UN Security Council Resolution 2372 of 2017, was African Union Mission to Somalia (AMISOM). This itself replaced a smaller previous effort, IGAD (Intergovernmental Authority on Development Protection and Training Mission), authorised by the AU in 2006 and receiving UN Security Council endorsement in 2007. This again was largely ineffectual, and was eclipsed hugely by the Ethiopian intervention from the end of 2006. In large part, AMISON was needed to counter a situation caused by this intervention—largely thought to have been instigated by US concerns over the rise of Islamic influence in Somalia, believing that to be jihadist influence and with the suspicion that al-Qaeda was gaining a clear foothold there. The formation of the Islamic Courts Union (also known as the Council of Islamic Courts), with its factions, some more radical than others, rang alarm bells for the US—even though the ICU was clearly succeeding in bringing at least some sense of uniform non-arbitrary justice to large parts of Somalia out of the reach of the Transitional Federal Government. The TFG was supported by the US, so there was a dual agenda: one of alarm over a perceived jihadist influence, and one of imposing TFG authority over a fractured country, especially after the ICU capture of Mogadishu in 2006. This prompted the US to encourage the Ethiopian invasion. It was a disaster.

Firstly, Ethiopian military strategy, notwithstanding the liberation of Ethiopia from the Stalinist Derg in 1987, still borrowed from the Soviet training and use of equipment from the time of the Derg. This was the Warsaw Pact strategy, whereby waves of armour were to overrun Western European defences and all else that stood in its way. Civilian collateral damage, cities, lives and livelihoods, would not stand in its way. Secondly, Ethiopia was perceived by many Somalis as their historical enemy—so the blitz and flatten approach of the Ethiopian invasion made new and confirmed old enemies. The destruction and lack of finesse in the use of tanks crushing all before was not a winning hearts and minds strategy.[14] The successful defeat of the Islamic Courts Union meant the dispersal of its factions that had been finely balanced, and the most radical of the factions, understanding no accommodation with the Transitional Federal government would be possible, became al-Shabaab—and it was against al-Shabaab that AMISOM was arrayed.

But al-Shabaab was not merely jihadist; it was canny enough to deploy traditional Somali motifs and characterise foreign intervention, even African intervention, as an attack against a cultural nationalism, never mind as foreign efforts to capture an already contested state.[15] In other words, even al-Shabaab had a sense of thought about nationalism. Because it is a jihadist group, al-Shabaab has, with its own factions and nuances, often been misunderstood,[16] viewed under a very visible cloak of atrocity and fundamentalism. AMISOM was not only against al-Shabaab; it was an instrument to help create a non-failed state in Somalia that would be a state in the image of AMISOM members—no matter what the artificiality of such a state might be.[17] With so many variants of 'stateness' within the AMISOM members there was no single applicable model, so the mission was something that was against an enemy and not fully calibrated towards what would take the place of al-Shabaab, except that it should in some way be recognisable as a state with a government having secular organs.

Nevertheless, the Ethiopians were already committed, and the Kenyans, to the south of Somalia, clearly saw al-Shabaab as a direct security threat. So Kenya became a leading military actor in AMISOM, in the process also inviting al-Shabaab retaliation against Kenyan targets, even in the heart of Nairobi,[18] prompting some loss of freedom for comment, dissent or even journalistic coverage on the grounds of national security.[19] It was all certainly, however, if nothing else, a robust upscaling of AU interventionist operations.[20]

But this upscaling on the Kenyan part, with an army experienced in peacekeeping but not in peace-making in the sense that it required war-making, fell into exactly the same trap Ethiopian military strategy did in the same theatre. Operations moved behind a huge artillery barrage. Civilian casualties were unavoidable. Each casualty fostered the image that Kenya was making war on Somalis and brought recruits to the al-Shabaab banner to wage war against Kenya. The upscaling had not come with any revision and redevelopment of military doctrine, and certainly none that suited a new era of peacekeeping and its extension into peace-making.

The added problem was that both Kenya and Ethiopia based their operations from their own territories, so that, except for a heavily (but not impregnably) fortified Mogadishu, non-al-Shabaab territory in southern and western Somalia is that territory adjacent to its Kenyan and Ethiopian borders. Sanitary buffer zones have been established, though not fail-safe ones, and the bulk of Somalia outside the autonomous efforts of Somaliland and Puntland to the north remains within or close to within al-Shabaab jurisdiction. In short, AMISOM may be seen as having accomplished nothing long-lasting and perhaps even nothing tangible.[21] It is not certain it has even led to a review of strategic thought and doctrine.

The French-led intervention may not have accomplished anything long-lasting in Mali either, the state being seen as failing in many of its duties to its citizens,[22] but they can say they certainly—for a time—rolled the Islamic insurgency of 2013 back on its heels. That insurgency swept down from the north of the country with a ferocity and, above all, a speed that caught government forces flat-footed. Intelligence of a forthcoming attack had led to the planned deployment of an AU rapid response force. But it was open knowledge as to when the deployment was planned—it was anything but rapid—so the insurgents struck well before that time; and did so with such modern equipment, based upon Toyota pickups moving at speeds far faster and more flexibly than tanks, that the government defence forces with heavy equipment were completely out-manoeuvred. The insurgents took Timbuktu (and did terrible damage to cultural heirlooms and historic buildings) and were sweeping upon the capital. The French intervention moved almost overnight and centred their response around their armoured cars that carried heavier weaponry than those of the insurgents—light cannon as opposed to machine guns—but moved as fast if not faster. But this meant an airlift of men and equipment at great speed, with immediate on-ground organisation and battle plans drawn up even before deployment.[23]

Basically, as more than one guerrilla general has explained to me, insurgent strategy is modelled on the doctrine of Clausewitz, the Prussian General who worked out why Napoleon was constantly defeating his forces—speed of concentration for attack *en masse* at the enemy's weakest point.[24] The emphasis is on the speed of concentration, before the speed of attack, with quite free-form formations, provided the speed and direction are there. This doctrine was used by German Panzer General Guderian against the static French Maginot lines in World War II and by Israeli generals against parade formation Egyptian lines in the 1967 Arab–Israeli war.[25] It is everything that is not drilled into officer cadets at war college.

It speaks to insurgent strategic thought being more advanced than official African military strategic thought and the sense that even robust peace-making (with force) is doctrinally different from counter-terrorism.[26] Thought about peace-making needs to go hand in hand with advances in strategic thought. But it also means that African defence thinking, the thought of high commands, needs to wean itself away from 'being like real armies and air forces' with heavy tanks and fighter aircraft and emphasise light armoured cars, attack helicopters and reliably maintained transport aircraft. It also means rethinking battle doctrine to suit the kind of warfare that uses mobility and speed. It is how ISIS smashed through the heavily-equipped and US-trained Iraqi army.[27] But it is also the chief element in French rapid mobilisation, as shown not only in Mali but in Ivory Coast in 2010 and Central African Republic in 2013, and that is not only doctrine that responds to fluidity but, by virtue absolutely of fluidity, all battle doctrine is flexible. African military thought is stolid by comparison.

* * *

Curiously, the only recent use of flexible doctrine by a non-insurgent force was Gaddafi's last stand against NATO, where he held out for six months despite overwhelming NATO air superiority and support for rebel forces on the ground.

Of course, all this raises the spectre of foreign intervention, not just French but, in the 2011 case of Libya, NATO as a combined intervention. Although it did try to broker some form of honourable compromise at the beginning of hostilities, the AU was powerless to prevent this.[28] The need for higher-level diplomacy from the AU in the face of the great powers in their militarised form is clearly at stake here—although, to be fair, the Western powers wrong-footed both Russia and China in the wording of the Security Council resolution under which NATO went to war in Libya. But it is precisely NATO that led the way, in Europe and not Africa, in the robustness of its rendition of 'Responsibility to Protect', the emerging norm in international relations and international law—applying this in Kosovo in 1998, justifying its military intervention by this norm, and without any recourse to a Security Council resolution.

As well as a more flexible strategy, the AU also needs the capacity to respond quickly, as one in humanitarian emergencies such as NATO deemed evident in Kosovo. But Kosovo was a mild humanitarian disaster compared to the festering sore in south-eastern Congo, where despite a clumsy and highly restricted UN peacekeeping force, no relief is in sight for communities that have suffered, by some estimates, 2 million fatalities, countless other casualties, and seen the advent of gendercide—mass rape—as a weapon of war.[29] Perhaps the Congo theatre is just too vast to encompass with limited military capacities by national armies and peacekeepers alike. But encompassing it in thought should be at least an AU priority. The responsibility to protect is enshrined in Article 4(h) of the AU's Constitutive Act. Enshrinement is one thing, observation of norms another, capacity to act still yet another—but the three together are the acid test of actual unity.

However, unity should not be manifested only in coming up to speed with work and standards elsewhere. It should be manifest in original leading of the way. As Marco Jowell has pointed out, almost all of the new peacekeeping academies in Africa for command-level officers utilise 'off-the-shelf' training programmes that are not fully bespoke to the particular difficulties, almost always different from conflict to conflict in different regions.[30] They give standard training to a uniform level and are good for officer credentialization and promotion purposes, but do not necessarily lead to better planning and command of peacekeeping. And, as Tim Murithi has pointed out, the entire field of conflict resolution needs an overhaul of its foundational principles and standard methodologies. This is where Africa can lead the way.[31] It can do so by taking into account how scarcity and problems of development can foster war and how long standing solutions need to be anchored in recognition of development needs.[32] As Susan Collin Marks indicates, conflict resolution during the often violent transition of South Africa from Apartheid to majority rule could not have been meaningful without fully recognising democracy's importance in the meaningful mediation of conflict.[33]

All this is to say that an Africa that is in turmoil is not an Africa that is in unity. Turmoil is not a basis for union. What are the key elements of concentrated African political thought required for that future pan-Africanism, for African renaissance?

1. If we deal with conflict, what is to be done with those who perpetuate violence and atrocity? It is true that the International Criminal Court is not perceived as a satisfactory site for the withdrawal of impunity. It can, at best, seem like distant justice.[34] It can even be an instrument, the use of which exacerbates conflict.[35] And yet, if the ICC is seen as distant, it is not as if Africa should tolerate impunity. The question is 'where is the African Union Criminal Court'—with its full working apparatus and fearlessness to indict even heads of state? The ICC is not alone in the international architecture of justice. UN tribunals such as the International Criminal Tribunal for the Former Yugoslavia, seated as with the ICC in The Hague, have indicted, tried and convicted far more white criminals of war—including a former President of Serbia who died in prison—than the ICC has ever tried and convicted Africans.[36]

2. Special consideration should be given for the prosecution of crimes of wartime rape against women. The use of gendercide is a shame to the idea of a united Africa composed of men and women. Something Thomas Sankara started has not yet been fully brought to fruition. And it is also something that emerging female leadership in Africa should forefront.

3. All the jurisprudential principles involved in a pan-African justice must, of course, be first rehearsed in national jurisdictions and constitutions. Here, much legal thought has been evident, stressing constitutional provision and guarantees of democracy, transparency, lack of arbitrariness, recourse against governments and protection under law. Work by scholars such as Chaloka Beyani[37] and Muna Ndulo[38] help to lead the way.

4. In the provision of guarantees under constitutions, what is the extent of pluralism possible under constitutional systems? In Somalia, for instance, with a huge number of often rival clans, do all groups—large or small—have the same rights? Do identity entities such as clans have the same legal personality as persons? We may ask this question about ethnicities and religions too. But it poses a challenge for African jurisprudence under which principles related to identity are problematically posed. Are there subsuming identities? In which case are all Africans equally African—whether from Somalia, Mauritius, Cape Verde, Nigeria or the remotest part of the Democratic Republic of Congo? What redress do people have under constitutions and under the African Union? And does the Afro-diaspora have the same rights under the African Union as continental Africans? All the questions raised by pan-Africanism come home to roost in areas not yet fully thought out.

5. Of special concern, and this is rightly the subject of an entirely other book: what is the place, rights and capacities of Islam—and Sharia law—under constitutional law, especially when claims are made that it is superior to constitutional law? And how does Africa deal with, outside of jurisprudence, but within doctrines of jihad, insurrection is waged against the state and across the borders of states—in the name of an Islam that finally claims its own pan-Africanism? A rival pan-Africanism?

These questions are posed to illustrate the thoughtfulness required of the road ahead. There are of course many more questions. But these, and the questions raised by the leaders and thinkers in this book, are the questions that concern Africa almost 140 years after the Congress of Berlin that divided the continent and imposed a unity based only on subjugation. What is the unity that comes from freedom? What is the free African identity?

Here, as a final word, the work of philosophers dealing with the nature of African knowledge and the nature of an African's self-knowledge resonates. The substance of self-knowledge was what colonialism ripped away. It led to what Ndlovu-Gatsheni called "the absent centre of ontology."[39] In terms of a continental representation, protection, and prosecution of the sense and responsibility of Africa, the African Union must not itself become an absent continental centre.

10

MALEDICTIONS OF THE POLITICAL ORDER

A SELECTION OF MODERN CHALLENGES

The Advent of Feminism

Apart from Thomas Sankara, who came to power in 1983, more than 20 years after the independence process had begun, few of the new leaders of Africa prioritised the equality of women, and very few accorded women even token representation in their first Cabinets. There were no female Cabinet Ministers in the new governments of Nkrumah, Nyerere and Kaunda. Even as late as 1994, with Mandela's first majority-rule government, there were only two female Cabinet Ministers.

This is not to say that women did not feature in African politics and society. Winnie Mandela is a case in point, but there is a question as to whether she could have had an impact if she had not been Nelson Mandela's wife as all looked to an eventual release of her husband. Often, however, women had to lead movements outside the mainstream of politics to have an impact. The charismatic church-based rebellion of Alice Lenshina against Kaunda's Zambia in the 1960s— savagely crushed by Kaunda[1]—prefigured the later uprising of the Acholi people in Uganda in the 1980s, led by the spiritual figure of Alice Lakwena.[2] Women as spiritual leaders and prophetesses of

179

rebellion seem not to suffer gender discrimination, but such discrimination has certainly disfigured the rise of women in politics.

Even years after Lenshina and Lakwena, the possibility of highest office often came about through marriage and the idea of succession. We have already discussed Grace Mugabe and her hopes of succeeding Robert Mugabe. Jacob Zuma's former wife, Nkosazana Dlamini-Zuma, although a female member of Mandela's Foundation Cabinet, and later Chair of the African Union—following a forceful campaign on her behalf by South Africa[3]—seemed to be in line to succeed her former husband as president,[4] with the assumption she would exonerate him on corruption charges.[5] She remains a Minister in Cyril Ramaphosa's Cabinet and is part of a continuing South African practice of family inheritance of liberation activity with entry into high politics: Lindiwe Sisulu, daughter of Walter Sisulu, is a current case in point. She certainly has liberation credentials of her own, and there is certainly a penchant for apparent dynasties in the USA, the Kennedy and Bush families being exemplars, as is Hillary Clinton. President Trump appointed his son-in-law and daughter to advisory positions, so familial 'insider trading' is not unusual. Still, the point is that no leaders of any opposition party or civil society movement against the political leaders discussed so far in this book have been women with their own power bases. There are, of course, significant female political theorists and philosophers in the US who speak to a moral foundation for politics and political rule, but their works are attached to the US political condition.[6] Such works are rarer but, as we shall see, not absent in African jurisdictions. The authors of such works may still, however, find themselves targeted as political enemies.

Familial links were apparent in Zimbabwe long before the advent of Grace Mugabe. Victoria Chitepo, the widow of Herbert Chitepo, the liberation leader controversially assassinated in Zambia,[7] became an early Minister. In Mugabe's first Cabinet, Teurai Ropa (later Joice Mujuru) was female. She was the wife of one of Mugabe's senior most Generals, Rex Nhongo (later Rex Mujuru, also later controversially assassinated),[8] but Teurai Ropa was at least acknowledged as having been a liberation war heroine in her own right. Amid the euphoria generated by independence, after a vicious struggle, many—in a rush to enjoy the fruits of majority rule—forgot those, not well connected, who had suffered and continued to suffer.

In a lengthy and detailed memoir, Eunice Chadoka King recounts the struggle from the point of view of a female fighter and cadre.[9] The use of the term 'tribulations' in her title is deliberate as the account, while heroic (and stoic), is also deeply ambivalent. Female fighters were not always treated well by their male comrades. And, while many were not frontline fighters, some certainly were. One day, when I began teaching civil servants from several African countries at my base in Zambia towards the end of 1980, a Zimbabwean female participant directly asked me if I would like to see her wounds. She lifted the front of her blouse, and the scar from the bullet's entry was clearly visible, though neat. Then she turned around. Of course, the exit scar was terrible as the bullet, which went right through her, splattered its way out. "It just missed the vital organs," she said. I nodded. In fact, by my estimate it had missed her spleen by a centimetre. She told me about her secondary school. "One day, the whole class, as one, without any prior agreement—it was like a mass understanding that it was time and that it was unavoidable—just stood up at our desks, put away our books, and we walked to Mozambique to join the guerrillas."

Many of those who survived were traumatised but not treated. The greatest novel of the Zimbabwean writer, the late Yvonne Vera, was of the trauma of a former guerrilla who expressed his mental disequilibrium by murdering and mutilating women.[10] Another great novel about the trauma of fighters who had to kill gratuitously and were haunted forever after was by Alexander Kanengoni.[11] It was not just the land that was inhabited by spirits. The spirits of those unjustly slain would return to haunt the killers, possess them, and drive them through stages of increasing lunacy to their own deaths.[12] In the case of Kanengoni's novel, it was the spirit, the *ngozi*, of an unjustly executed woman who returned to haunt the novel's protagonist, Manashe. The freedom struggle left physical and emotional scars on all who fought in it, but at least for Mugabe and his inner circle, there was the consolation of recognition, as he gained power and was lionised as a liberation hero across Southern Africa. Many of the men, but particularly the women who, unlike him, had picked up a gun in the name of Zimbabwe, were left to deal with their trauma and sacrifice in obscurity.

In some cases of course, female liberation fighters who married liberation leaders have gone on to attain huge success and carved out conspicuous reputations of their own. Graça Machel, a liberation fighter in her own right, married the first President of independent Mozambique, Samora Machel, and became the Minister of Education—transforming educational provision for girls during her tenure. After Samora's assassination, she married Nelson Mandela and now heads an international organisation promoting the education and welfare of girls and young women. Sometimes, it takes the intensity of struggle, and the intensity of relationships within them, to catalyse transformation for all. Even so, the very relationships and social context of being in a liberation army can be such that female combatants do not afterwards wish to demobilise. I recall in Eritrea in 1992, I was asked to write a summary document on demobilisation—something that for long years afterwards in a militarily paranoid Eritrea would have seemed fantastic—but the female fighters in the long war for independence said to me point-blank they would resist demobilisation. "Here, in the forces, we are free. Back in everyday society we would enter a world of subordination. We would lose our equality which we gained by risking our lives equally alongside the men. In those conditions, no one could deny us."

Was all feminism in Africa born of war or analogous extraordinary circumstances? The mother of Fela Kuti, the pioneering but dissident Nigerian musician, was killed by rampaging military government soldiers bent on teaching the very popular but problematic musician a lesson. It gave rise to Fela's perhaps greatest song, *Coffin for a Head of State*,[13] in which he describes taking his mother's body to the army barracks as a public display of continued defiance and to alert the public as to the brutality of military rule. But his mother, Funmilayo Ransome-Kuti, was widely regarded as Nigeria's pioneering feminist in the campaigns against colonial rule.[14] She was the first female student at her school and carried a lifelong dedication to women's education and the need for female representation in public life. She organised literacy classes for lower-income women, campaigned against unfair taxes on market women, and demanded voting rights for women. She was also involved in international campaigns for peace and women's rights. At one stage she led a protest march of 10,000 women against malpractice in local administration. She appealed primarily to an educated public, not reaching deeply, for instance, into the Islamic northern regions of Nigeria. She won the Lenin Peace Prize for her activism and leadership. Her own son, Fela, did not seem to practise gender equality in terms of the numerous 'wives' he kept in his 'independent republic' of a commune—that, all the same, was in its esoteric way an informal civil centre for human rights.

If we are looking for written works on feminism analogous to the output of feminists in the West, we should consider Sara Longwe of Zambia. Kenneth Kaunda, who held office from 1964 to 1991, had long emphasised respect for women. He instituted, for instance, paid days off for female employees at the peak of their periods. He courted female membership of his ruling party and stressed the importance of the party's Women's League as a mobilising device for it. Women rose to important positions in the national system of politics and public administration, but this had to be closely tied to membership and seniority in the single party. In this way, 'feminism' was an organised but restrained force, in some ways well-meaning but condescending, and did not necessarily impact everyday relationships or cultural practices in which women were very often subordinate creatures. Curiously, the cross-cultural nature of Christian churches, with a plethora of denominations—including home-grown charismatic denominations—helped spread a curious equality. If a female preacher could speak in tongues and heal the sick, if she was in this way touched by God, no one was going to object to her promotion to Bishop.[15] Within the ecumenical and umbrella United Church of Zambia,[16] this became common enough not to be remarked on. But Longwe, a University of Zambia academic, spoke a secular and modern—an international—language of equality and freedom. It had to be international as she criticised global agencies such as OXFAM as well as local practices. Her 'moment of radicalisation' occurred as a young school teacher in the Kaunda era, where she was denied maternity leave—which she vigorously and successfully protested, securing maternity leave as a universal right for all female teachers. She also demanded the right to wear trousers in the schools where she taught. This engendered a controversy that had to be decided at the very top of the Ministry of Education—in her favour. But her work with scholars of development at the University of Zambia profoundly influenced her own thought that women were the forgotten subjects of development theory and practice. Through her work in development, and through civil society groups, some of which she helped to found, she became an intellectual and lobbying force in Zambia.

The 1991 elections ended the one-party rule of Kenneth Kaunda. There was much national rejoicing that greater political pluralism and freedom had finally come. But Longwe pointed out that a multi-party system did not, in itself, transform the position of women in society.[17] And nor did it, even in terms of successful female candidatures in elections that followed; these remained much lower in number than successful male candidates even ten years later.[18] Longwe had been active in the campaign for gender equality long before 1991. Her work had been already internationally recognised,[19] and it came to a peak with the development of her Women's Empowerment Framework of 1990. This Framework continues to be influential to this day. It is a core reference point in international training and evaluation programmes for working with women, fielded by the International Labour Organization[20] and the World Bank.[21]

Basically, the Framework has five levels of equality, of which all development planners and aid agencies should be aware: welfare, access, 'conscientization', participation, and control. Empowerment is required in each of these levels. Welfare concerns basic needs; access concerns ability to use resources such as credit, land and education; 'conscientization' is almost a feminist version of Nkrumah's Consciencism, whereby self-awareness of oneself as female but within a realm of equality is key, i.e. it acts against self-denigration and self-complicity in accepting subjugation in a man's world, and it requires constant vigilance and constant thought; participation requires women to become equal to men in decision-making; and this leads finally to equal control in the balance of power between the genders.

From precisely the adoption of this Framework by agencies such as the ILO and World Bank, it can be seen that it was applicable to women everywhere. It was not peculiarly 'African'. Indeed, albeit with exceptions, African traditions habitually rendered women unequal. The Framework was against this in Africa, but also against this anywhere. The Framework was hugely influential in both the

Millennium Development Goals and the Sustainable Development Goals and has been applied in Asia and Latin America as well as in Africa. In short, there was something universal at stake here, and required political thought on the African condition to be also, in key respects, appreciative of global conditions. Women should be seen as members of a modern equality, one within developmental and economic codes of practice and regard.

As well as her international work, Longwe continued to work as a local activist. In 1992 she successfully sued Lusaka's Intercontinental Hotel—where Thabo Mbeki used to stay when visiting the ANC in Zambia—for refusing women entrance to its bar unless accompanied by a man. And she continued to write on educational parity for young women.[22] Longwe saw a universal feminism, but also one where developmental problems and inequalities have a pronounced disadvantage to women. Insofar as she was vocal and active on local issues as well as international ones, the Zambian state became mindful of her influence and did not always look kindly on it, threatening once to deport her expatriate husband—both for his success as a political satirist,[23] but also as a lever against her own work.

* * *

Times have moved on a little. There have now been three female Presidents in Africa—Liberia and Malawi—with executive, head-of-government capacities; and a ceremonial female President in Ethiopia. In Liberia, Ellen Johnson Sirleaf was President from 2006–18, emerging into the role after the terrible civil war and the Presidency of Charles Taylor, who has been convicted for his participation and leading role in propagating the war and its atrocities. There were several women's groups who protested the war and conducted campaigns for peace, and Johnson Sirleaf shared the Nobel Peace Prize in 2011 for involving women in the peace process, which she helped oversee although it is well to remember that women too were involved in the fighting and some of the atrocities. Stephen Ellis wrote about the condensed and not fully accurate initiation and indoctrination of young men in the coming-of-age rituals known as *poro*. They meant that however young in actual years, they were now ceremonially adult and could now fight and kill. Young women caught up in the violence, and seeking to fight, also sought the blessings of tradition and the safeguards against harm it was meant to bring. Excluded from the male-only *poro* rituals, the girls and young women turned to what were called *sande* rituals, which have their own esoteric elements to be sure, but which in the context of war can also be seen as a deliberate effort to parallel the rushed process to come of age and fight as an endorsed adult that had been open only to boys and young men. [24] In short, in the effort to appropriate the blessings of 'authenticity', there was an ingenious reinvention of tradition, and, for the young women, there was the re-gendering of the reinvention.

This sort of deep backdrop eluded the jury for the Nobel Peace Prize, but the prize was deserved, as the administration of Johnson Sirleaf did oversee the end of the war and gave greater opportunities, including political opportunities for women. [25] Even so, the majority of her Cabinets were men and, while she represented a first for women in Africa by becoming President, she did not successfully prosecute other social issues. She herself had an elite formation, educated at Harvard and working for Citibank. She was seen as the kind of technocratic figure that could revive Liberia's fortunes and, above all, in a desolate but war-weary country, she was seen as someone not at all like Charles Taylor, who had led the country into an era of atrocity. Simply being the technocratic alternative was not enough in itself, and she was constrained in many parts of her agenda by conservatism in the political institutions around her. Despite announcing, for instance, her intention to decriminalise homosexuality, huge domestic pressure forced her never to repeal existing laws against it.

After her Presidency, she has become an elder stateswoman. She was the leader of the main US observer group to the 2018 post-Mugabe Zimbabwean elections, and she sits on the Advisory Board of the Brenthurst Foundation—instigated by the Oppenheimer family who also hosted the Brenthurst fireside chats for Nelson Mandela—which both accomplishes exceptional Track 2 diplomatic work, but which also allows former Presidents and Prime Ministers to reinvent or add to their legacies. The Chair of the Board is Olusegun Obasanjo, the target of Fela's rage in *Coffin for a Head of State*, who was also probably the best of the Nigerian Presidents despite a range of controversies. The Brenthurst Foundation may be best described as an 'elders' type of group, an assemblage of the great and good who once held power but who had recognised technocratic skills and forms of democratic record. It believes in democratic empowerment and, with it, the economic empowerment of those left out by development orthodoxies—believing entrepreneurship should be encouraged and facilitated. Someone with a Citibank background would feel at home with this emphasis.

Similarly, Joyce Banda has endorsed the Foundation's work and its recent book, with Obasanjo as a co-author, on an alternative development model for Africa. "I wish I had this handbook when I was President of Malawi."[26]

She has published her own short book on the need to educate girls and of the importance of the first ten years of their lives.[27] The concern for particularly young girls was also that of Mandela's widow, Graça Machel, herself a former liberation fighter and conscious of the harm done to children by war.[28]

Joyce Banda was President of Malawi in 2012–14 and was thus Africa's second female President—although, unlike Johnson Sirleaf, she never won an election. She was Vice President when the incumbent President died. Constitutionally, she was in line to take over as President, but a combination of party factional and personal politics intruded. It was only when the army commander sided with Banda—and the constitution—that she attained the Presidency. She was defeated heavily in the next elections—the results of which she tried, unsuccessfully, to annul—so her accomplishments are not necessarily to do with democracy. And, precisely because of party politics, her Cabinet reshuffles were frequent and prevented any clear judgement as to whether or not they sought to promote women into senior roles. That she played a part in the long-running saga to bring a sense of stability and norm-driven governance to a Malawi still not fully recovered from the constraints and repressions of Hastings Banda, almost 20 years after his tenure as a 'little Big Man', is undeniable. But she broke no new ground, neither for women nor on the issue of homosexuality. She did seek to decriminalise homosexuality but, as with Johnson Sirleaf, this came to nothing. It is very much in her self-reinvention after holding office, through vehicles like the Brenthurst Foundation, that she remains known as a female political voice of reason. Still, it is hard to say exactly how she should be remembered in terms of accomplishments while in office—except the fact of stability in Malawi is an accomplishment in itself; yet the political intrigue within a small country was such that 'palace politics' consumed much of her time and that of her rivals. Not as well educated as Johnson Sirleaf, she did leave an abusive marriage and was very mindful of the suffering that frequently accompanied the efforts of women to achieve equality in relationships. As a successful independent businesswoman, she became an exemplar to other women and, as noted above, is committed to the education of young females.

A case where the latter-day phenomenon of women in high office may be seen both as some extension of history and as part of an across-the-board political dispensation is in Ethiopia. Women featured in Ethiopian mytho-history as greatly wise, as in the case of Magda (the Queen of Sheba), who travelled to Solomon's court, not just to experience his wisdom, but to test her own wisdom and knowledge against his. In more recent times, women warriors were a recorded feature of the 1896 Battle of Adwa, in which Ethiopian forces defeated the invading Italian army. Taytu Betul, the Empress from 1898 to 1913, was herself a successful and innovative General.[29] And the military overthrow of the Stalinist Derg, after a long war which achieved victory in 1991, also featured—as it did on the side of the allied Eritrean forces—female combatants. So that the sweeping reforms of Prime Minister Abiy Ahmed in 2018—which included appointing a female President, Chief Justice, and half his Cabinet Ministers—were meant to signal a grand reform of the country that nevertheless was in line with history.

It didn't necessarily mean a dramatically freer country. Government—by the same party—since 1991 has been authoritarian, though not tyrannical in the mode of the predecessor Derg and not feudal as in the Derg's own predecessor empire. But it is hard to envisage the overthrow by peaceful or violent means of this entrenched government. And it is better able to control the population than before. Ahmed is PhD-educated with degrees in, among other things, encryption. He understands what being 'wired up' entails, and also how to benefit from that as a government. Even so, what we have in the case of Ethiopia is an attempt to be a *modern* government, and female political emancipation—insofar as that means parity in high political office—is part of that. His greatest accomplishment, for which he won the Nobel Peace Prize, has been ending the bitter war with Eritrea—which began shortly after the overthrow of the Derg by combined Ethiopian and Eritrean forces and which lasted a quarter-century.[30] His boldness in conceding disputed territory to Eritrea was a true act of political courage, especially given how many men and women had died in that war. Of course, the civil war within Ethiopia that erupted towards the end of 2020, with its atrocities and slaughters, has greatly tarnished the reputation of Ahmed and, by extension, that of his government. The question is whether the representation of women alone prevents war—as in the case of war against Tigray—or repression, as in Rwanda, where there is a constitutional requirement that women should hold 30% of the parliamentary seats. Women have won up to 50% of the seats, yet extensive evidence has continued to be published on the totalitarianism embedded in the very powerful executive Presidency of Paul Kagame.[31]

Women are becoming, if not Presidents, leading opposition figures—often imprisoned for their activism on behalf of human rights. Stella Nyanzi in Uganda is a case in point,[32] as is Diane Rwigara in Rwanda.[33] As pointed out above, quotas of women are not in themselves necessarily meaningful in an authoritarian country, where official participation is possible only through concurrence with official policy, and where parliaments in any case are relatively powerless in the face of strong, centralised executive presidencies. Even Sudan, under President Bashir, had a quota system that guaranteed women in parliament.[34] My sense of it as an official observer at the 2010 elections was that Bashir was using the device as a means of courting the West, which had ostracised him over his repression in Darfur. Even with the best will in the world, however, such provision, whether decorative or not, does not mean that ordinary women can lead equal lives with equal opportunities. In Julius Nyerere's seemingly once idealistic country, Tanzania, the slide into today's neo-authoritarianism had the late President Magufuli banning pregnant schoolgirls from continuing their education.[35] And, of course, 'traditional' and 'authentic' practices like female genital mutilation are still common in many parts of Africa. Whether by 'Christian' disapproval of unmarried pregnancies or by 'traditional' practice, women are still inhibited from achieving equality, even if slowly this is changing at some of the highest levels.

The third female executive president is John Magufuli's successor in Tanzania. In 2021 she became the first Islamic female president in Africa. Samia Suluhu Hassan, having been Magufuli's vice president, was constitutionally his successor. Whether she will be in due course elected, or chosen as her party's official presidential candidate at the end of what would have been Magufuli's term in 2025, remains to be seen; as does whether she will seek consciously and deeply to improve the lot of women in Tanzania.

We cannot transform the lot of women throughout Africa only by legislation and constitutional provision. As Awino Okech has pointed out in her keenly researched book, women and property rights—indeed women as property, albeit with varying forms of agency—form cornerstones of much traditional culture. The struggle for equality has implications for questions of custom and at least local 'authenticities'.[36] There is also the ongoing and increasingly populated debate on not African feminism, but African feminisms, the plural representing the continent's diversity. What this means for women in various locations throughout Africa, and what it means in terms of a global sisterhood where Western feminism often fails to grasp the lived experience of women outside the West, remains an open question.[37] But it proposes far greater demands on any female President—to have policies congruent with the needs of political unity, economic development, national female emancipation and equality, and global cooperation and communion, together with reforming tradition without totalitarianism—than would face male presidents. The leverage to accomplish all of this will depend in any location on political party support.

The question precisely of accepted leadership of a dominant political party may be the key turning point in how efficacious women can be in the highest office. Despite the succession to President Mugabe being won finally by Emerson Mnangagwa in Zimbabwe, the contestation beforehand for this position between Mugabe's wife, Grace Mugabe, and the vice president, Joice Mujuru—the former liberation war heroine, Teurai Ropa—was also one of contestation to lead the powerful ruling party. If Grace Mugabe had won, the party would have most probably continued as the authoritarian power-centralising institution it had long been. If Mujuru had won, but Grace Mugabe ensured she did not, the party may have slowly been made to change—to the extent that dominance with a lighter touch may be regarded as change.[38] This sort of observation nuances the analysis of power—not just women in the top offices of the land, but at the top of the determining party apparatus. The power behind the throne, in these terms, can limit the power of the throne itself. In addition, of course, insofar as a dominant political party echoes, with carefully plotted but limited points of openness, the hegemony of the old one-party states, the party seeks to suborn to itself the free space that is sought by civil society—so that there is a tension, to the point of competition, between a party feminism and the sorts often espoused in civil societies.

But, insofar as it concerns parties, it may not be determined only by the smoke-filled rooms of party barons and baronesses. As evidenced most recently in Namibia, a new generation of younger female Ministers and Parliamentarians may start to change the practice of representation without effect.[39] It interacts far more with civil society, but it remains change led at the top, in systems where those at the bottom hold up half of the sky as a burden.

For the feminist thinkers of the present day and the future, this means a linkage between top and bottom, so that feminism is not an elite expression. It means taking seriously the intersection of civil society—both as a participant in development in the manner Sara Longwe meant and, in a way not able to be derived from Western templates of civil society, in the tension between traditional beliefs and constraints on the one hand and a problematic appropriation of modernity on the other. Western civil society is secular, but throughout Africa it includes church, mosque and other social organisations—some of which advance profoundly conservative values as well as emancipatory ones. We have mentioned how certain charismatic forms of Christianity can empower women because God first empowered female bishops. Whether equivalent empowerment can emanate from Islamic teachers and mosques remains to be seen. Certainly, it makes the advent of Tanzanian President Samia Suluhu Hassan a moment that could become a touchstone for much else. Beyond the importance of education for girls and young women, what kinds of society will their educations prepare them for?

If it is hard for women, even thought on equality, perhaps even toleration of homosexuality, is harder. Here the rule of the 'authentic' becomes the rule of iron even in churches that preach God's love. It is here that the link between sexual equality and sexual preference can be lost.

The Repression of Gays

In many countries, public opinion remains strongly against the decriminalisation of homosexuality. South Africa has led the way with its majority-rule constitution, where both gender and sexual preference rights are enshrined and participate in a range of constitutional equalities.

Of the other countries we have discussed thus far in this book, with leaders or dissidents who established reputations for their thought, homosexuality remains illegal in Senegal, Ghana, Zambia, Tanzania, Nigeria and Zimbabwe. It is not unlawful in, of all places, the Democratic Republic of Congo. It is legal in Guinea Bissau, and the other former Portuguese colonies of Angola and Mozambique; and in Madagascar where Thomas Sankara received some of his formation. It is tolerated in Sankara's Burkina Faso, in Rwanda, and in Namibia—though sodomy remains a crime in the latter. Homosexuality has full protections in Cape Verde—evoking a difference between protection, decriminalisation, tolerance and legal limbo.[40]

Africa is, in short, a site of ambivalence when it comes to homosexuality and, even if tolerated, it is discouraged from being expressed in the public domain. Homosexuality generally lacks equality in the sphere of rights pertaining to heterosexuality and, in its expression, generally lacks the freedom to do so. There is a double constraint at work: firstly, there is the assertion that homosexuality is a condition or practice absent in traditional African culture; secondly, it is prohibited and damnable in the Christian faith. Of the first, many have pointed out exceptions to this 'rule'.[41] Of the second, in a so-called postcolonial world, the power of Christianity in its literal iteration and, increasingly in a world of global penetrations of faith and its precepts, the power of particularly US churches in discouraging a whole range of sexual practices—premarital heterosexual sex alongside homosexuality—has been immense.

This has been vivid in Uganda, where anti-homosexuality laws, and the extended, often hostile Parliamentary debate on them between 2009 to 2014, was seen as closely linked to US Christian pressure.[42] And, in Zambia in 2019, a remark by the US Ambassador that sentences passed on a gay couple seemed disproportionately harsh evoked a huge public backlash, with President Lungu demanding (and receiving) the recall of the Ambassador to the USA,[43] on the grounds that Zambia had been offended as a constitutionally Christian nation. Lungu was prepared even to risk the significant foreign aid from the US, largely devoted in fact to the health sector and its fight against HIV, to prove his point. In an exchange with the Ambassador that grew progressively more heated, Lungu said: "We frown on it… the practice… most of us think it's wrong… it's un-Biblical and un-Christian… and we don't want it."[44]

In this kind of heated and intimidating atmosphere, to speak of one's gayness is to court reprobation and retribution. So it is one thing for Ngũgĩ wa Thiong'o, as we shall see below, to lambast corruption and bad faith in Kenya, but perhaps for those who identify as gay, it is in some ways more courageous to speak of their gayness. Ngũgĩ always had a hinterland of support, even when he was imprisoned. Many Kenyans felt he told the truth about the country's political condition. To speak of one's gayness is often to speak alone, and even those who wish to offer support often dare not. The open admission by Kenyan writer Binyavanga Wainaina that he was gay was defiant, but he too had an international support base denied most others.[45] Wainaina made this statement in 2014, at a time when it seemed some progress towards decriminalisation was possible. This was curtailed by the 2019 Kenya High Court ruling that the colonial laws against homosexual acts should be retained.[46] Wainaina died three days before the High Court ruling.[47] He was HIV Positive, but his death at the age of 48 was due to a stroke.[48] He had been named in April 2014 by TIME magazine as one of the '100 Most Influential

People in the World'. This was partly because of his essay, 'How to write about Africa', which remains his most provocative and astounding legacy.[49] It is short but slams into the exoticised Africa of European dreams, including the evocation of its landscapes and even the romantic view of Mandela's Rainbow Nation; and of ideas of African Renaissance. In capsule form, it is an African statement not unrelated to Edward Said's critique of Orientalism, the exoticisation of the East and of the colonial subject generally.

If Wainaina's international reputation offered a degree of protection in Kenya, this is not afforded to all writers. Even so, expression through creative writing, the imaginative word, has long been a recourse for the offering of critical comment in authoritarian and restrictive regimes. The question of what is fiction and what is directly critical has provided a space of ambiguity in which writers can shelter, but their readers can interpret meanings that accord with their daily lives and perceptions. Insofar as international reputations can add to a writer's protection, this has meant writing in metropolitan languages. Wainaina's 'How to write about Africa' was written in English. This raises a profound question about writing in vernacular languages and directly reaching those not fully literate in English, French or Portuguese. As we have seen, Ngũgĩ raised this very question, although more in terms of the transmission of meaning through language, but the question of access to literature and, through literature, currents of dissent, is an important one in resistance to colonialism and to postcolonial repression.

The Imaginative Word

Not that all vernacular literature waxed against colonialism in obvious ways. Precisely because in vernacular, one could inject all manner of subtleties, all manner of inflexions and nuances that a non-native reader might pass over without full appreciation. Something could be satirical without being obvious even to those trained in the language but un-acculturated to the social context of the words—or not be obvious in any way in translation. This was the case with the Zambian author, Stephen Mpashi, writing in Bemba in what was then called Northern Rhodesia. But Mpashi also used his works to demonstrate a kind of cosmopolitanism. Born in 1920, he worked in menial jobs in Tanganyika (now Tanzania) but joined the imperial army in 1941, serving in Egypt, Somaliland and Palestine, rising to Sergeant. But this meant he accumulated experience in different locations and cultures, and understood the British mode of military organisation. When he was discharged, he found work in publishing—a publishing bureau controlled by the colonial authorities—and started writing himself. He won a year's scholarship to study English and Literature at Exeter University but continued writing in Bemba, his linguistic nuances circumventing colonial censorship. But his first novel, written even before going to Exeter, *Cekesoni Aingila Ubusoja* (first published 1950), is based on his own experiences in other parts of Africa and the Middle East. The young soldier who is depicted as travelling to these areas returns home, wiser, appreciating his own culture in the light of the cultures of others, but also knowing that the future was destined to be cosmopolitan with the need for cultural adjustments and adaptations. The term *ubusuma* describes the values that emerged from his writing. It is a Bemba term that links goodness and truth,[50] and it is something that encompasses both the cosmopolitan and the local.

If something like *ubusuma* reflects or inflects an ethical value, it suggests discourse, debate and even disputation over the nature of good and truth as well as their intersections. In short, the language has its own epistemological depths and, of course, subtleties. This is seen also in Kikuyu writing, appearing in Kenya as the country worked towards independence. People like Kenyatta are praised for their leadership roles, but others who laboured to convince Kikuyu-speaking people of the justice of the nationalist cause, in their own language, have often been forgotten. The writings of Henry Muoria are now available in facing-page translation, i.e. the original Kikuyu is given on one page and its English translation on the other.[51] In an essay in the Muoria volume, John Lonsdale noted the debates on meaning in the nationalist circles—much to do with European vs Kikuyu learning, Biblical meaning and Kikuyu wisdom. Muoria proposed a fusion in which European learning should be something of which no one should feel inferior. There were tools of understanding that could render the best of European and Kikuyu learning—rendering Kikuyu learning on a par with that of Europe.[52] This of course also means that Ngũgĩ's much later work on *Decolonising the Mind*[53] was not a sudden personal decision, but was part of a long debate in Kikuyu circles from the time of colonialism into the independent epoch.

Muoria also made what Lonsdale calls 'moral' or 'moralist' arguments—better viewed as ethical propositions and positions. The one that follows is not unusual in his extensive *oeuvre*, but is set in a lengthy essay in which knowledge and epistemology are debated, in public as opposed to academic language, but with sophistication.

> If there is anything to make us hate them (white people), let it be spoken of openly, with finality, and then forgotten. Let us think about the days ahead and how we can develop the country together. Happiness will prevail and poverty and ignorance will be eradicated. These things are impossible without the unity of all. For hatred achieves nothing good, only misery and pain.[54]

Ngũgĩ wa Thiong'o (b. 1938) achieved fame as a novelist and playwright, writing at first in English—and continuing to use epigrams in his novels from poets such as W.B. Yeats who, as an Irishman, had his own problems with British colonialism. Ngũgĩ's famous novel, *Petals of Blood*,[55] makes much use of Yeats's poem, *The Second Coming*, of the rough beast slouching towards Bethlehem—to indicate an imminent rebirth. Stanzas from this poem punctuate the saga of a group of outlaws and exiles from mainstream Kenyan society, making their way to Nairobi to protest the failures of independence, as does work from Walt Whitman. He decided in 1967 to begin a transition to writing in Kikuyu, notwithstanding an academic formation in the UK and later exile academic positions in the USA. Quite apart from his view that the choice of language is also a choice of reasoning, a choice of epistemologies, what he also wanted was, like Muoria, an epistemological equality. But the question of equality is problem-strewn.

Firstly, if it is to be an expression of modernity, language cannot be simply traditional. New scientific terms and concepts, new borrowings into language, and new modes of expression are unavoidable. Language becomes a series of intersections.

Secondly, insofar as Kikuyu and other African languages were first rendered literate by missionaries—who did seek to be accurate in order better to deliver the Biblical message—there is, despite good intentions, the possibility of inflexions from metropolitan languages into aspects of grammar not fully understood by those missionaries. Thirdly, not everyone can read even vernacular language. The project of literacy is not complete and, where people are literate, they are often so in an 'official' language, e.g. English, which they learned in school, and not in their 'native' language.

Fourthly, in a 1983 interview, Ngũgĩ maintained that language penetration among peasants was important, even if coverage of penetration was uneven. "In class terms it is better to reach a single peasant than not to reach any peasant at all."[56] It is not clear what he here means by 'class', nor of any scale of differentiation, he is implying between an elite city dweller and a peasant, both speaking Kikuyu.

Fifthly, in the same interview he maintains that translation from one indigenous language to another would build solidarity among different peasant groups who would feel: "Oh, so we are the same, we have the same problems."[57] But that is manifestly not sustainable, as the problems of a Tuareg nomad peasant are very different to those of a settled Kenyan peasant. And, even with religious affinities, and still using the Tuareg example, Tuareg men wear the veil and women do not, marking a difference with other Islamic societies. As Ngũgĩ himself said, culture is reflected in language, so translation is not free from the same difficulties as those between English and Kikuyu.

Sixthly, there is an ethnolinguistic impediment to full understanding between language groups. Within an ethno-competitive Kenya, as in the 2007 electoral riots—and even if those riots were incited by political figures for political ends—language becomes a tool for division.

So, the rhetorical benefit of language, while important for the sense of pride and in overcoming any sense of inferiority, encounters real problems in the practices of a very diverse continent which is also a part, however problematically, of a globalised world.

Nevertheless, Ngũgĩ's earlier works, not just in his novels and plays, were powerful indictments not of elite metropolitan language but of elite corruption and theft from what was meant to be the nation's public wealth. In those denunciations, and in the negative aspects of tradition, e.g. forcing women to marry against their will, Ngũgĩ appeared to be a champion of the underclass and women.[58]

Ngũgĩ is sometimes referred to as a Fanonian Marxist, although this is a complex attribution.[59] Insofar as Fanon was a Marxist, it is by means of identification with the *dependencia* school that analysed uneven and exploitative global accumulation. Certainly Fanon's views on the necessity and inescapability of violence within just rebellion were clear in Ngũgĩ's mind—although he stopped short of advocating the violent overthrow of the Kenyan postcolonial state. He did, however, attack its corrupt foundations in denunciations so fierce that the Kenyan Government considered him an enemy of the state and, after time in prison,[60] Ngũgĩ went into voluntary exile. But he did celebrate outstanding figures in the liberation of Kenya from British colonial rule—figures who led violence against that rule—such as Dedan Kimathi.[61] He believed in the public role of writers and intellectuals and, in a volume on that theme, his celebrated essay in which he channelled Kim Chee Ha's 'Five Bandits', lambasting South Korean corruption, showed how writers in prison everywhere shared the same solidarity.[62] But that is the point entirely: in the face of corruption, the freedom and equality of the underclass; in the face of exploitation, equality of emerging nations; in the face of modernity, equality of those wishing to catch up on their own terms. Here, language may (or may not) play a pivotal role. The psychology of survival and emergence—a key theme of Fanon's when discussing the infliction of colonial violence—is certainly pivotal. It is something present in Ngũgĩ's work, but it is very evident in the work of his contemporary, Wole Soyinka.

Soyinka was in fact Fela Kuti's first cousin. Both were middle class, if somewhat different, dissidents and public actors. Soyinka won the Nobel Literature Prize in 1986, remaining the only black African writer to do so (although Ngũgĩ is repeatedly nominated). Soyinka's acceptance lecture stressed that the African past must be able to address the condition of Africa and Africans in the present.[63] Among other things, the lecture denounced Apartheid, then still raging and destabilising all of Southern Africa, but it also denounced Islamic insurrections used against other Africans who held a different religion. And he was almost at pains, as did Fanon, to cite Hegel and his view of history as something that led forwards. There was nothing curatorial for its own sake in his lecture. Yet, Soyinka could appeal to the values and motifs of traditional African religion and culture as well as anyone. His volume of poetry, in which he depicts and evokes the ancient Nigerian spiritual cosmos and gods, is strikingly powerful.[64] At the same time, he was able to deploy satire against the fetishisation of superstitions and the priests who specialise in it.[65]

His concern for the condition of the present led to him being, like Ngũgĩ, imprisoned. This was for two years from 1967 during the Nigerian civil war. There is an apocryphal story that his name derives from his time in prison and means 'shit inka', meaning ink made out of his own faeces, with which he continued writing on toilet paper while incarcerated. Certainly he somehow wrote while in prison.[66] But he has over many years produced many writings laying into not just Nigerian, but African-wide, corruption and dictatorship. Despite suffering at the hands of dictatorship, he was able to look back with a light touch in the aftermath.[67] This is a measure of the man, but his writings nevertheless became an extended testament to his sense that both the continent and its past mean less than they could in the face of modern evil. He was able to criticise corruption both with satire,[68] and by denunciatory essay.[69] But in many ways his most powerful works are to do with psychological adjustment to the emptiness that comes with failure of the moral project. He wrote mostly essays and plays but, of his two novels, *Season of Anomy*, reflecting his time in prison, deals plangently with the need to be moral, almost religiously, in the face of evil and wrong.[70] However, the feeling of psychological disjuncture in the adjustment to modernity within a state of constant change and lack of a mental or political map is found in his other novel, *The Interpreters*, and this may yet remain one of his finest works.[71] This sense of disjuncture is what faces a small group of young friends about to embark on adult life. They come into a Nigeria not marked by its traditional past as much as its uncertain modern future. How to deal with the future in moral and balanced terms, while being politically and socially critical, are the hallmarks of Soyinka's career.

Modernity demands an engagement that is not antique. It does not repudiate antiquity, tradition and its siren songs of certainty and safe haven—these are psychological needs—but uncertainty is itself ameliorated if not abolished by transparency and participation in transparent processes. In the productive African literary world these are key themes. Certainly freedom from trauma and psychological disjuncture was found in the work of the two Zimbabwean novelists mentioned earlier, Yvonne Vera and Alexander Kanengoni, and disjuncture was undoubtedly a hallmark both in the life and the writing of perhaps the greatest Zimbabwean writer, Dambudzo Marechera—Oxford-trained and Oxford-expelled—he epitomised an unease with accepting the world with its restraints of conventions, rituals and politics. His finest (and esoteric) work, *The House of Hunger*,[72] continued to lend its title years afterwards to the condition of dissatisfaction with the nation that Robert Mugabe claimed to have created.[73]

But Mpashi, Muoria and Ngũgĩ aside, all the writers mentioned here wrote in metropolitan languages. In so doing, they achieved not only a distinctive African voice in world literature, they created modern intersections with other literature and with the wider world. They sought equality with the wider world. Soyinka demonstrated that equality by winning the Nobel Literature Prize. The same aspiration might be said of the philosophers and thinkers of the late 20th century and 21st century.

The New Thinkers

There was a need, even in the period of independence, but certainly as the century wore on and the new African states began to give rise to feelings of disappointment, for more complex and sometimes radical forms of thought. One of the pioneers of radicalism was Samir Amin.

This Egyptian thinker has long been associated with the cause of Africa and the emerging world in general. For some time (1963–70), he was the Executive Secretary of the Council for the Development of Social Science Research in Africa (CODESRIA),which he helped to found, headquartered in Dakar and one of the most important pan-African think tanks and research institutes. He died in 2018.[74] He made a huge international impression with two books in particular, the French editions of both appearing in 1985 and 1988 respectively, in English entitled *Delinking*[75] and *Eurocentrism*.[76]

He continued writing well into his later years; his 2010 book, *Global History: A View from the South*,[77] being a case in point. In this book he examined not so much Africa, but the historical development of world systems in the Middle East, South Asia and East Asia. In this he followed upon his thoughts in *Eurocentrism*, in which he criticised the bias towards a centralisation of Western history and thought in the contemplation of history. But it was his book on *Delinking* which gave rise to a range of imaginations as to how the South could assert its independence from the North—even go its own way into an international socialist system separated from Western and Northern capitalism. Amin acknowledged this would be hard and, indeed, devotes his last chapter to the question posed by fundamental Islam in the Middle East and Africa—which could jeopardise any delinking's effort to be progressive. But, although Amin was a pioneer in the thought of delinking, the effort towards a practice of delinking was made by Julius Nyerere—not in his writings, but in his mobilisation of others as a statesman. Because Nyerere's efforts failed, it is the writing of Amin that lingers.

In 1979 the fifth round of the UN Conference on Trade and Development (UNCTAD) negotiations was held in Manila. For years, countries of the South had sought to use these negotiations to persuade mainly the West (in the parlance of the time, the North West) to make more humane and compassionate, fairer, the international capitalist order. Rumblings began to be sounded about the need—as it came particularly to be called in 1980 with the findings of the Brandt Commission—for a New International Economic Order (NIEO).[78] But, before then, before the effort to propose an amelioration of the economic order, Nyerere contemplated breaking away from it entirely. At a summit of the G77 (Group of 77, the emerging nations of the UN General Assembly) in Tanzania before the Manila meeting, Nyerere basically demanded change from the North West, saying that Manila was its last chance before a rupture began in the international economic system.

Now, in fact, the North West was prepared to call Nyerere's bluff. The February 1975 Dakar Declaration of 110 nations had basically adopted a formal *dependencia* position, no doubt influenced by thinkers like Amin, who was in Dakar at that period, and used terms such as 'imperialism' and 'neocolonialism' in its critique of the international economic system. But a bare month later, in March 1975, the Lima Declaration sought a greater share for the emerging world in global industrialisation—but succeeded simultaneously in revealing how weak its industrial base was.[79] The onus was on the North West to cede to the South, meaning the North West held more cards than the South. Indeed, on the eve of Manila, I was secretary of a large international conference in Colombo, Sri Lanka, which among other things, acted as a stopover and rehearsal location for delegations bound for Manila. I was astounded very late one evening being approached, quite discreetly, by a particular small Ministerial delegation—who sheepishly asked if I could draft its Manila position paper for them. To my genuinely puzzled expression, they responded that there was no one in their government apparatus who had been able to do that for them. I remember hastily cannibalising bits and pieces of my own earlier papers and giving it to them. They were happy not to have to go into the meeting naked, without a written position, but I wondered how many of those upon whom Nyerere counted went to Manila under improvisations. In any case, no stand was successfully made against *dependencia* at Manila, there was no delinking, and the next step was the reformative report of the Brandt Commission— business as usual, but perhaps in a nicer manner. But it meant that the work of thinkers was not in itself enough. Accompanying the thought had to be batteries of technocratic data and argument.

The work of the Malawian economist Thandika Mkandawire, who died in 2020, seeks to address this and stands out for its being grounded in data. Well known as a public intellectual concerned with development issues such as gender and language,[80] he was also long associated with CODESRIA.[81] However, it must be said that, even with CODESRIA-style biases against the 'Washington consensus' and neoliberalism, his work with data makes him stand out—not only in proposing practical ways forward for Africa and the South but in disentangling the vocabulary of *dependencia* and allied schools of thought and allocating to the component parts specific and measurable quantities. As an economist, his *oeuvre* included a host of edited books but, above all, consisted of technical papers. These have not had the same wide readership as exhortatory, and more clearly Marxist or neo-Marxist, books and speeches. However, in something like the use of the term, 'neopatrimonialism', long used to encompass the process of elite accumulation as if it were a fixed, class-based right, there have been few studies seeking to measure such acquisition and accumulation and to define precisely what a neo-patrimonial class consists in and what it must precisely do to be that class and be sustained as that class. To say simply, "they steal at others' expense", may or may not be true; to add "in a systemic" or even "structural" manner even more perhaps true; and to add the flourish "in a class-based system" may make it seem obvious and convincing; but none of these is a scientific statement. What Mkandawire does is attempt a scientific statement.

I will take three of his recent articles as examples. The first is indeed on neo-patrimonialism and proposes his critical reflections. What he sets out to do is to recognise the benefits and generalities of the term. It is a short-hand, but the long-hand is not always spelt out. The term has become a "convenient, all purpose, and ubiquitous moniker for African governance." It is in widespread use, not only in serious work but in popular reportage. It has

> assumed politically and economically exigent status. The school identifies causal links between neopatrimonialism and economic performance, and makes predictions drawing from what is referred to as the 'logic of neopatrimonialism.' Neopatrimonialism is said to account for trade policies, hyperinflation, economic stagnation, low investment in infrastructure, urban bias, and ultimately, the lack of economic development in Africa.

In short, the term carries too much of a burden by itself, especially without extensive definition and measures by which it can be assessed. This is especially true when the unspecified and unmeasurable term is used as a starting point for policy prescriptions—even if diagnoses and critiques based on it are more common than detailed prescriptions and programmes. He

> argues that while descriptive of the social practices of the states and individuals that occupy different positions within African societies, the concept of neopatrimonialism has little analytical content and no predictive value with respect to economic policy and performance.[82]

The bulk of his paper goes on to propose the need for such analytical content and predictive value. This starts to enter a seemingly dry and technical realm, and it is not the purpose here to explicate it—but certainly to say that, as an economic and development economic tool, this kind of work is essential and has all too often been missing in African thought, to the extent that diagnoses and critiques are themselves remiss—even if persuasive in the round.

Others have also worked on applying econometrics to the concept and practice of neo-patrimonialism, also noting that neopatrimonialism would often work differently in, say, the agricultural as opposed to an industrial sector.[83] Even so, the econometric data is essential both for analysis and for modelling in any and all sectors. There is an entire range of factors involved. Mushtaq Khan outlined how they were deployed in Palestine,[84] and his delineations and methodology have been applied to Africa.[85]

So that a commitment to vocabulary by itself can not only dissuade one from specificity of measure and thus scientific weighing of evidence and variables, it can act as a deterrent to recognition as to how schools of thought change and adapt according to world conditions, pressures and opportunities. To give *dependencia* class labels is simultaneously to be denunciatory of some of them and make them impediments to any vision of a pure world. Mkandawire looks instead at how, perhaps stealthily but clearly, African economic thought and practice have evolved over the years. Without fully giving cognisance to this, every such developed policy might be seen as the collaboration of a 'class enemy' with metropolitan dominance. However, it is the case that economic ideas and policymaking in Africa have changed over the last few decades. He writes that he discusses

> the ways in which the focus of economists working on Africa has moved from the structuralist-developmentalist and neo-Marxist perspectives of the 1960s and 1970s, through a neoliberal phase of the 1980s and 1990s, to a more eclectic combination of neo-institutionalism, growth orientation, and welfarist interests in poverty and redistribution issues. These shifts in development thinking, while not unique to Africa, have not been the subject of much debate in Africa. The article argues that such a debate is long overdue, including an interrogation not only of the leverage of foreign interests, but also of the profession of economics itself and the implications of its material underpinnings and social construction on the integrity and credibility of its research.[86]

He is not here endorsing necessarily what has happened, what has evolved, but he stresses the need to be mindful of it and interrogate it to further develop economic planning. And the opportunity for such planning, revitalised perhaps with African values in mind and African development and welfare truly at heart might lie in the present moment. Writing shortly after the end of the first decade of the 21st century, he said: "For more than a decade, African policy making was limited to a narrow space prescribed by the Washington Consensus. Things are changing now, facilitated by the collapse of that doctrine."[87] But, without knowing where one has got to, dispassionately, technically, one can exploit no weakness in the other side.

Mkandawire uses a full economic vocabulary and range of concepts, together with data. None of this is 'un-African' because it is not drawn from traditional knowledge. It is an engagement with terms and technicalities, methodologies and calculations of modernity. Like every economist, he references others in a proper interdiscursivity. This is also possible when it comes to philosophical work, as the case of Achille Mbembe shows. Here we have work that is properly discursive. While it rejects a simple reliance on Western metropolitan philosophical and theoretical thought, it shows itself a master of such thought redirected towards an original African critique of politics, political culture and society.

We have already had a look at the work of Mbembe, originally from Cameroon but now resident in South Africa, though much in demand internationally. We have mentioned his work on the carnivalesque and the necropolis. But the idea of the necropolis might be fairly ascribed as Mbembe's particular application of Foucault to Africa. Foucault's account of the public death of Damien as a spectacle, drawn from Foucault's classic work, *Discipline and Punish*,[88] is essentially retold by Mbembe in a host of African examples of tyranny. Foucault wrote of a slow death with carefully crafted and premeditated pain. This tyranny, however, has its own spectacular feature of 'drunkenness', of excess, of theatricality, ceremony and the intimacy of tyranny—the last term meaning that the subjects of tyranny, in cooperation with tyranny even only for the sake of survival, are obliged to internalise its signs and make them 'normal'. They become part of the state's carnival. The term carnival is derived from the Russian thinker Bakhtin and his work on the Russian author, Dostoevsky.[89] But Mbembe reverses the application of this term.

Whereas Dostoevsky meant that resistance could be polyphonic, occur on so many planes and through so many modalities that the tyrannical order could not keep up, Mbembe means that African tyranny seeks to seize this space of imagination. If it succeeds, it constitutes a tyranny that is terrible and terrifyingly dangerous.[90]

The point is that Mbembe's critique is made the more powerful, particularly to an outside world whom he wishes to alert to the depravity of the necropolis in Africa. But it would be wrong to consider he was intrinsically dependent on thinkers such as Foucault and Bakhtin. In his book, *Critique of Black Reason*, he gives one of the most stirring and evocative accounts of racial subjugation that certainly I have ever read[91]—but then proceeds to give an account of the emancipatory work of great black thinkers such as Césaire, Fanon, Mandela—and taking in Blyden, Garvey, Senghor and Martin Luther King—so that the thoughtful seeds of rebellion to an extent give rise to 'authentic' trees and flowers, even though, as we have seen, these pioneering thinkers themselves encompassed many influences, and some never made it to Africa.[92] The title of the book is of course a riff off Kant's *Critique of Pure Reason* and, although it is written in a very different register to Kant's work, in a way far more literary than philosophical, it is all the same a challenge, a declaration of a form of thoughtful equivalence, of equality.

Someone perhaps seeking a deeper blend of international thought and African thought that existed before the advent of missionaries and the international in Africa is the Congolese thinker, Valentin Mudimbe (b. 1941), with his Belgian university formation and French influences from the time of Sartre and afterwards, he has also been someone daring enough to propose an 'unknowingness' as a form of knowledge. That is simple enough to say, but Mudimbe is very complex in his argument.[93] He is sometimes likened to Edward Said in that his book, *The Invention of Africa*,[94] was seen to perform the same function as Said's *Orientalism*, i.e. declaring an unshackling of self-regard from the imposed and exoticising gaze of the imperial metropolis. But Said never attempted the extent of Mudimbe's work.

Mudimbe uses phenomenology and structuralism in what might be said to be 'the French mode' but also delves into myth and linguistics. His teaching range as a Professor extends to ancient Greek history and culture. He brings a basically polymathic capacity to his work. His book is not about African thought *per se*, but how it has been represented or reconstructed in Western thought, starting with missionary accounts of Africa and their translation of African languages, and later by Africanist disciplines in Western universities. In the global world, construction and reconstruction have been fed back to African scholars in Africa itself, and, at first sight, there would seem no escape from this. But Mudimbe argues that the African scholars do 'write back', even if that means they have to exceed the limits of imposed languages and epistemological frameworks.

In saying this, he does, however, make use of Foucault's idea of the archaeology of knowledge.[95] He does this by an 'excavation' of the power relationships within the disciplines that have been used to investigate Africa. He tears through a huge array of sources in several languages. But this means he deciphers a plenitude of modes of interpretation. He doesn't dismiss these in any peremptory fashion but, and this is where his contribution to thought is both stirring, provocative, and delving into what is 'unknowable' except through a form of intuition. It is something mere power cannot reach. Mudimbe writes about an esoteric knowledge (using the Greek term), *gnosis*, a knowledge that has an implied spiritual form and spiritual quality.

But *how* can African scholars write back? Ngũgĩ tried it by writing in his own language. But are there procedures that are true to that knowledge? Mudimbe does not give us a methodology. He insists that what Western-based disciplines have done in contemplating Africa is incomplete and probably distorted. And he is not sparing of his contemporaries and immediate forebears. Even those who worked intellectually to create, e.g. a *negritude* or a science of 'Africanness', like Senghor and Diop, basically essentialise Africa by perhaps unconscious use of intellectual disciplines and approaches they have internalised. Basically, Mudimbe leaves us with a rigorous negative critique. In the face of this, the hope is that one day, almost mystically, the true *gnosis* will arise.

It is impossible to read Mudimbe, or try to read him, without being shaken by his learning, but also left with a form of hopelessness. If the authentic cannot be 'known', on what foundations can Africa be built? Of course that was the rationalising question behind so much of the African political thought discussed in this book. If what is intrinsic is a domain of uncovered *gnosis*, can the extrinsic be, after all, the binding force? Is there nothing possible that is African without being simultaneously pan-African? Without in fact being simultaneously black, i.e. encompassing the entire black diaspora, so that African thought has a hinterland, a bridge on something of its own terms to the outside world?

Ali Mazrui writes of a great Afro-black trans-Atlantic cross-fertilisation.[96] And certainly, in the progress of this book, we can see how the slave trade changed, even if problematically, the Americas. Once there, black people from Blyden on through Garvey, black Americans, have looked to Africa as some kind of at least spiritual home—even though living conditions in Africa might be extremely difficult for many black Americans. African rhythms helped establish American jazz and the export of the technology of instruments such as saxophones helped develop and change African music. In the intellectual context that developed around such musical and artistic expression, via vehicles such as *negritude*, black Americans found a way to be proud in the 'black is beautiful' movement that accompanied the drive for civil rights. But in the development of, for example, jazz musicians into icons who, all the same, like Miles Davis, had to seek refuge from US racism by exiling himself to Paris, and being an adjunct to *Racing Club Paris* jazz that influenced African music just as much,[97] if not in places like Congo even more, than New Orleans jazz, and given the little known story of icons like Louis Armstrong sending his own trumpet in the 1950s to South African trumpeter Hugh Masekela as a gesture of solidarity, we see an endless circle. We see an affirmation if not always an explicit philosophical explanation of something great and significant.

Not that anything is as yet near completion. Contemporary scholars like Ndlovu-Gatsheni say more needs to be done to complete the project of intellectual and cultural freedom.[98] But what we have tried to establish in this chapter is that the project is complex, and complexity cannot be wished away in a mere political flourish. And perhaps the project is not to make Africa into a monastery of its own thought, but thoughtfully to nourish the world and be nourished by it in a sphere of equality.

NOTES

PREFACE

1. Jean-Paul Sartre, 'Preface' to Frantz Fanon, *The Wretched of the Earth*, London: Penguin, 1967, p. 15.

1. ANTECEDENTS: RACE AND ROMANTICISM

1. E.g. Henry Morton Stanley, *Through the Dark Continent: Or, The Sources of the Nile Around the Great Lakes of Equatorial Africa and Down the Livingstone River to the Atlantic Ocean*, San Bernardino: Ulan Press, 2012.
2. Homer (trans. Robert Fagles), *The Odyssey*, NY: Viking, 1996, p. 78.
3. Edward Wilmot Blyden, *Christianity, Islam and the Negro Race* (in full facsimile form), Mansfield CT: Martino Fine Books, 2016.
4. "Elections in Liberia", African Elections Database, http://africanelections.tripod.com/lr.html. Last Updated: 25 November 2011. Downloaded 10 March 2020.
5. John Iliffe, *Honour in African History*, Cambridge: Cambridge University Press, 2005, e.g. Chapters 3 & 6.
6. W.E.B. Du Bois, *The Souls of Black Folk*, Oxford: Oxford University Press, 2008.
7. For an account of this quarrel, see Thomas Aiello, 'The First Fissure: The Du Bois—Washington Relationship 1898–1899, *Phylon*, 51:1, 2014, pp. 76–81.
8. For a documentary history, see George Padmore (ed.), *Colonial and Coloured Unity—A Programme of Action—History of the Pan-African Congress*, London: Hammersmith Bookshop, 1947.
9. W.E.B. Du Bois, "To the Nations of the World", address given in London, 1900, https://warwick.ac.uk/fac/arts/english/currentstudents/undergraduate/modules/fulllist/second/en213/syllabus2017–18/dubois_tothenations.pdf. Downloaded 21 December 2020.

10. Letter from W. E. B. Du Bois to President Woodrow Wilson, ca. November 1918. W. E. B. Du Bois Papers (MS 312). Special Collections and University Archives, University of Massachusetts Amherst Libraries, https://credo.library.umass.edu/view/full/mums312-b013-i174. Downloaded 21 December 2020.

11. P.M.H. Bell, *A Certain Eventuality: Britain and the Fall of France*, London: Saxon House, 1974, pp. 220–225.

12. See Hakim Adi, Marika Sherwood, George Padmore, *The 1945 Manchester Pan-African Congress revisited*, London: new Beacon, 1995.

13. C.L.R. James, *The Black Jacobins: Toussaint L'Ouverture and the San Domingo Revolution*, London: Penguin, 2001.

14. See Martin O. Ijere, 'W.E.B. Du Bois and Marcus Garvey as Pan-Africanists: A Study in Contrast', *Presence Africaine*, 89, 1974, pp. 188–206.

15. Marcus Garvey (ed. Amy Jacques-Garvey), *Philosophy and Opinions of Marcus Garvey*, in *The Journal of Pan African Studies*, 2009, p. 26.

16. See Ali Mazrui, *Cultural Forces in World Politics,* London: James Currey, 1990, Chapter 7.

17. Ali Rahnema, *An Islamic Utopian: A Political Biography of Ali Shari'ati*, London: I.B. Tauris, 2000.

18. George Cole, 'Miles Davis: a love affair with Paris', *The Guardian*, 10 December 2009.

19. Obituary for 'Aimé Césaire', *The Times*, 18 April 2008.

20. Kaye Whiteman, 'Obituary—Leopold Senghor', *The Guardian*, 21 December 2001. https://www.theguardian.com/news/2001/dec/21/guardianobituaries.books1. Downloaded June 2021.

21. Ebou Dibba, 'Leopold Sedar Senghor—A Taga', *West Africa*, 18–24 November 1996, pp. 1790–1791.

22. Ali Mazrui, *Cultural Forces in World Politics*, London: James Currey, 1990, Chapter 7.

23. Author's discussion with Malcolm MacDonald, London, 1978. We were both committee members in the Royal Commonwealth Society at the time.

2. NATIONAL CONSCIOUSNESS, INTERNATIONAL STRUGGLE: CABRAL, KAUNDA AND THE THOUGHT OF LIBERATION

1. Susan Sontag, 'Some Thoughts on the Right Way (for us) to Love the Cuban Revolution', *Ramparts*, April 1969, pp. 6–19.

2. Robert F. Kennedy, *13 Days: The Cuban Missile Crisis October 1962*, London: Pan, 1969.

3. Graham T. Allison, *Essence of Decision: Explaining the Cuban Missile Crisis*, NY: Little Brown, 1971.

4. For extracts from Guevara's African diaries, see https://www.theguardian.com/books/2000/aug/12/cuba.artsandhumanities, 12 August 2000.

5. https://www.thecubanhistory.com/historical-pages-of-cuba/cuban-presidents/jose-marti-y-perez/. Downloaded 21 December 2020.

6. http://www.socialsciencecollective.org/poetry-agostinho-neto-bursts-book-fair/ downloaded 21 December 2020.

7. See Reddit thread: https://www.reddit.com/r/portugal/comments/e9507h/haq_houve_um_escravo_negro_a_ascender_%C3%A0_condi%C3%A7%C3%A3o/. Downloaded 21 December 2020.

8. Antonio Tomas, *Amílcar Cabral: The Life of a Reluctant Nationalist*, London: Hurst, 2021.

9. The following comments are drawn from Amílcar Cabral's speech to the conference, January 1966, *The Weapon of Theory* https://www.marxists.org/subject/africa/cabral/1966/weapon-theory.htm downloaded 21 December 2020.

10. Amílcar Cabral, *History is a Weapon* February 1970 https://www.historyisaweapon.com/defcon1/cabralnlac.html downloaded 21 December 2020.

11. David Birmingham, *A Concise History of Portugal*, Cambridge: Cambridge University Press, 1971. David Birmingham, *Frontline Nationalism in Angola & Mozambique*, London: James Currey, 1992.

12. See P.L. Ehioze Idahosa, 'Going to the People: Amílcar Cabral's Materialist Theory and Practice of Culture and Ethnicity', *Lusotopie: Portugal, une identité dans la longue durée*, n°9, 2 September 2002, pp. 29–58.

13. Lutz Marten & Nancy Kula, 'Zambia, One Zambia, One nation, many Languages', in Andrew Simpson (ed.), *Language and National Identity in Africa*, Oxford: Oxford University Press, 2008.

14. Yuyi K. Libakeni, *They Built Zambia: Zambia's hundred graduates at independence*, Lusaka: the author, 2008. Peter Desmond Snelson, *To Independence and Beyond: Memoirs of a Colonial Commonwealth*, London: Radcliffe. 1993, Chapters 4 & 5.

15. See Stephen Chan, *Southern Africa: Old Treacheries and New Deceits*, New Haven: Yale University Press, 2011, Chapter 1.

16. I lived in Zambia for a large part of the 1980s, when South African destabilisation of the region was at its height. Before that had been Rhodesian destabilisation. Many of my insights derive from long conversations with members of the Zambian High Command.

17. My accounts of Kaunda's mediation and negotiations are in Stephen Chan, *Kaunda and Southern Africa: Image and Reality in Foreign Policy*, London: I.B. Tauris, 1992.

18. See Douglas G. Anglin, *Zambian Crisis Behaviour: Confronting Rhodesia's Unilateral Declaration of Independence*, Montreal & Kingston: McGill-Queen's University Press, 1994.
19. General Lungu's own account to me in Lusaka.
20. Richard Hall, *The High Price of Principles: Kaunda and the White South*, London: Penguin, 1973.
21. As recounted to me by both Zambian and Zimbabwean soldiers, and by Mujuru's biographer, Blessing Miles Tendi.
22. Kenneth D. Kaunda (ed. Colin Morris), *On Violence*, London: Harper Collins, 1980; Published in the USA as *The Riddle of Violence*, San Francisco: Harper & Row, 1981.
23. E.g. see the review by Anani Dzidzienyo Brown University, https://scholarscompass.vcu.edu/cgi/viewcontent.cgi?article=1043&context=ess 1982.
24. Frederic Hunter, 'An African leader's sensitive message to the West; The Riddle of Violence, by Kenneth Kaunda' *Christian Science Monitor*, 18 February 1981. https://www.csmonitor.com/1981/0218/021802.html
25. Kenneth Kaunda, *On Violence*, p. 58.
26. Christopher Cviic, 'The Politics of the World Council of Churches', *The World Today*, 35: 9, 1979, pp. 369–376.
27. Kenneth Kaunda, *On Violence*, pp. 121–2.
28. *Ibid.*, p. 164.
29. *Ibid.*, p. 173.
30. Stephen Chan and Ranka Primorac, 'The Exile's Spirit of Bravado: Lewis Nkosi (1936–2010), *The Journal of Commonwealth Literature*, 46:1, 2011, pp. 183–4.
31. In Lindy Stiebel & Liz Gunner (eds.), *Still Beating the Drum: Critical Perspectives on Lewis Nkosi*, Amsterdam: Rodopi, 2005, pp. 130–1.
32. *Ibid.*, p. 181.

3. THE NEW AFRICAN MAN: THE POLITICAL THOUGHT OF TRANSFORMATION

1. David Armstrong, *The Rise of the International Organisation: A Short History*, London: Macmillan, 1982, pp. 30–33.
2. See John Henrik Clarke, 'Kwame Nkrumah: His Years in America', *The Black Scholar*. 6:2, 1974, pp. 9–16.
3. See https://www.lincoln.edu/about/history (downloaded 21 December 2020).
4. See Abdullai Haroon, *Pan-Africanism Then and Now, and African Political Thought*, Tamale: Muetpress, 2013. This small book, written by my

successful PhD student, was a side-project to his main thesis—but expresses concisely and well a linked genealogy of thought and influence from one generation to another.

5. See https://www.history.com/topics/roaring-twenties/harlem-renaissance (downloaded 21 December 2020).

6. Ian Duffield, 'Marcus Garvey and Kwame Nkrumah', *History Today*, 31:3, 1981; and Mark Christian, 'Marcus Garvey and African Unity: Lessons for the Future from the Past', *Journal of Black studies*, 39:2, 2008, pp. 316–331.

7. Sebastiane Ebatamehi, 'Dr Nnamdi Azikiwe: The Man Who Shaped Nkrumah's Perspective on Pan-Africanism', *The African Exponent*, 21 December 2020, https://www.africanexponent.com/post/9966-the-man-who-influenced-pan-african-hero-kwame-nkrumah.

8. P. Kiven Tunteng, 'George Padmore's Impact on Africa: A Critical Appraisal', *Phylon*, 35:1, 1974, pp. 33–44.

9. Ayi Kwei Armah, *The Beautyful Ones Are Not Yet Born*, London: Heinemann, 1969, p. 82. Henry Bienen, *Tanzania: Party Transformation and Economic Development*, Princeton: Princeton University Press, 1967, p. 212.

10. See David Birmingham, *Kwame Nkrumah*, London: Cardinal/Sphere, 1990, Chapter 1.

11. Kat Eschner, 'Martin Luther King and Gandhi Weren't the Only Ones Inspired By Thoreau's "Civil Disobedience"', *Smithsonian Magazine*, 12 July 2017, https://www.smithsonianmag.com/smart-news/martin-luther-king-and-gandhi-werent-only-ones-inspired-thoreaus-civil-disobedience-180963972/ (downloaded 15 June 2021).

12. Henry David Thoreau, *Essay on Civil Disobedience*, available at https://users.manchester.edu/Facstaff/SSNaragon/Online/texts/201/Thoreau,%20CivilDisobedience.pdf. First published 1849. Downloaded 29 March 2020.

13. David Birmingham, *Nkrumah*, Chapter 2.

14. Kwame Nkrumah, *African Socialism Revisited*, 1967 conference paper delivered in Cairo, available at https://www.marxists.org/subject/africa/nkrumah/1967/african-socialism-revisited.htm. First published by Peace and Socialism Publishers, Prague, 1967, in "Africa: National and Social Revolution".

15. Kwame Arhin, 'The Structure of Greater Ashanti (1700– 1824)', *The Journal of African History*, 8:1, 1967, pp. 65–85.

16. Jefrey Herbst, *The Politics of Reform in Ghana, 1982–1991*, Berkeley: University of California Press, 1993, pp. 20–23.

17. Kwame Nkrumah, *Consciencism: Philosophy and Ideology for Decolonization and Development with Particular Reference to the African Revolution*, NY: Monthly Review Press, 1964.

18. V.Y. Mudime, *The Invention of Africa: Gnosis, Philosophy and the Order of Knowledge*, Bloomington: Indiana University Press, 1988.

19. See https://africaunbound.org/index.php/aumagazine/issue-1/item/ edward-blyden-on-the-struggle-for-african-liberation-2.html (downloaded 24 December 2020).

20. See Kwame Botwe-Asamoah, *Kwame Nkrumah's Politico-Cultural Thought and Policies*, NY: Routledge, 2005, Chapters 4 & 5.

21. Kwame Gyekye, *An Essay on African Philosophical Thought: The Akan Conceptual Scheme*, Cambridge: Cambridge University Press, 1987, Chapter 3.

22. See Faisal Fatehali Devji, 'Subject to translation: Shakespeare, Swahili, Socialism', *Journal of Postcolonial Studies*, 3:2, 2000, pp. 181–9.

23. Alamin M. Mazrui, 'Shakespeare in Africa: Between English and Swahili Literature', *Research in African Literatures*, 27:1, 1996, pp. 64–79.

24. Ibid., p. 68.

25. T.O. Ranger, *Dance and Society in Eastern Africa 1890–1970: The Beni Ngoma*, London: Heinemann, 1975.

26. Thomas Molony, *Nyerere: The Early Years*, Oxford: James Currey, 2016.

27. Susan C. Crouch, *Western Responses to Tanzanian Socialism 1967–83*, Aldershot: Avebury, 1987.

28. Available at https://www.marxists.org/subject/africa/nyerere/1967/ arusha-declaration.htm (downloaded 31 March 2020).

29. Isaria N. Kimambo, *Penetration and Protest in Tanzania*, London: James Currey, 1991, Chapter 9.

30. Christos A. Frangonikolopoulos, 'Tanzanian Foreign Policy: The proportions of autonomy', *The Round Table*, 307, 1988, pp. 276–292.

31. Samuel Sitta, Willibrod Slaa & John Cheyo, *Bunge Lenye Meno: A Parliament with Teeth for Tanzania*, London: Africa Research Institute, 2008.

32. Thomas Fuller, 'British Images and Attitudes in Colonial Uganda', *The Historian*, 38:2, 1976, pp. 305–318.

33. John Iliffe, *Honour in African History*, Cambridge: Cambridge University Press, 2005.

34. Garth Glentworth & Ian Hancock, 'Obote and Amin: Change and Continuity in Modern Ugandan Politics, *African Affairs*, 72:288, 1973, pp. 237–255.

35. Available at https://otoascrapnotes.wordpress.com/2012/05/22/dr-apollo-milton-obotes-common-mans-charter/ (downloaded 24 December 2020).

36. *Daily Monitor*, 'Was Obote's nationalisation drive in 1970 a necessary evil?', 26 August 2012, https://www.monitor.co.ug/uganda/special-reports/uganda-50/was-obote-s-nationalisation-drive-in-1970-a-necessary-evil--1524116 (downloaded 24 December 2020).

37. Ancietos Mwansa, 'Barotseland and the advocacy for statehood: a case entailing the complexities of statehood and state recognition in public international law', *African Journal of Political Science and International Relations*, 11:11, 2017, pp. 317–338.

38. For my account of 'humanism', see Stephen Chan, *Kaunda and Southern Africa: Image and Reality in Foreign Policy*, London: I.B. Tauris, 1992, pp. 18–32.

39. See his work on Kaunda: John Hatch, *Two African Statesmen*, London: Secker & Warburg, 1976; privately republished in part in Zambia in 1981 as *Kaunda of Zambia*.

40. I was resident in Zambia throughout this time, and was familiar both with Hatch and the student leaders, including some of those Kaunda had imprisoned, and Kaunda's chief of staff who had in fact signed the detention orders.

41. Stephen Chan, *Issues in International Relations: A View from Africa*, London: Macmillan, 1987, Chapter 5.

42. See the report of the *New York Times*, 13 August 1964, about the demise of the Lumpa church's uprising: https://www.nytimes.com/1964/08/13/archives/rhodesia-holds-leader-of-cult-kaunda-says-alice-lenshina-calls-for.html (downloaded 15 June 2021).

43. See John M. Mwanakatwe, *End of the Kaunda Era*, Lusaka: Multimedia, 1994, Chapters 5–9.

44. A list of his most important books may be found in the Bibliography at the end of this book.

45. Vatican summary of missionary reports from circa. 1590, in John Iliffe, *The African Poor—A History*, Cambridge: Cambridge University Press, 1987, p. 52.

4. 'BIG MEN': THE LIMITATIONS IN THOUGHT OF MOBUTU AND BANDA

1. Achille Mbembe, *Critique of Black Reason*, Johannesburg: Wits University Press, 2017.

2. Achille Mbembe, 'Power and Obscenity in the Post-Colonial Period: The Case of Cameroon', in James Manor (ed.), *Rethinking Third world politics*, London: Longman, 1991, pp. 166–182.

3. Richard Gray, 'A Kongo Princess, the Kongo Ambassadors and the Papacy', *Journal of Religion in Africa*, 29:2, 1999, pp. 140–154.

4. Adam Hochschild, *King Leopold's Ghost: A Story of Greed, Terror and Heroism in Colonial Africa*, London: Macmillan, 1999.

5. Flora Dury, 'EXCLUSIVE: Crumbling in the Jungle', *Mail Online*, 7 June 2016, https://www.dailymail.co.uk/news/article-3629030/Crumbling-

Jungle-Eerie-dictator-s-palace-Muhammed-Ali-trained-fight-life-alongside-African-despot-insisted-right-deflower-virgins-drank-human-blood.html (downloaded 15 June 2021). This is a sensationalistic account, but gives the number of gratuitous executions as 100. This *Chicago Tribune* account, from 29 April 1997, is less sensationalistic: www.chicagotribune.com, ct-xpm-1997–04–29–9704290128-story. My own figure of 200 is an estimate given me by exiles from Mobutu's rule and, although it should be treated with caution, is all the same from non-sensationalistic people.

6. Cited in Marvine Howe, 'Mobutu Is Building an 'Authentic' Zaire', *New York Times*, 23 June 1972, https://www.nytimes.com/1972/06/23/archives/mobutu-is-building-an-authentic-zaire.html (downloaded 15 June 2021).

7. Jean-Jacques Wondo Omanyundu, 'The urgency of a mental decolonization of the Congolese: reread Mabika Kalanda', 24 May 2017, http://desc-wondo.org/lurgence-dune-decolonisation-mentale-des-congolais-relire-mabika-kalanda-jj-wondo/ (downloaded 15 June 2021).

8. Mabika Kalanda, *The questioning. Basis of mental decolonization*, Brussels: African Note, 1967.

9. Emmanuel Kabongo Malu, "Culture, conscience and development. Mabika Kalanda: the paradigm of Congolese cultural decline", in José Tshishungu Wa Tshisungu (ed.), *De La mental decolonization: Mabika Kalanda and the XXIth Century Congolese*, Toronto: Editions Glopro, 2016, p. 154.

10. Frantz Fanon, *Communication to the Second Congress of Black Writers and Artists*, Rome, 1959.

11. Anthony W. Gambino, *Congo: Securing Peace, Sustaining Progress*, NY: Council on Foreign Relations, 2008. It has not greatly improved since the year of publication.

12. Zoe Marriage, *Formal Peace and Informal War: Security and Development in Congo*, London: Routledge, 2013.

13. Kristof Titeca and Tom de Herdt, 'Real governance beyond the "failed state": negotiating education in the Democratic Republic of Congo', *African Affairs*, 110:439, 2011, pp. 213–231.

14. Gerald Horne, *The United States and the War against Zimbabwe, 1965–1980*, Chapel Hill: University of North Carolina Press, 2001, pp. 97 & 302.

15. Vera Chirwa, *Fearless Fighter: An Autobiography*, London: Zed, 2007, pp. 198–201.

16. Kenneth R. Ross (ed.), *Christianity in Malawi*, Geru: Mambo Press, 1996.

17. Jack Mapanje, *And Crocodiles are Hungry at Night*, Banbury: Ayebia Clarke, 2011.
18. Jack Mapagange, *Skipping Without Ropes*, Newcastle-Upon-Tyne: Bloodaxe, 1998, p. 14.
19. Jack Mapange, 'Prisons That Still Choke Us Cold', in *Beasts of Nalunga*, Tarset: Bloodaxe, 2007, p. 20.
20. Jack Mapagange, 'When You've Never Lived under a Despot' in *Beasts of Nalunga*, p. 23.

5. THE COUP 'ARTISTS' AND THE NEW NATIONALISMS ON COMMAND: RAWLINGS AND SANKARA

1. 'Den Kaiser—diese Weltseele—sah ich durch die Stadt zum Rekognoszieren hinaus reiten; es ist in der Tat eine wunderbare Empfindung, ein solches Individuum zu sehen, das hier auf einen Punkt konzentriert, auf einem Pferde sitzend, über die Welt übergreift und sie beherrscht.' Hegel, letter of 13 October 1806 to F. I. Niethamme.
2. The classic work on military coups: S.E. Finer, *The Man on Horseback: The Role of the Military in Politics*, London: Pall Mall, 1962.
3. Stephen Chan, *Grasping Africa: A Tale of Tragedy and Achievement*, London: I.B. Tauris, 2007, p. 53.
4. Although the following novel caught the sense of a man of great volatility, rather than madness deserving ridicule: Giles Foden, *The Last King of Scotland*, London: Faber and Faber, 2007.
5. Brian Titley, *Dark Age: The Political Odyssey of Emperor Bokassa*, Montreal & Kingston: McGill-Queens University Press, 2002.
6. Stephen Ellis, *The Mask of Anarchy: The Destruction of Liberia and the Religious Dimension of an African Civil War*, London: Hurst, 1999.
7. For a naked satire, notwithstanding any technocracy, see Wole Soyinka, *King Baabu*, London: Methuen, 2002. But see also Kunle Amuwo, Daniel C. Bach and Yann Lebeau (eds.), *Nigeria During The Abacha Years (1993–1998)*, Ibadan: IFRA, 2002.
8. Max Siollun, *Nigeria's Soldiers of Fortune: The Abacha and Obasanjo Years*, London: Hurst, 2019. For Obasanjo's second incarnation as Nigerian President, this time as an elected civilian, and his wise conduct of foreign policy, see Steve Itugbu, *Foreign Policy and Leadership in Nigeria: Obasanjo and the Challenge of African Diplomacy*, London: I.B. Tauris, 2017. For Obasanjo's subsequent career and his work as one of the world's wise great and good, see Greg Mills, Olusegun Obasanjo, Jeffrey Herbst and Dickie Davis, *Making Africa Work: A handbook for economic success*, Cape Town: Tafelberg, 2017.
9. A. Zack-Williams and Stephen Riley, 'Sierra Leone: The Coup and Its Consequences', *Review of African Political Economy*, 56, 1993, pp. 91–98.

10. Brooks Marmon, '25 years after his demise, Samuel Doe continues to cast a long shadow across Liberian politics', *African Arguments*, 9 September 2015, https://africanarguments.org/2015/09/09/25-years-after-his-demise-samuel-doe-continues-to-cast-a-long-shadow-across-liberian-politics/ (downloaded 15 June 2021).

11. Kwesi Botchwey, *Transforming the Periphery: A study of the struggle of social forces in Ghana for democracy and national sovereignty*, NY: United Nations, 1981.

12. Reginald H. Green, 'Reflections on Economic Strategy, Structure, Implementation and Necessity: Ghana and the Ivory Coast, 1957–1960', in Philip Foster & Aristide Zolberg (eds.), *Ghana and the Ivory Coast: Perspectives on Modernization*, Chicago: University of Chicago Press, 1971, pp. 251–60.

13. Jeffrey Herbst, *The Politics of Reform in Ghana, 1982–1991*, Berkeley: University of California Press, 1993.

14. Kwaku Osei-Hwedie & Yaw Agyeman-Badu, *Essays on the Political Economy of Ghana*, Lawrenceville: Brunswick, 1987, Chapter 2.

15. ODI Briefing Paper, *Adjustment in Africa: Lessons from Ghana*, London: Overseas Development Institute, July 1996, available at https://www.odi.org/sites/odi.org.uk/files/odi-assets/publications-opinion-files/2634.pdf.

16. Sérgio Pereira Leite, Anthony Pellechio, Luisa Zanforlin, Girma Begashaw, Stefania Fabrizio, and Joachim Harnack, Ghana: Economic Development in a Democratic Environment, Occasional Paper 199, Washington DC: IMF, 2000, available at: https://www.imf.org/external/pubs/nft/op/199/.

17. See http://www.presidentrawlings.com/pgs/recoverygrowth2.php (downloaded 7 April 2020).

18. Ivor Agyeman-Duah, *Between Faith and History: A Biography of J. A. Kufuor*, Trenton: Africa World Press, 2003.

19. Mohammed Awai & Jeffrey Paller, *Who Really Governs Urban Ghana?*, London: Africa Research Institute, 2016.

20. See interview with Explo Nani-Kofi: 'Against the Odds: Rawling and Radical Change in Ghana', *Review of African Poltical Economy*, 1 December 2016, http://roape.net/2016/12/01/odds-rawlings-radical-change-ghana/ (downloaded 15 June 2021).

21. BBC News, 'Burkina Faso's war against militant Islamists', 30 May 2019, https://www.bbc.co.uk/news/world-africa-39279050 (downloaded 15 June 2021).

22. Thomas Sankara, *Women's Liberation and the African Freedom Struggle*, Atlanta: Pathfinder, 2007.

23. See Maureen Covell, *Madagascar: Politics, Economics and Society*, London: Frances Pinter, 1987.

24. Daryl Glaser. 'African Marxism's Moment', in Daryl Glaser & David M. Walker (eds.), *Twentieth-Century Marxism: A Global Introduction*, London Routledge, 2007, p. 130.

25. Ali Rahnema, *An Islamic Utopian: A Political Biography of Ali Shari'ati*, London: I.B. Tauris, 2000.

26. Jean-Paul Sartre, *Existentialism & Humanism*, London: Methuen, 1948.

27. Anthony Brewer, *Adam Smith's Stages of History*, 2008, https://ideas. repec.org/p/bri/uobdis/08–601.html (downloaded 25 December 2020).

28. W.W. Rostow, *The Stages of Economic Growth: A Non-Communist Manifesto*, Cambridge: Cambridge University Press, 2008.

29. Georg Wilhelm Friedrich Hegel, 1824a., *Reason in History, A general introduction to the philosophy of history*, New York: Liberal Arts Press, 1953; Hegel, 1824b., *The Philosophy of History*, New York: Dover Publications, 1956.

30. Jean-Paul Sartre, 'Materialism and Revolution', in Sartre's *Literary and Philosophical Essays*, London: Hutchinson, 1968, p. 227.

31. Francis Fukuyama, *The End of History and the Last Man*, NY: Free Press, 1992.

32. William S. Lewis, *Louis Althusser and the Traditions of French Marxism*, Lanham: Lexington, 1971.

33. Arthur Hirsh, *The French New Left: An Intellectual History from Sartre to Gorz*, Boston: South End, 1981.

34. Simone de Beauvoir, *The Second Sex*, London: Vintage, 1997; first published in French in 1949, the year of Sankara's birth.

35. Joel Gordon, *Nasser's Blessed Movement: Egypt's Free Officers and the July Revolution*, Oxford: Oxford University Press, 1997.

36. Alexandra Reza, 'Sankara and Mitterrand', *London Review of Books*, 36:23, 2014, https://www.lrb.co.uk/the-paper/v36/n23/alexandra-reza/short-cuts (downloaded 15 June 2021).

37. The film by Robert Guédiguian, *The Last Mitterrand* (2005), was acclaimed for capturing this complexity.

38. Thomas Sankara, 'Against those who exploit and oppress us—here and in France', in *Thomas Sankara Speaks: The Burkina Faso Revolution 1983–87*, Atlanta: Pathfinder, 2007, pp. 325–334

39. Many of these collections overlap so that some speeches and writings are found in more than one volume.

40. *United Nations General Assembly Official Records, 20th Plenary Meeting, Thursday, 4 October 1984, at 10.40 a.m., New York*, (A/39/PV.20), pp. 405–410.

41. See https://www.youtube.com/watch?v=sli38RMGgbk (downloaded 15 June 2021).

42. See http://www.thomassankara.net/sankara-et-cuba-articles-et-pho-tos-de-la-presse-cubaine/ (downloaded 9 April 2020).

43. See http://www.thomassankara.net/the-heirs-of-thomas-sankaras-revolution/?lang=en (downloaded 25 December 2020).

44. Ernesto 'Che' Guevara, *The Motorcycle Diaries*, London: Harper, 2003.

45. E.g. Mamadou Diallo, 'Thomas Sankara and the Revolutionary Birth of Burkina Faso', *Viewpoint Magazine*, 1 February 2018, https://www.viewpointmag.com/2018/02/01/thomas-sankara-revolutionary-birth-burkina-faso/ (downloaded 15 June 2021).

46. Nicholas A. Jackson & Amber Murrey, 'The Lives and Afterlives of Thomas Sankara', https://www.plutobooks.com/blog/lives-after-lives-thomas-sankara/ (downloaded 9 April 2020). See also Amber Murrey (ed.), *A Certain Amount of Madness: The Life, Politics and Legacy of Thomas Sankara*, London: Pluto, 2018.

6. THE LEGACY OF FANON

1. Elaine Mokhtefi, *Algiers, Third World Capital: Freedom Fighters, Revolutionaries, Black Panthers*, London: Verso, 2018.

2. Eldridge Cleaver, *Soul on Ice*, London: Delta, 1999 (first published 1968).

3. Frantz Fanon, *The Wretched of the Earth*, NY: Grove, 1963.

4. Frantz Fanon, *Les damnés de la terre*, Paris: La Découverte, 2002 (first published 1961).

5. See https://www.gauteng.net/pages/trevor_huddleston (downloaded 1 May 2020).

6. Associated Press, 'How Louis Armstrong Passed his Trumpet to Hugh Masekela', *Wall Street Journal*, 21 March 2014, https://www.wsj.com/articles/how-louis-armstrong-passed-his-trumpet-to-hugh-masekela-1395426385 (downloaded 15 June 2021).

7. Jon Pareles, 'Taking Africa With Her', *New York Times*, 10 November 2008, https://www.nytimes.com/2008/11/11/arts/music/11appr.html (downloaded 15 June 2021).

8. Tyler Fleming, 'A marriage of inconvenience: Miriam Makeba's relationship with Stokely Carmichael and her music career in the United States', *Safundi: The Journal of South African and American Studies*, 17:3, 2016, pp. 312–338.

9. William Galvez, *Che Cuevara's Congo Diary*, London: Ocean Press, 1999; Ernesto 'Che' Guevara, *The African Dream: The Diaries of the Revolutionary War in the Congo*, NY: Grove, 2001.

10. Stokely Carmichael (ed. Charles V. Hamilton), *Black Power: The Politics of Liberation in America*, NY: Vintage, 1992.

11. Ahmed Sékou Touré, *Guinea Conakry: Democratic Governance, A History*, Morrisville: Lulu Press, 2017.

12. Lewis R. Gordon & LaRose T. Parris, 'Frantz Fanon's Psychology of Black Consciousness', in: Suman Fernando & Roy Moodley (eds), *Global Psychologies*, London: Palgrave Macmillan, 2018, pp. 215–228.

13. See Xolela Mangcu, Biko: A Life, London: I. B.Tauris, 2014.

14. Donald Woods, *Biko*, London: Paddington Press, 1978, p. 36.

15. Paul B. Rich, *White power and the liberal conscience: racial segregation and South African liberalism, 1921–60*, Manchester: Manchester University Press, 1984.

16. Qama Qukla, 'Zille recounts exposing cover-up around Steve Biko's death—"I was terrified", CapeTalk, 12 September 2019, http://www.capetalk.co.za/articles/360620/zille-recounts-exposing-cover-up-around-steve-biko-s-death-i-was-terrified (downloaded 2 May 2020).

17. BBC News, 'South Africa opposition party suspends Helen Zille over colonialism tweets', 3 June 2017, https://www.bbc.co.uk/news/world-africa-40143710 (downloaded 15 June 2021).

18. See Robert J C Young, 'Fanon and the turn to armed struggle in Africa', *Wasafiri*, 20:44, 2005, pp. 33–41.

19. Stephen Chan, 'Fanon: The Octogenarian of International Revenge and the Suicide Bomber of Today', *Cooperation and Conflict*, 42:2, 2007, pp. 151–168.

20. R.C. Keller, 'Clinician and revolutionary: Frantz Fanon, biography and the history of colonial medicine', *Bulletin of the History of Medicine*, 81, 2007, pp. 823–841; R.C. Keller, *Colonial Madness: Psychiatry in French North Africa*, Chicago: University of Chicago Press, 2007.

21. Frantz Fanon (eds. Jean Khalifa & Robert J. C. Young), *The Psychiatric Writings from Alienation and Freedom*, London: Bloomsbury, 2020.

22. Lou Turner & Helen Neville, *Frantz Fanon's Psychotherapeutic Approaches to Clinical Work: Practising internationally with Marginalized Communities*, London: Routledge, 2019.

23. Frantz Fanon, *Black Skin, White Masks*, London: Penguin, 2020 (first published 1952).

24. David Macey, *Frantz Fanon: A Biography*, NY: Picador, 2000.

25. See https://www.youtube.com/watch?v=vhhoS3zOskE (downloaded 15 June 2021).

26. Stephen Chan, *Exporting Apartheid: Foreign Policies in Southern Africa 1978–1988*, London: Macmillan, 1990.

27. See the transcript of an interview with French Colonel Mathieu: https://www.democracynow.org/2005/11/9/the_battle_of_algiers_1966_film (downloaded 3 May 2020).

28. Achille Mbembe, *Critique of Black Reason*, Johannesburg: Wits University Press, 2017, p. 169. See pp. 165–170.

29. Jean-Paul Sartre, 'Preface' to Frantz Fanon, *The Wretched of the Earth*, p. xx.
30. From Aimé Césaire's collection, *Les Armees miraculeuses*, Paris: Gallimard, 1970, pp. 73–4, translation David Macey.
31. Recounted by David Macey, *Frantz Fanon*, pp. 294–5.
32. See Benjamin Graves, 'The Master-Slave Dialectic: Hegel and Fanon', http://www.postcolonialweb.org/sa/gordimer/july6.html (downloaded 2 May 2020).
33. Frantz Fanon, *Black Skin, White Masks*, pp. 216–222.
34. Frantz Fanon, *Ibid.*, on Freud, e.g. pp. 13 & 165; on Jung, e.g. p. 190; on Adler, pp. 210–16.
35. Erica Burman, 'Fanon's Lacan and the Traumatogenic Child: Psychoanalytic Reflections on the Dynamics of Colonialism and Racism', *Theory, Culture & Society*, 33:4, 2016, pp. 77–101.
36. Derek Hook, 'Fanon's Lacan', Backdoor Broadcasting Company, 27 June 2018, https://backdoorbroadcasting.net/2018/06/derek-hook-fanons-lacan/ (downloaded 15 June 2021).
37. Françoise Vergès, 'Creole Skin, Black Mask: Fanon and Disavowal', *Critical Inquiry*, 23:3, 1997, pp. 578–596.
38. Jean-Paul Sartre, *Critique of Dialectical Reason*, London: Verso (Volume 1) 2004, (Volume 2) 2006. (First published in French 1960).
39. Cited in Macey, *Frantz Fanon*, p. 435.
40. Macey, *Ibid.*, p. 478.
41. Jean-Paul Sartre, 'Materialism and Revolution', republished in Jean Paul Sartre, *Literary and Philosophical* Essays, London: Hutchinson, 1968, pp. 189–239.

7. THE OLD LIBERATIONIST: ROBERT MUGABE

1. Stephen Chan, *The Commonwealth Observer Group in Zimbabwe: A Personal Memoir*, Gweru: Mambo Press, 1985.
2. Stephen Chan, *Robert Mugabe: A Life of Power and Violence*, Ann Arbor: University of Michigan Press, 2003 & London: I.B. Tauris, 2003 & 2019; (ed. With Ranka Primorac), *Zimbabwe in Crisis: The International Response and the Space of Silence*, London: Routledge, 2007; (ed. With Ranka Primorac), *Zimbabwe since the Unity Government*, London: Routledge, 2013; (With Julia Gallagher, *Why Mugabe Won: The 2013 Elections in Zimbabwe and Their Aftermath*, Cambridge: Cambridge University Press, 2017.
3. Stephen Chan, *Exporting Apartheid: Foreign Policies in Southern Africa 1978–1988*, London: Macmillan, 1990; (ed. With Vivienne Jabri), *Mediation in Southern Africa*, London: Macmillan, 1993; (With Moises Venancio et al.), *War and Peace in Mozambique*, Houndmills: Macmillan, 1998; *Southern*

Africa: Old Treacheries and New Deceits, New Haven: Yale University Press, 2011.

4. E.g. Meredith Blair, *Mugabe: Power and Plunder in Zimbabwe*, Oxford: Public Affairs, 2002; David Blair, *Degrees in Violence: Robert Mugabe and the Struggle for Power in Zimbabwe*, London: Continuum, 2002.

5. E.g. Sarah Rich Dorman, *Understanding Zimbabwe: From Liberation to Authoritarianism*, London: Hurst, 2016.

6. E.g. Ibbo Mandaza (ed.), *Zimbabwe: The Political Economy of Transition 1980–1986*, Dakar: CODESRIA, 1987; Brian Raftopoulos, *Race and Nationalism in a Post-colonial State*, Harare: SAPES, 1996.

7. Samir Amin, *Eurocentrism*, London: Zed, 1988.

8. E.g. Sabelo J. Ndlovu-Gatsheni & Pedzisai Ruhanya (eds.), *The History and Political Transition of Zimbabwe: From Mugabe to Mnangagwa*, Basingstoke: Palgrave Macmillan, 2020.

9. Matthew Weaver & Paul Owen, 'Nelson Mandela's memorial service: as it happened', *The Guardian*, 10 December 2013, https://www.theguardian.com/world/blog/2013/dec/10/nelson-mandelas-memorial-service-live-updates (downloaded 15 June 2021).

10. Stephen Chan, 'Robert Mugabe: Ruthless president of Zimbabwe once hailed as a beacon of African liberation who bankrupted the country he fought for', *The Guardian*, 7 September 2019, pp. 8–10.

11. Ronald, H. Chilcote, *The Portuguese Revolution: State and Class in the Transition to Democracy*, Lanham: Rowan & Littlefield, 2010, p. 39.

12. Immanuel Wallerstein, *The Capitalist World Economy*, Cambridge: Cambridge University Press, 1975.

13. Terence Ranger, *Peasant Consciousness and Guerrilla War in Zimbabwe*, London: James Currey, 1985.

14. David Lan, *Guns and Rain: Guerrillas and Spirit Mediums in Zimbabwe*, Berkeley: University of California Press, 1985.

15. Norma J. Kriger, *Zimbabwe's Guerrilla War: Peasant Voices*, Cambridge: Cambridge University Press, 2008.

16. Billy Mukamuri, *Making Sense of Social Forestry: A Political and Contextual Study of Forestry Practices in South Central Zimbabwe*, Tampere: University of Tampere, 1995.

17. Jeremy Youde, 'Why Look East? Zimbabwean Foreign Policy and China', *Africa Today*, 53.3, 2007, pp. 3–19; Victor Ojakorotu & Rumbidzai Kamidza, 'Look East Policy: The Case of Zimbabwe–China Political and Economic Relations Since 2000', *India Quarterly*, 74:1, 2018, pp. 17–41.

18. *The Seoul Times*, 'Korean Messages Greet Chinese Visitors for Embarrassment', n.d., https://theseoultimes.com/ST/?url=/ST/db/read.php%3Fidx=4721&PHPSESSID=b224d1ec27fa6b7fbb466e3ccf27eff4 (downloaded 11 April 2020).

19. See Stephen Chan (ed.), *The Morality of China in Africa: The Middle Kingdom and the Dark Continent*, London: Zed, 2013, for both my and the Deputy Chair's recollections.

20. Lucy Corkin, *Uncovering African Agency: Angola's Management of China's Credit Lines*. Farnham: Ashgate, 2013.

21. Fantu Cheru & Cyril Obi (eds.), *The Rise of China and India in Africa: Challenges, Opportunities and Critical Interventions*, London: Zed, 2012.

22. Arkebe Oqubay, *China-Africa and an Economic Transformation*, Oxford: Oxford University Press, 2019.

23. Stephen Chan, *Citizen of Africa: Conversations with Morgan Tsvangirai*, (No publisher credited, but many citations reference the Cape Town-based Fingerprint Cooperative who were the printers) 2005.

24. Stephen Chan, *Citizen of Zimbabwe: Conversations with Morgan Tsvangirai*, Harare: Weaver Press, 2010. There were also pirate editions, notably in the USA. The book earned me an interrogation or two with the Zimbabwean secret police.

25. E.g. Lily Kuo, 'There's legitimate suspicion that China approved of Zimbabwe's coup,' QZ, https://qz.com/africa/1132281/did-china-approve-of-zimbabwes-coup/, 17 November 2017, downloaded 25 December 2020.

8. THE MORAL AFRICAN AND THE AFRICAN RENAISSANCE: THABO MBEKI

1. Penny Dale, 'The man who taught Mandela to be a soldier', BBC News, 9 December 2013, https://www.bbc.co.uk/news/world-africa-23515879, downloaded 12 April 2020.

2. *Irish Times*, 'Father of South African President Mbeki Dies', https://www.irishtimes.com/news/father-of-south-african-president-mbeki-dies-1.394809, 30 August 2001, downloaded 15 June 2021.

3. Commonwealth Group of Eminent Persons, *Mission to South Africa: The Commonwealth Report*, Harmondsworth: Penguin, 1986.

4. Olivia B. Waxman, 'The U.S. Government Had Nelson Mandela on Terrorist Watch Lists Until 2008. Here's Why', https://time.com/5338569/nelson-mandela-terror-list/, 18 July 2018.

5. Conversation with Mosiuoa Lekota, Lake Como, 7 October 2012.

6. 2009: Directed by Clint Eastwood, starring Morgan Freeman as Mandela and Matt Damon as a South African rugby star coming to understand the moral dimension of Mandela's time in prison. It was a good film with typical fast and unfussy Eastwood direction. Freeman made a passable Mandela. The film didn't really care about rugby and the scenes where the national team plays rugby are unforgivably ridiculous.

7. Conversations with Sydney Mufamadi in Johannesburg, 2007–9.

8. I am relying on accounts given to me by one of the participants.
9. Merle Lipton, *Capitalism and Apartheid*, Aldershot: Gower, 1985; Lipton later problematized the entire transition period and whose 'truth' about history could emerge: Merle Lipton, *Liberals, Marxists, and Nationalists*, NY: Palgrave Macmillan, 2007.
10. In fact, an IMF loan did have to be taken out on the eve of majority rule. Looking back on the ambivalence and uncertainty about how to go ahead, see former ANC Minister, Ronnie Kasrils, 'How the ANC's Faustian pact sold out South Africa's poorest', *The Guardian*, 24 June 2013.
11. See Mac Maharaj, *The ANC and South Africa's Negotiated Transition to Democracy and Peace*, Berlin: Berghof, 2008, Chapter 4. Susan Boyson, 'Changing relations of political power in South Africa's transition: the politics of conquering in conditions of stalemate', *Politikon*, 19:3, 2007, pp. 64–80.
12. Years later I published a long poem about this; it was, when I first wrote it, the most 'rational' account I could devise in the face of a mounting irrationality in terms of black cohesion in the face of the die-hard white negotiators: Stephen Chan, 'Body Count in Natal', *Alternatives*, 25, 2000.
13. R.W. Johnson & Lawrence Schlemmer (eds.), *Launching Democracy in South Africa: The First Open Election, April 1994*, New Haven: Yale University Press, 1996; Andrew Reynolds (ed.), *Elections '94 South Africa: The campaigns, results and future prospects*, London: James Currey, 1994.
14. For good histories of the country, see: Robert Ross, *A Concise History of South Africa*, Cambridge: Cambridge University Press, 1999; T.R.H. Davenport, *South Africa: A Modern History*, Houndmills: Macmillan, 1977.
15. See https://www.justice.gov.za/trc/ (downloaded 25 December 2020).
16. I would host Sachs at SOAS which, for some time, was part of his lecture circuit. He would always repeat the 'Henry' story.
17. E.g. Nompumelelo Mungi Ngomane, *Everyday Ubuntu: Living Better Together, the African Way*, London: Bantam, 2019.
18. Leyla Tavernaro-Haidarian, *A Relational Model of Public Discourse. The African Philosophy of Ubuntu*, London: Routledge, 2018 (Kindle edition).
19. See Alexander Johnston, *Inventing the Nation South Africa*, London: Bloomsbury, 2014, Part Three.
20. Adam Habib, *South Africa's Suspended Revolution: Hopes and Prospects*, Johannesburg: Wits University Press, 2013.
21. H.W. van der Merwe, *Peacemaking in South Africa: A Life in Conflict Resolution*, Cape Town: Tafelberg, 2000, Chapter 11.

22. See https://www.sahistory.org.za/article/delegations-and-dialogue-between-anc-and-internal-non-government-groups   (downloaded 13 April 2020).

23. Stephen Chan, *Exporting Apartheid: Foreign Policies in Southern Africa 1978–1988*, London: Macmillan, 1990.

24. Stephen Chan, 'Fidel Castro and the Moment of Change in Africa', in Sabella Ogbobode Abidde & Charity Manyeruke, *Fidel Castro and Africa's Liberation Struggle*, Lanham: Lexington, 2020.

25. Chris Sandys, 'Nelson Mandela death: Somerset's part in South African history', BBC News, https://www.bbc.co.uk/news/uk-england-somerset-22990166, 5 December 2013.

26. William Mervin Gumede, *Thabo Mbeki and the Battle for the Soul of the ANC*, London: Zed, 2005.

27. Gumede described to me, on more than one occasion in Johannesburg and London, the reprobation and hate mail he received.

28. Brian Pottinger, *The Mbeki legacy*, Cape Town: Zebra, 2008; Mark Gevisser, *Thabo Mbeki: The Dream Deferred*, Johannesburg: Jonathan Ball, 2007.

29. Hugh Macmillan, *The Lusaka Years: The ANC in Exile in Zambia, 1963–1994*, Johannesburg: Jacana, 2013.

30. For his exile years see Mark Gevisser, *Thabo Mbeki: The Dream Deferred*, Johannesburg: Jonathan Ball, 2007, Part Four.

31. John Toye & Richard Toye, 'The Origins and Interpretation of the Prebisch-Singer Thesis', *History of Political Economy*, 35:3, 2003.

32. Although I did celebrate it, and proposed a moral equivalent when I delivered the Third Hans Singer Memorial Lecture at the German Development Institute in Bonn: Stephen Chan, *Mercy and the Structures of the World*, Bonn: German Development institute, 2011.

33. Probably the best and most even-handed treatment of Gandhi, including his attitudes to black South Africans, is Ramachandra Guha, *Gandhi Before India*, London: Allen Lane, 2013.

34. Tim Rogan, *The Moral Economists: R. H. Tawney, Karl Polanyi, E. P. Thompson, and the Critique of Capitalism*, Princeton: Princeton University Press, 2018.

35. For an account of the economic policies see Brian Pottinger, *The Mbeki Legacy*, Cape Town: Zebra, 2008, Part II.

36. Brian Pottinger, *The Mbeki Legacy*, pp. 214–221.

37. See the projections and figures I present in Stephen Chan, 'Free and Fair? Observation of Selected African Elections', *Journal of African Elections*, 18:1, 2019, pp. 6–8.

38. Jeffrey Davidow, *A Peace in Southern Africa: The Lancaster House Conference on Rhodesia, 1979*, Boulder: Westview. 1984; Stephen Chan, *The*

Commonwealth in World Politics: A Study of International Action 1965to 1985, London: Lester Crook, 1988, Chapter 4.

39. For my account see Stephen Chan, *Southern Africa: Old Treacheries and New Deceits*, New Haven: Yale University Press, 2011, Chapter 8.

40. Stephen Chan, 'Free and Fair? Observation of Selected African Elections', pp. 10–11.

41. My discussions with Nkosana Moyo, Harare, 2008.

42. Tamuka Chekero & Shannon Morreira, 'Mutualism Despite Ostensible Difference: HuShamwari, Khanyisani and Conviviality Between Shona Zimbabweans and Tsonga South Africans in Giyani, South Africa', *Africa Spectrum*, pp. 1–17 of first online publication (13 April 2020).

43. Ruby Magosvongwe, 'Shona philosophy of *Unhu/Hunhu* and its onomastics in selected fictional narratives', 10:2, 2016, pp. 158–175.

44. Stephen Chan, 'Abuja and After: The Case for Change in the Commonwealth Secretariat', *The Round Table*, 93:374, 2004, pp. 239–246.

45. See my account in Stephen Chan, *Southern Africa: Old Treacheries and New Deceits*, pp. 68–72.

46. Ngũgĩ wa Thiong'o, *Decolonising the Mind*, London: Heinemann, 1986. This book was first rehearsed as the Robb Lectures at the University of Auckland, on the invitation of Professors Michael Neil and the late Sebastian Black.

47. I describe these newsletters in Stephen Chan, *Southern Africa; Old Treacheries and New Deceits*, pp. 73–76.

48. Including by his own brother, Moletsi Mbeki, writing in 2000. See http://www.columbia.edu/cu/ccbh/souls/vol2no2/vol2num2art8. pdf (downloaded 26 December 2020).

49. Itumeleng Mekoa, 'African Renaissance—Thabo Mbeki's "African Renaissance": a critique of its theory and practice', *African Renaissance*, 15:1, 2018, pp. 9—28.

50. Cheikh Anta Diop, *Towards the African Renaissance: Essays in African Culture and Development, 1946–1960*, London: Karnak House, 1996.

51. See John Henrik Clarke, 'The Historical Legacy of Cheikh Anta Diop: His Contributions to a New Concept of African History', *Presence Africaine*, 149/150, 1989, pp. 110–120.

52. Sabelo Ndlovu-Gatsheni, *Epistemic Freedom in Africa: Deprovincialization and Decolonization*, London: Routledge, 2018.

53. Kwame Gyekye, *An Essay on African Philosophical Thought: The Akan Conceptual Scheme*, Cambridge: Cambridge University Press, 1987, Chapter 2.

54. See https://www.sahistory.org.za/article/bikos-imprisonment-death-and-aftermath (downloaded 26 December 2020).

55. Adam Habib, *South Africa's Suspended Revolution: Hopes and Prospects*, Johannesburg: Wits University Press, 2013; John S. Saul, *A Flawed Freedom: Rethinking Southern African Liberation*, London: Pluto, 2014, Chapter 4; imaginatively, on possible futures without the ANC, certainly in its present form, Frans Cronje, *A Time Traveller's Guide to Our Next Ten Years*, Cape Town: Tafelberg, 2014.

56. Achille Mbembe, *Critique of Black Reason*, Durham: Duke University Press, 2017, 'Epilogue'.

9. THE RESPONSIBILITY TO BE FREE: THE UNTAPPED POTENTIAL OF A NEW PAN-AFRICANISM

1. Themon Djaksam, 'Conflict and Unity: Towards an Intellectual History of the Forebears of the OAU', *India Quarterly*, October–December, 1990, pp. 41–90.

2. Zdenek Cervenka, *The Unfinished Quest for Unity: Africa and the OAU*, London: Julian Friedmann, 1977.

3. A.H. Akiwumi, 'The Economic Commission for Africa', *Journal of African Law*, 16:3, 1972, pp. 254–261.

4. Rose M. D'Sa, 'The Lagos Plan of Action--Legal Mechanisms for Co-operation between the Organisation of African Unity and the United Nations Economic Commission for Africa', *Journal of African Law*, 27:1, 1983, pp. 4–21.

5. *The Economist*, 'A political union for East Africa?', 9 February 2019, https://www.economist.com/middle-east-and-africa/2019/02/09/a-political-union-for-east-africa (downloaded 15 June 2021).

6. Gwyneth Williams, *Third World Political organizations*, London: Macmillan, 1981, pp. 52–4; Kweku Ampiah, *The Political and Moral Imperatives of the Bandung Conference of 1955: The Reactions of the US, UK and Japan*, Folkestone: Global Oriental, 2007, pp. 84–8.

7. Paul D. Williams, 'From Non-intervention to Non-indifference: The Origins and Development of the African Union's Security Culture', *African Affairs*, 106:423, 2007, pp. 253–279.

8. Information supplied to me by high-level South African sources meeting directly with President Bashir of Sudan, 2007.

9. My discussion with ZamBat non-commissioned officer, Lusaka, 2010.

10. My discussion with Maj.Gen. Martin Luther Agwai, London, 2007.

11. There is a slightly garbled account of part of my intervention in Paul Moorcraft, *Inside the Danger Zone: Travels to Arresting Places*, London: Biteback, 2010, pp. 397–8. Paul had no idea I had also conspired to present my case to the People's Liberation Army.

12. Gaafar Karrar Ahmed, *The Chinese Stance on the Darfur Conflict*,

Johannesburg: South African Institute for International Affairs (Occasional Paper 67), 2010.

13. I was able to gain several insights about this from my conversation with China's Ambassador-at-large to Africa, and senior emissary to Sudan, Liu Guijin, London, 2010.

14. Abdi Ismail Samatar, 'Ethiopian Invasion of Somalia, US Warlordism and AU Shame', *Review of African Political Economy*, 34:111, 2007, pp. 155–165.

15. Mohamed Haji Ingiriis, 'The Invention of Al-Shabaab in Somalia: Emulating the Anti-colonial dervishes', *African Affairs*, 117:467, 2018, pp. 217–237.

16. Stig Jarle Hansen, *Al-Shabaab in Somalia: The History and Ideology of a Militant Islamist Group, 2005–2012*, London: Hurst, 2013; Devon Knudsen, 'Better understanding of al Shabaab's plans for the region must be global priorities, *African Arguments*, 30 Septmeber 2013, https://africanarguments.org/2013/09/30/better-understanding-of-al-shabaabs-plans-for-the-region-must-be-global-priorities-by-devon-knudsen/.

17. Jonathan Fisher, 'AMISOM and the regional construction of a failed state in Somalia', *African Affairs*, 118:471, 2019, pp. 285–306.

18. David M. Anderson & Jacob McKnight, 'Kenya at war: Al-Shabaab and its enemies in Eastern Africa', *African Affairs*, 114:454, 2015, pp. 1–27; Jeremy Lind, Patrick Muthahi & Marjoke Oosterom, *Tangled Ties: Al-Shabaab and Political Volatility in Kenya*, Brighton: IDS (Evidence Report 130), 2015; also IDS, *Understanding Insurgent Margins in Kenya, Nigeria and Mali*, Brighton: IDS (Rapid response Briefing 10), 2015.

19. Devon Knudsen, 'A New Wave of African Counterterrorism Legislation: Contextualizing the Kenyan Security Laws', *Georgetown Journal of International Affairs*, 10 June 2015.

20. Dawit Yohannes Wondemagegnehu & Daniel Gebregziabher Kebeade, 'AMISOM: charting a new course for African Union peace missions', *African Security Review*, 26:2, 2017, pp. 199–219.

21. Peter Albrecht & Cathy Haenlein, 'Fragmented Peacekeeping: The African Union in Somalia', *RUSI Journal*, 161:1, 2016, pp. 50–61.

22. Jaimie Bleck & Kristin Michelitch, 'The 2012 crisis in Mali: Ongoing empirical state failure', *African Affairs*, 114:457, 2015, pp. 598–623.

23. Michael Shurkin, *France's War in Mali: Lessons for an Expeditionary Army*, Santa Monica; Rand Corporation, 2013.

24. Karl von Clausewitz, *On War*, Oxford: Oxford University Press, 2008.

25. Sydney Bailey, *Four Arab-Israeli Wars and the Peace Process*, Houndmills: Macmillan, 1990, Chapter 3.

26. See https://www.oxfordresearchgroup.org.uk/blog/the-french-inter-

vention-in-mali-an-interview-with-bruno-charbonneau, 28 March 2019.

27. For my descriptions and analysis of this, see Stephen Chan, *Spear to the West: Thought and Recruitment in Violent Jihadism*, London: Hurst, 2019, Chapter 7.

28. Horace Campbell, *Global NATO and the Catastrophic Failure in Libya: Lessons for Africa in the Forging of African Unity*, NY: Monthly Review, 2013, Chapter 12.

29. Georgina Holmes, '"Living on gold should be a blessing, instead it is a curse": Mass rape and genocide in the Democratic Republic of Congo', *The RUSI Journal*, 157:6, 2012, pp. 62–6; Georgina Holmes, *Women and War in Rwanda: Gender, Media and the Representation of Genocide*, London: I.B. Tauris, 2013, Chapter 6.

30. Marco Jowell, *Peacekeeping in Africa: Politics, Security and the Failure of Foreign Military Assistance*, London: I.B. Tauris, 2018.

31. Tim Murithi, *The Ethics of Peacebuilding*, Edinburgh: Edinburgh University Press, 2009.

32. Roger Mac Ginty and Andrew Williams, *Conflict and Development*, Abingdon: Routledge, 2009.

33. Susan Collin Marks, *Watching the Wind: Conflict Resolution During South Africa's Transition to Democracy*, Washington DC: US Institute for Peace, 2000.

34. Phil Clark, *Distant Justice: The Impact of the International Criminal Court on African Politics*, Cambridge: Cambridge University Press, 2018.

35. Nicholas Waddell and Phil Clark (eds.), *Courting Conflict: Justice, Peace and the ICC in Africa*, London: Royal Africa Society, 2008.

36. Ivo Josipovic, *The Hague: Implementing Criminal Law*, Zagreb: Hrvatski Pravni Centar, 2000.

37. Chaloka Beyani, *Protection of the Right to Seek and Obtain Asylum Under the African Human Rights System*, Leiden: Martinus Nijhoff, 2013.

38. John Hatchard, Muna Ndulo & Peter Slinn, *Comparative Constitutionalism and Good Governance in the Commonwealth: An Eastern and Southern African Perspective*, Cambridge: Cambridge University Press, 2004.

39. Sabelo J. Ndlovu-Gatsheni, *Empire, Global Coloniality and African Subjectivity*, NY: Berghahn, 2013, p. 105.

10. MALEDICTIONS OF THE POLITICAL ORDER: A SELECTION OF MODERN CHALLENGES

1. Andrew Roberts, *The Lumpa Church of Alice Lenshina*, Lusaka: Oxford University Press, 1972.

2. Heike Behrend, *Alice Lakwena and the Holy Spirits: War in Northern Uganda,*

1985–97, London: James Currey, 1999. For my fictional recreation, see Stephen Chan, *Joseph Kony and the Titans of Zagreb*, London: Nth Position, 2012, Book One.

3. Stephen Chan, 'Dlamini-Suma's awful AU legacy', *The Africa Report*, 82–83, 2016, pp. 44–5.

4. Mark Anderson, 'South Africa: Battle Lines', *The Africa Report*, 87, 2017, pp. 42–3.

5. See https://www.africa-confidential.com/article/id/12192/A_fight_to_the_photo-finish, 15 December 2017.

6. E.g. Martha C. Nussbaum, *The Monarchy of Fear*, Oxford: Oxford University Press, 2018—which deals with the Trump administration.

7. Luise White, *The Assassination of Herbert Chitepo: Texts and Politics in Zimbabwe*, Bloomington: Indiana University Press, 2003.

8. Blessing-Miles Tendi, *The Army and Politics in Zimbabwe: Mujuru, the Liberation Fighter and Kingmaker*, Cambridge: Cambridge University Press, 2020.

9. Eunice Chadoka King, *In My Tribulations Lies my Great Victory*, London: GlobalKing, 2016.

10. Yvonne Vera, *The Stone Virgins*, Harare: Weaver, 2002.

11. Alexander Kanengoni, *Echoing Silences*, Harare: Baobab, 1997.

12. For my essay on Vera and Kanengoni's work, see Stephen Chan, 'The Memory of Violence: trauma in the writings of Alexander Kanengoni and Yvonne Vera and the idea of unreconciled citizenship in Zimbabwe', *Third World Quarterly*, 26:2, 2005, pp. 369–382.

13. See https://www.youtube.com/watch?v=Q021-VyLzpk.

14. Cheryl Johnson-Odim & Emma Mba, *For Women and the Nation: Funmilayo Ransome-Kuti of Nigeria*, Urbana: University of Illinois Press, 1997.

15. Chammah J. Kaunda & Mutale Kaunda, 'Pentecostalism, Female Spirit-Filled Politicians, and Populism in Zambia', *International Review of Mission*, 107:1, 2018, pp. 23–32.

16. Paul Gifford, *African Christianity: its Public Role*, London: Hurst, 1998, Chapter 5; *The Basis of Union and Constitution of the United Church of Zambia*, Lusaka: United Church of Zambia, 1965.

17. Sara H. Longwe & Roy Clarke, *A gender perspective on the Zambian general election of October 1991*, Lusaka: Zambia Association for Research and Development, 1991.

18. Mutumba M. Bull, 'The Gender Dimension of the 2001 Zambian elections: Before, During and After', *African Social Research*, 45/46, 2001, espec. pp. 121–2.

19. See https://genderlinks.org.za/who-we-are/board-of-directors/sara-longwe/ (downloaded 20 April 2020).

20. See https://www.ilo.org/public/english/region/asro/mdtmanila/training/unit1/empowfw.htm (downloaded 20 April 2020).
21. See http://siteresources.worldbank.org/INTGENDER/Resources/GenderEvaluation.pdf (downloaded 20 April 2020).
22. Sara H. Longwe, 'Education for women's empowerment or schooling for women's subordination?, *Gender and Development*, 6:2, 1998, pp. 19–26.
23. Roy Clarke and Trevor Ford, *The Worst of Kalaki and the Best of Yuss*, Lusaka: Bookworld, 2004.
24. Stephen Ellis, *The Mask of Anarchy: The Destruction of Liberia and the Religious Dimension of an African Civil War*, London: Hurst, 2001, Chapter 6, espec. pp. 225–8.
25. Veronika Fuest, '"This is the Time to get in Front": Changing Roles and Opportunities for Women in Liberia', *African Affairs*, 107:427, 2008, pp. 201–224.
26. Greg Mills, Olusegun Obasanjo, Jeffrey Herbst, Dickie Davis, *Making Africa Work: A handbook for economic success*, Cape Town: Tafelberg, 2017. (The book was also endorsed by 2 other former prime ministers, 2 leaders of the opposition, and senior African civil servants, but Banda's endorsement featured on the cover above the book's title.)
27. Joyce Banda, *From Day One: Why Supporting Girls Age 0 to 10 is Critical to Change Africa's Path*, Washington DC: Center for Global Development, 2018.
28. Graça Machel, *The Impact of War on Children*, London: Hurst, 2001.
29. Paulos Milkias and Getachew Metaferia (eds.), *Battle of Adwa: Reflections on Ethiopia's Historic Victory Against European Colonialism*, NY: Algora, 2005.
30. I was involved in trying to mediate between the two sides as the war began, absolutely to no avail. What followed in terms of loss of life on both sides, and political repression in Eritrea, was tragic.
31. See Michela Wrong, *Do Not Disturb: The Story of a Political Murder and an African Regime Gone Bad*, London: 4ᵗʰ Estate, 2021.
32. Samuel Okiror, 'Stella Nyanzi marks release from jail in Uganda with Yoweri Museveni warning', *The Guardian*, 21 February 2020, https://www.theguardian.com/global-development/2020/feb/21/stella-nyanzi-marks-release-from-jail-in-uganda-with-yoweri-museveni-warning (downloaded 15 June 2021).
33. See https://edition.cnn.com/2018/11/07/africa/rwanda-diane-rwigara-trial-asequals-intl/index.html, 7 November 2018.
34. I was an observer at the 2009 Sudan elections, immaculately conducted by a regime tarnished by human rights abuses and war in Darfur but, at every single polling station, even in the most remote areas, voters

were handed an array of voting slips including one for female Parliamentarians.

35. Karen McVeigh, 'World Bank pulls $300m Tanzania loan over pregnant schoolgirl ban', *The Guardian*, 15 November 2018, https://www.theguardian.com/global-development/2018/nov/15/world-bank-pulls-300m-tanzania-loan-over-pregnant-schoolgirl-ban.

36. Awino Okech, *Widow Inheritance and Contested Citizenship in Kenya*, London: Routledge, 2019.

37. Gabeba Baderoon & Alicia C. Decker (eds.), *African Feminisms: Cartographies for the Twenty First Century*, in a special issue of *Meridians*, 17:2, 2018.

38. Simukai Tinhu, 'Joice Mujuru: the woman threatening to topple Robert Mugabe's ruling party', *The Guardian*, https://www.theguardian.com/world/2015/sep/28/zimbabwe-joice-mujuru-mugabe, 28 September 2015.

39. Carien du Plessis, 'Namibia's youngest MP enters the crucible as Africa's youth lead the way', *The Guardian*, https://www.theguardian.com/global-development/2020/apr/17/namibias-youngest-mp-enters-the-crucible-as-africa-youth-lead-way-emma-theofelus.

40. See https://www.amnesty.org.uk/lgbti-lgbt-gay-human-rights-law-africa-uganda-kenya-nigeria-cameroon, 31 May 2018; https://outrightinternational.org/region/africa?gclid=EAIaIQobChMI8p3h4dL7 6AIVzuvtCh2ohQuUEAAYASAAEgJBjfD_BwE (both downloaded 22 April 2020).

41. Bisi Alimi, 'If you say being gay is not African, you don't know your history', *The Guardian*, 9 September 2015, https://www.theguardian.com/commentisfree/2015/sep/09/being-gay-african-history-homosexuality-christianity.

42. Rahul Rao, *Out of Time: The Queer Politics of Postcoloniality*, Oxford: Oxford University Press, 2020.

43. BBC News, 'US recalls ambassador to Zambia after gay rights row', https://www.bbc.co.uk/news/world-africa-50901537, 24 December 2019.

44. Alex Crawford, 'US ambassador "shocked" by Zambian president's antigay comments', Sky News, https://news.sky.com/story/us-ambassador-shocked-by-zambian-presidents-anti-gay-comments-11876681, 2 December 2019.

45. Binyavanga Wainaina, "I am a homosexual, mum" (essay). *Africa is a Country*, 19 January 2014. Reprinted in *The Guardian*, 21 January 2014.

46. See https://www.hrw.org/news/2019/05/24/kenya-court-upholds-archaic-anti-homosexuality-laws-0, 24 May 2019.

47. Alison Flood, 'Binyavanga Wainaina, Kenyan author and gay rights

activist, dies aged 38', *The Guardian*, 22 May 2019, https://www.the-guardian.com/books/2019/may/22/binyavanga-wainaina-kenyan-author-and-gay-rights-activist-dies-aged-48.

48. Margaret Busby, 'Binyavanga Wainana obituary', *The Guardian*, https://www.theguardian.com/books/2019/jun/02/binyavanga-wainaina-obituary, 2 June 2019.

49. *Granta*, 92, 2005, https://granta.com/how-to-write-about-africa/.

50. Kalunga Lutato & Ranka Primorac, 'Our greatest writer?', *The Bulletin & Record*, May 2013, pp. 30–1.

51. Wangari Muoria-Sal, Bodil Folke Frederiksen, John Lonsdale and Derek Peterson, *Writing for Kenya: The Life and Works of Henry Muoria*, Leiden: Brill, 2009.

52. John Lonsdale, 'Henry Muoria: Public Moralist', *Ibid.*, espec. pp. 44–8.

53. Ngũgĩ wa Thiong'o, *Decolonising the Mind: The Politics of Language*, London: Heinemann, 1986.

54. Henry Muoria, 'What should we do, our people?', *Ibid.*, p. 161.

55. Ngũgĩ wa Thiong'o, *Petals of Blood*, London: Penguin 1977. This was the same year as *I Will Marry When I Want*, f/n below) and helped earn Ngũgĩ prison time.

56. G.G. Darah, 'To Choose a Language Is to Choose a Class: Interview with Ngũgĩ wa Thiong'o', in Reinhard Sander & Bernth Lindfors (eds.), *Ngũgĩ wa Thiong'o Speaks*, Oxford: James Currey, 2006, p. 191.

57. *Ibid.*

58. Ngũgĩ wa Thiong'o and Ngũgĩ wa Mini, *I Will Marry When I Want* (originally *Ngaahika Ndeenda*), London: Heinemann, 1982 (first performed in 1977).

59. Richard Lane, *The Postcolonial Novel*, Cambridge: Polity, 2006, p. 58.

60. Ngũgĩ wa Thiong'o, *Detained: A Writer's Prison Diary*, London: Heinemann, 1981.

61. Ngũgĩ wa Thiong'o & Micere Githae Mugo, *The Trial of Dedan Kaminthi*, London: Heinemann, 1976.

62. Ngũgĩ wa Thiong'o, *Writers in Politics*, London: Heinemann, 1981, p. 114.

63. See https://www.nobelprize.org/prizes/literature/1986/soyinka/lecture/, downloaded 24 April 2020.

64. Wole Soyinka, *Ogun Abibiman*, London: Rex Collings, 1976.

65. Wole Soyinka, *The Trials of Brother Jero*, Oxford: Oxford University Press, 1969.

66. Wole Soyinka, *The Man Died: Prison Notes*, London: Arrow, 1985 (first published 1971).

67. *Financial Times*, 'Nigerian writer Wole Soyinka on coup culture and challenging Castro', https://www.ft.com/content/c436336e-beed-11e7-9836-b25f8adaa111 3 November 2017.

68. Wole Soyinka, *King Baabu*, London: Methuen, 2002.

69. Wole Soyinka, *The Open Sore of a Continent: A Personal Narrative of the Nigerian Crisis*, Oxford: Oxford University Press, 1996.

70. Wole Soyinka, *Season of Anomy*, Bury St Edmunds: Arena, 1988 (first published 1973).

71. Wole Soyinka, *The Interpreters*, London: Heinemann, 1970.

72. Dambudzo Marechera, *The House of Hunger*, London: Heinemann, 2009 (first published 1978).

73. E.g. Brian Raftopoulos, *Beyond The House of Hunger: The Struggle for Democratic Development in Zimbabwe*, Harare: ZIDS, 1991.

74. See https://www.codesria.org/spip.php?article2870, downloaded 25 April 2020.

75. Samir Amin, *Delinking*, London: Zed, 1990.

76. Samir Amin, *Eurocentrism*, London: Zed, 1989.

77. Samir Amin, *Global History: A View from the South*, Cape Town: Pambazuka, 2011.

78. Willy Brandt (Chair), Independent Commission on International Development Issues, *North-South: A Programme for Survival*, London: Pan, 1980. Over Christmas 1979 and New Year 1980, my office was immediately next door to those of the Secretariat of the Brandt Commission. There was a genuine, if technocratic, idealism afoot as the report was drafted. For some of the technical data used, see GJW Government Relations (Foreword by Willy Brandt), *Handbook of World Development: The Guide to the Brandt Report*, London: Longman 1981.

79. For the state of negotiations in this period, into the early 1980s, see Stephen Chan, 'A new economic order: A humanised dependency?', *New Zealand International Review*, IX:4, 1984, pp. 9–14; and Stephen Chan, *Issues in International Relations: A View from Africa*, London: Macmillan, 1987, Chapter 15.

80. Thandika Mkandawire (ed.), *African Intellectuals: Rethinking Politics, Language, Gender and Development*, London: Zed, 2005. In this volume he brings together people like Ngũgĩ wa Thiong'o to illustrate the breadth of development concerns among African intellectuals.

81. Ibbo Mandaza, 'Incorrigible Visionary', *The Africa Report*, https://www.theafricareport.com/25501/thandika-mkandawire-an-intellectual-giant-and-incorrigible-pan-african/, 1 April 2020.

82. Thandika Mkandawire, 'Neopatrimonialism and the political economy of economic performance in Africa: critical reflections', *World Politics*, 67:3, 2015, pp. 563–612.

83. E.g. Pierre Englebert, *State Legitimacy and Development in Africa*, Boulder: Lynne Rienner, 2000.

84. Mushtaq Khan, 'Markets, States and Democracy: Patron-Client

Networks and the Case for Democracy in Developing Countries', *Democratization*, 12:5, 2005, pp. 1–21.

85. Pritish Behura, Lars Buur & Hazel Gray', 'Studying Political Settlements in Africa', *African Affairs*, 116:464, 2017, pp. 508–525.

86. Thandika Mkandawire, 'The spread of economic doctrines and policy-making in postcolonial Africa', *African Studies Review*, 57:1, 2014, pp. 171–198.

87. Thandika Mkandawire, 'Can Africa turn from recovery to development', *Current History*, 113:763, 2014, p. 171–177.

88. Michel Foucault, *Discipline and Punish: The Birth of the Prison*, London: Penguin, 1991 (first published in French in 1975).

89. Mikhail Bakhtin, *Problems of Dostoevsky's Poetics*, Minneapolis: University of Minnesota Press, 1984.

90. A capsule summary of these influences on him can be found in Achille Mbembe, 'Power and Obscenity in the Post-Colonial Period: The Case of Cameroon', in James Manor (ed.), *Rethinking Third World Politics*, London: Longman, 1991, pp. 166–182.

91. Achille Mbembe, *Critique of Black Reason*, Durham: Duke University Press, 2017, Chapter 5.

92. Achille Mbembe, *Ibid.*, Chapter 6.

93. He did sometimes try to express it straightforwardly. See the interesting debate: https://www.youtube.com/watch?v=87TmAnmSGrI&t= 120s, 4 February 2014.

94. V.Y. Mudimbe, *The Invention of Africa: Gnosis, Philosophy and the Order of Knowledge*, Bloomington: Indiana University Press, 1988.

95. Michel Foucault, *The Archaeology of Knowledge*, London: Routledge, 2002 (first published in French 1969).

96. Ali Mazrui, *Cultural Forces in World Politics*, London: James Currey, 1990.

97. Pim Higginson, *Scoring Race: Jazz, Fiction, and Francophone Africa*, Woodbridge: James Currey, 2017.

98. Sabelo J. Ndlovu-Gatsheni, 'African Decolonization's Past and Present Trajectories', *Current History*, May 2020, pp. 188–193.

SELECT BIBLIOGRAPHY

Below are the key works by the major African political leaders and intellectuals featured in this book:

Amin, Samir, *Delinking: Towards a Polycentric World*, London: Zed, 1990.
—— *Eurocentrism*, London: Zed, 1989.
—— *Ending the Crisis of Capitalism or Ending Capitalism*, Cape Town: Pambazuka, 2011.
—— *Global History: A View from the South*, Cape Town: Pambazuka, 2011.
Armah, Ayi Kwei, *The Beautyful Ones Are Not Yet Born*, London: Heinemann, 1969.
Azikiwe, Nnamdi, *Renascent Africa*, London: Frank Cass, 1968 (first published 1937).
Biko, Steve, *I Write What I Like: Selected Writings*, Chicago: University of Chicago Press, 2002.
Blyden, Edward Wilmot, *Christianity, Islam and the Negro Race* (facsimile edition), Hartford CT: Martino Fine Books, 2016 (first published 1887).
—— *The Negro in Ancient History* (facsimile edition), Hartford CT: Martino Fine Books, 2020 (first published 1869).
Cabral, Amílcar, *Return to the Source: Selected Speeches*, NY: Monthly Review Press, 1973.
Césaire, Aimé, *Discourse on Colonialism*, NY: Monthly Review Press, 2000 (first published 1950).
—— *Journal of a Homecoming / Cahier d'un retour au pays natal*, Durham, N. Carolina: Duke University Press, 2017 (first published 1939).
Diop, Cheikh Anta, *The Cultural Unity of Black Africa: The Domains of Patriarchy and of Matriarchy in Classical Antiquity*, London: Karnak House, 1989 (first published 1963).
—— *Towards the African Renaissance: Essays in Culture and Development, 1946–1960*, London: Karnak House, 1996.

SELECT BIBLIOGRAPHY

Du Bois, W.E.B., *The Souls of Black Folk*, New Haven: Yale University Press, 2015 (first published 1903).

—— *The Talented Tenth*, NY: Nook Press, 2018 (first published 1903).

—— *The Philadelphia Negro*, Philadelphia: University of Pennsylvania, 1899.

—— *Black Reconstruction in America 1860–1880*, NY: Free Press, 1999 (first published 1935).

Fanon, Frantz, *The Wretched of the Earth*, London: Penguin, 2001 (first published 1961).

—— *Black Skin, White Masks*, London: Penguin, 2021 (first published 1952).

—— *Toward the African Revolution*, NY: Grove Press, 1994 (first published 1964).

—— *Alienation and Freedom*, London: Bloomsbury, 2018 (previously unpublished as a single volume).

—— *A Dying Colonialism*, NY: Grove Press, 1994 (first published 1959).

Garvey, Marcus, *Selected Writings and Speeches of Marcus Garvey*, NY: Dover, 2005.

—— *The Tragedy of White Injustice: Garvey's Epic Poem*, Trenton, NJ: Black Classic Press, 2016 (first published 1927).

Garvey, Marcus & Amy Jacques Garvey, *Philosophy and Opinions of Marcus Garvey* (two volumes published in one facsimile edition), Hartford CT: Martino Fine Books, 2014 (first published 1923).

Gyekye, Kwame, *An Essay on Akan Philosophical Thought: The Akan Conceptual Scheme*, Cambridge: Cambridge University Press, 1987.

James, C. L. R., *The Black Jacobins: Toussaint L'ouverture and the San Domingo Revolution*, London: Penguin, 2001.

Kaunda, Kenneth, *Zambia Shall be Free*, London: Heinemann, 1962.

Kaunda, Kenneth (ed. Colin Legum), *Zambia, independence and beyond: The speeches of Kenneth Kaunda*, London: Nelson, 1966.

Kaunda, Kenneth D., *A Humanist in Africa: Letters to Colin M. Morris*, London: Longmans, 1966.

—— *Letters to my Children*, NY: Prentice Hall, 1973.

—— *The Riddle of Violence*, NY: Harper & Row, 1981.

Kaunda, Kenneth D. (ed. Colin Morris), *Kaunda on Violence*, NY: Harper Collins, 1980.

Mandela, Nelson, *The Struggle is My Life*, Atlanta: Pathfinder, 1991.

—— *Long Walk to Freedom*, London: Abacus, 1995.

—— *No Easy Walk to Freedom: Speeches, Letters and Other Writings*, London: Penguin, 2002.

Mbeki, Thabo, *Africa—The Time Has Come: Selected Speeches*, Cape Town: Tafelberg, 1998.

—— *Africa—Define Yourself*, Cape Town: Tafelberg, 2002.

—— *Letters from the President: Articles from the First 100 Editions of ANC Today*, Johannesburg: ANC Communications Unit, 2003.

Mbembe, Achille, *On the Postcolony*, Berkeley: University of California Press, 2001.

—— *Critique of Black Reason*, Durham NC: Duke University Press, 2017.

—— *Necropolitics*, Durham NC: Duke University Press, 2019.

Mkandawire, Thandika & Charles C. Soludo, *African Voices on Structural Adjustment*, Trenton NJ: Africa World Press, 2003.

Mkandawire, Thandika (ed.), *African Intellectuals: Rethinking Politics, Language, Gender and Development*, London: Zed, 2005.

Mkandawire, Thandika, *Africa Beyond Recovery*, Oxford: African Books Collective, 2015.

Mapanje, Jack, *Skipping Without Ropes*, Newcastle-Upon-Tyne: Bloodaxe, 1999.

—— *And Crocodiles are Hungry at Night*, Banbury: Ayebia Clarke, 2011.

Mudimbe, V.Y., *The Invention of Africa: Gnosis, Philosophy and the Order of Knowledge*, Oxford: James Currey, 1990.

Ndlovu-Gatsheni, Sabelo J., *Coloniality of Power in Postcolonial Africa: Myths of Decolonization*, Dakar: CODESRIA, 2013.

—— *Empire, Global Coloniality and African Subjectivity*, NY: Berghahn, 2015.

—— *Epistemic Freedom in Africa: Deprovincialization and Decolonization (Rethinking Development)*, London: Routledge, 2018.

—— *Decolonization, Development and Knowledge in Africa: Turning Over a New Leaf (Worlding Beyond the West)*, London: Routledge, 2020.

Ngũgĩ wa Thiong'o, *Decolonising the Mind: The Politics of Language in African Literature*, Oxford: Heinemann, 1986.

—— (eds. Reinhard Sander & Bernth Lindfors), *Ngũgĩ wa Thiong'o Speaks*, Oxford: James Currey, 2006.

Nkrumah, Kwame, *Africa Must Unite*, London: Heinemann, 1963.

—— *Consciencism: Philosophy and Ideology for Decolonization*, NY: Monthly Review Press, 1996 (first published 1970).

—— *Neo-Colonialism: The Last Stage of Imperialism*, Bedford: Panaf, 1974.

Nyerere, Julius K., *Ujamaa: Essays on Socialism*, Oxford: Oxford University Press, 1971.

—— *Freedom and Socialism—Uhuru na Ujamaa*, Oxford: Oxford University Press, 1970.

—— *On Socialism*, Oxford: Oxford University press, 1970.

—— *Man and Development*, Oxford: Oxford University Press, 1975.

—— *Freedom and Unity: A Selection from Writings and Speeches, 1952–1965*, Oxford: Oxford University Press, 1971.

Obasanjo, Olusegun, *My Command*, Oxford: Heinemann, 1981.

—— *My Watch* (three volumes), Lagos: Kachifo, 2014–15.

Padmore, George (ed.), Hakim Adi & Marika Sherwood, *The 1945*

SELECT BIBLIOGRAPHY

Manchester Pan-African Congress Revisited: With Colonial and Coloured Unity, London: New Beacon, 1995.

Rodney, Walter, *How Europe Underdeveloped Africa*, London: Verso, 2018 (first published 1972).

Sankara, Thomas, *Women's Liberation and the African Freedom Struggle*, Atlanta: Pathfinder 2007.

—— *Thomas Sankara Speaks: The Burkina Faso Revolution 1983–1987*, Atlanta: Pathfinder, 2007.

—— *We are the Heirs of the World's Revolutions: Speeches from the Burkina Faso Revolution 1983–1987*, Atlanta: Pathfinder, 2007.

Senghor. Leopold Sedar, *Nocturnes*, New Rochelle: Opaku, 1971.

—— *Ethiopiques*, Paris: Seuil, 1956.

Soyinka, Wole, *The Open Sore of a Continent: A Personal Narrative of the Nigerian Crisis*, NY: Oxford University Press, 1997.

Soyinka, Wole, *The Man Died: The Prison Notes of Wole Soyinka*, NY: Noonday, 1988.

—— *Season of Anomy*, London: Rex Collins, 1973.

—— *The Interpreters*, Oxford: Heinemann, 1970.

INDEX

INDEX

INDEX

INDEX

INDEX